Trevor Frankland
Between Clarity and Mystery

For Dorothy, wife, artist and companion.

Trevor Frankland

Trevor Frankland

Between Clarity and Mystery

Simon Fenwick

Sansom & Company

First published in 2010 by Sansom & Company Ltd.,
81g Pembroke Road, Bristol BS8 3EA

0117 9737207
www.sansomandcompany.co.uk
info@sansomandcompany.co.uk

ISBN 978-1-906593-20-9

British Library Cataloguing-in-Publication Data. A catalogue record for this book is available from the British Library

Designed by Jane Humphrey

Printed and bound in the Czech Republic via Akcent Media

Illustration dimensions are width before height.

An Appreciation

The paintings of Trevor Frankland sing with a precious dialogue between interior and exterior space where guests have been invited. They are magical invitations, their shapes colours and light cadences create patterns – melodies of clock-ticking moments of the present, of yesterday and dream-like murmurings of far away places. They are indeed between clarity and mystery.

In his painting *Summer Evening* the long rectangle of the canvas, almost a double square in proportion, is lit up by a narrow door-way view of a southern Romanesque church on a hill under a vibrating cobalt evening sky – bleaching the church in resonating orange-tinted harmonies. We descend by glittering poplars to firs, almost silver-white under the heat blaze, to a carved horizontal hand rail bordering a white lemon sun-splashed ochre path. Then to darker shaded ochre steps and a wider lemon ochre path.

So to the splendid foreground interior with its lyrical bell-like intervals of long verticals of various widths and complementary compact horizontal and vertical patterns of smaller units. The major colour chords and harmonies are deep low-toned wine-red, dark olive green and near black, which create a magical mood of peace and rest. The long vertical orange forms framed in black rising from the blue settee chime with the church beyond. I love the glowing cadences of light passing upwards along the half-closed window shutters creating a glorious melody of colour and light. This combination of colour and light intermingled in differing related harmonies and intensities is a vital aspect of the whole painting, giving it an enchantment which continues to grow the longer we view the painting – how beautiful.

Looking at Trevor Frankland's paintings gives me enormous pleasure.

Leonard McComb RA November 2009

Contents

Introduction

In the summer of 2006, at the end of three years as President of the Royal Watercolour Society, Trevor Frankland asked me if I would be interested in writing an account of his life and his work. However it was not until more than a year later that I began writing. During much of the two years I spent my time at Bankside Gallery raising funds for a new room for the Society's library and archives. I had been complaining to Trevor, who was then still President, about the lack of space in my office and had remarked to him, flippantly, that the only way to expand was upwards by creating a mezzanine floor. Somewhat to my surprise, not to mention alarm, he told me to go ahead and do something about it. After very, very many meetings, phone-calls, letters and e-mails the money was raised, the extension built and opened in 2008. For me it all proved an interesting experience. The project reflected Trevor's own considerable concern for the Society in particular and his interest in art history in general; for his constant enthusiasm and encouragement I remain deeply grateful.

Earlier in his presidency my bicentennial history of the Royal Watercolour Society, *The Enchanted River*, had been published by John Sansom, and it seemed appropriate that I should now turn to Trevor Frankland's own story. This he envisioned as a progressive and almost logical – and he is nothing if not logical – narrative. It was to be the tale of a young man from the provinces who becomes a student first at the Laird School of Art in Birkenhead and then at the Royal Academy Schools in London. The young man goes on to combine life as a creative artist with that of a teacher. In the fullness of time he is elected to various art societies of long standing. Then he eventually serves as President of the second oldest in the kingdom, the Royal Watercolour Society, an honour in itself and the fulfilment of an ambition he had held since his youth.

My additional thanks to Dorothy Frankland for her unfailing hospitality, to Jane Humphrey the designer of this book, and to John Sansom its publisher.

Simon Fenwick
Hampstead, November 2009

1

In conversation with the painter and writer André Marchand, Henri Matisse said that you have only one idea, you are born with it, and all your life you develop your fixed idea, you make it breathe. He continued, 'I believe that in drawing I have been able to say something, I have worked a lot with that problem.'

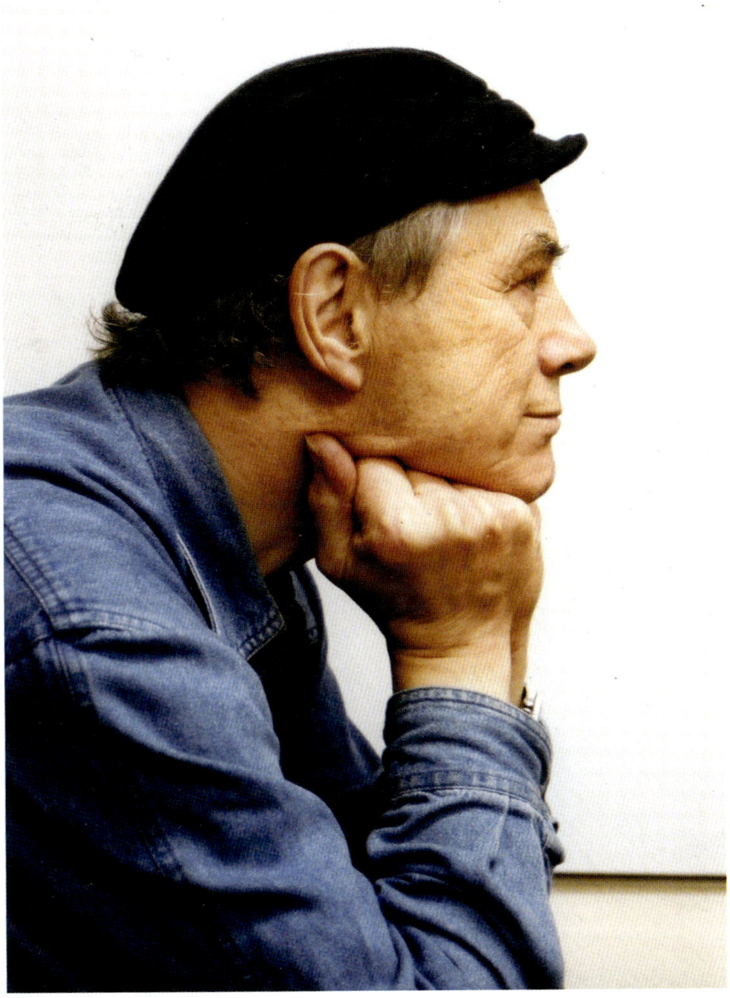

A logical development, step by step, manner might be thought necessary to the creation of an artist's 'signature' or style and yet Trevor Frankland's work has appeared to change radically over the past decades. But what he calls his life-long interest in creating a balance between clarity and mystery has provided the constant underlying framework for all his work. Even while still a student at the Royal Academy Schools his approach towards the objects he drew or painted was more than just academic, and a decade later his work had changed to one based on a modular unit incorporating a strong element of optical illusion.

He likes the word 'fuseki' to describe his approach to the creation of a modular composition. This is the word given to the initial layout of the pieces in the Japanese board game 'Go' where 'fuseki' means preparing for action when lack of information prevents the taking of rational decisions. It is however a springboard for intuition – the structured beginning from which to develop an intuitive approach to an idea. It is also similar to Stravinsky's description of how, paradoxically, in his compositions restraints allowed him greater freedom to compose.

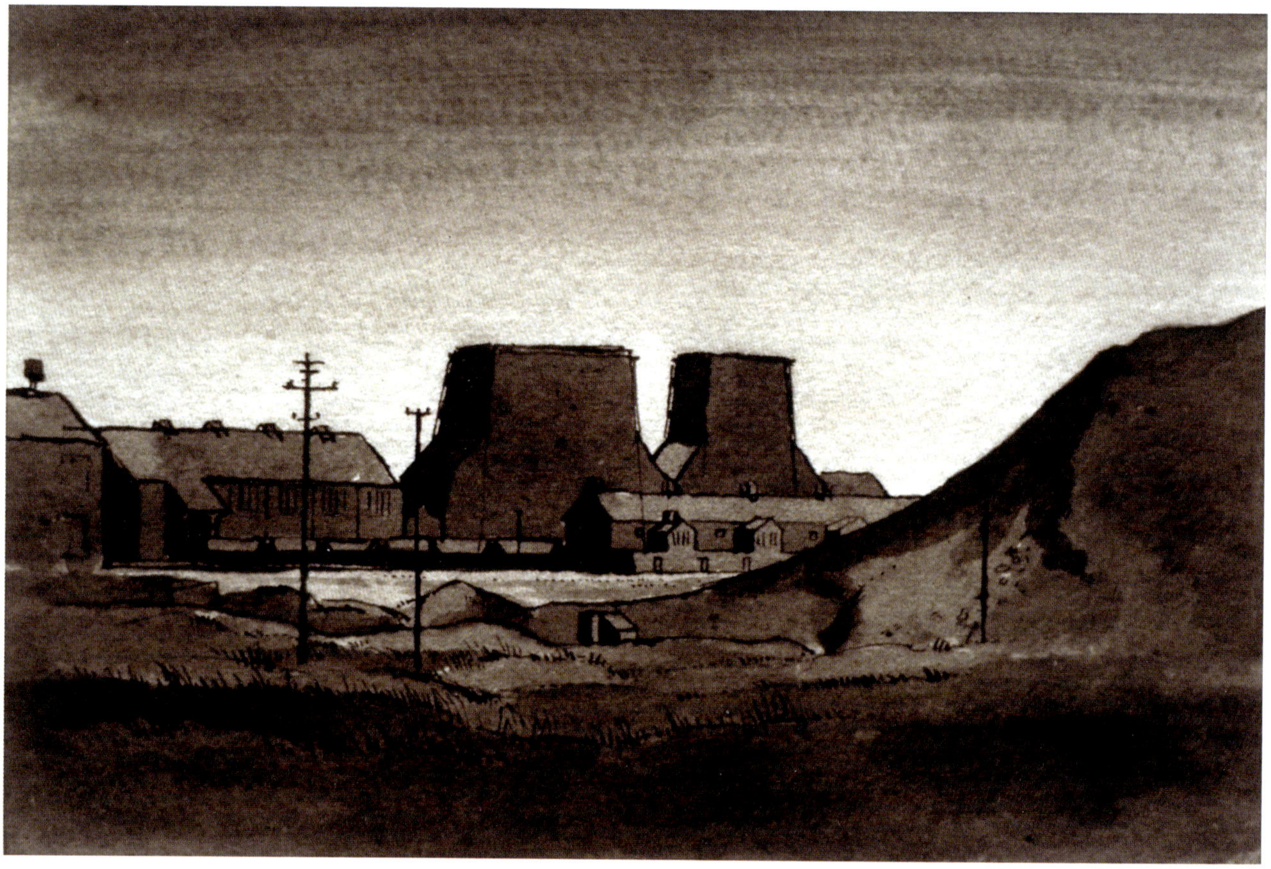

Southbank Teesside Industrial Workings
200 x 140 mm, pen and wash

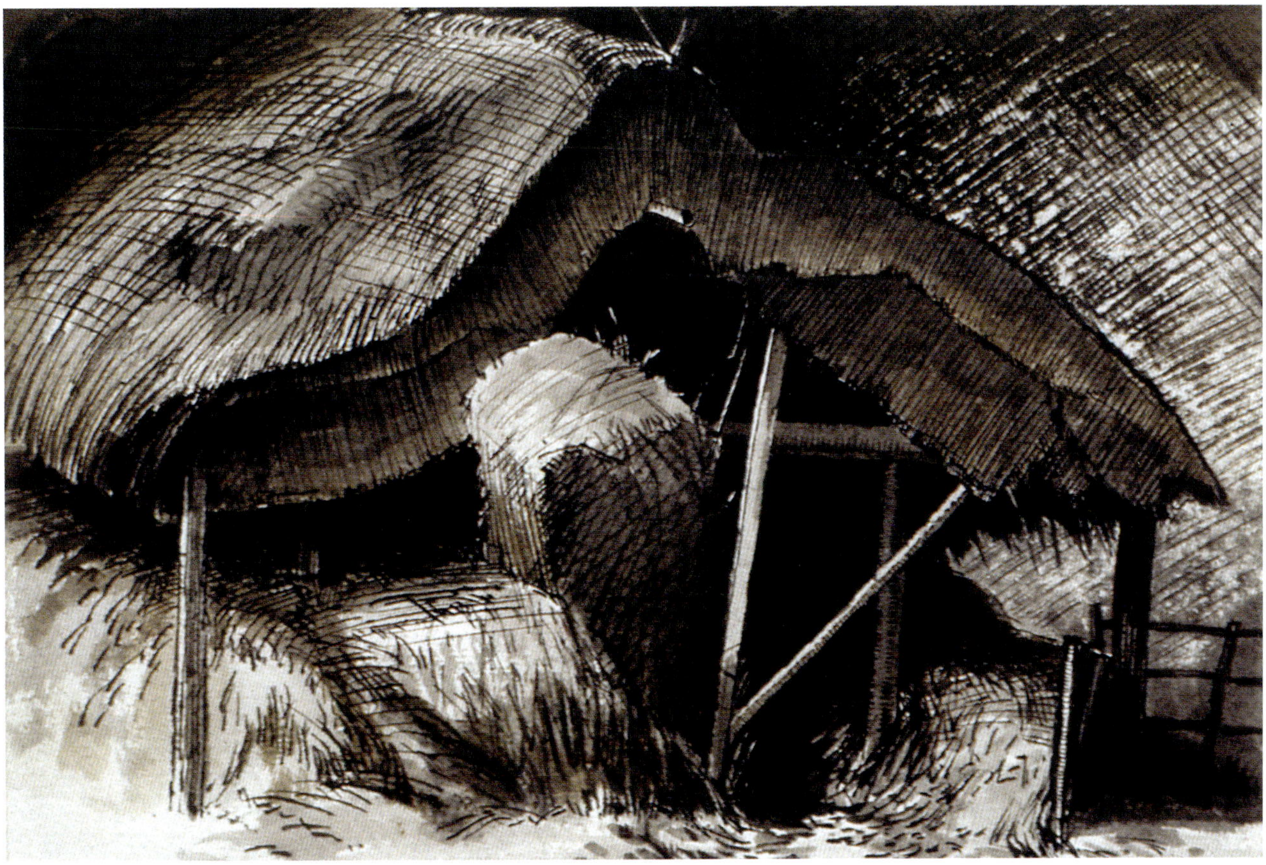

Farmyard
190 x 140 mm, pen and wash

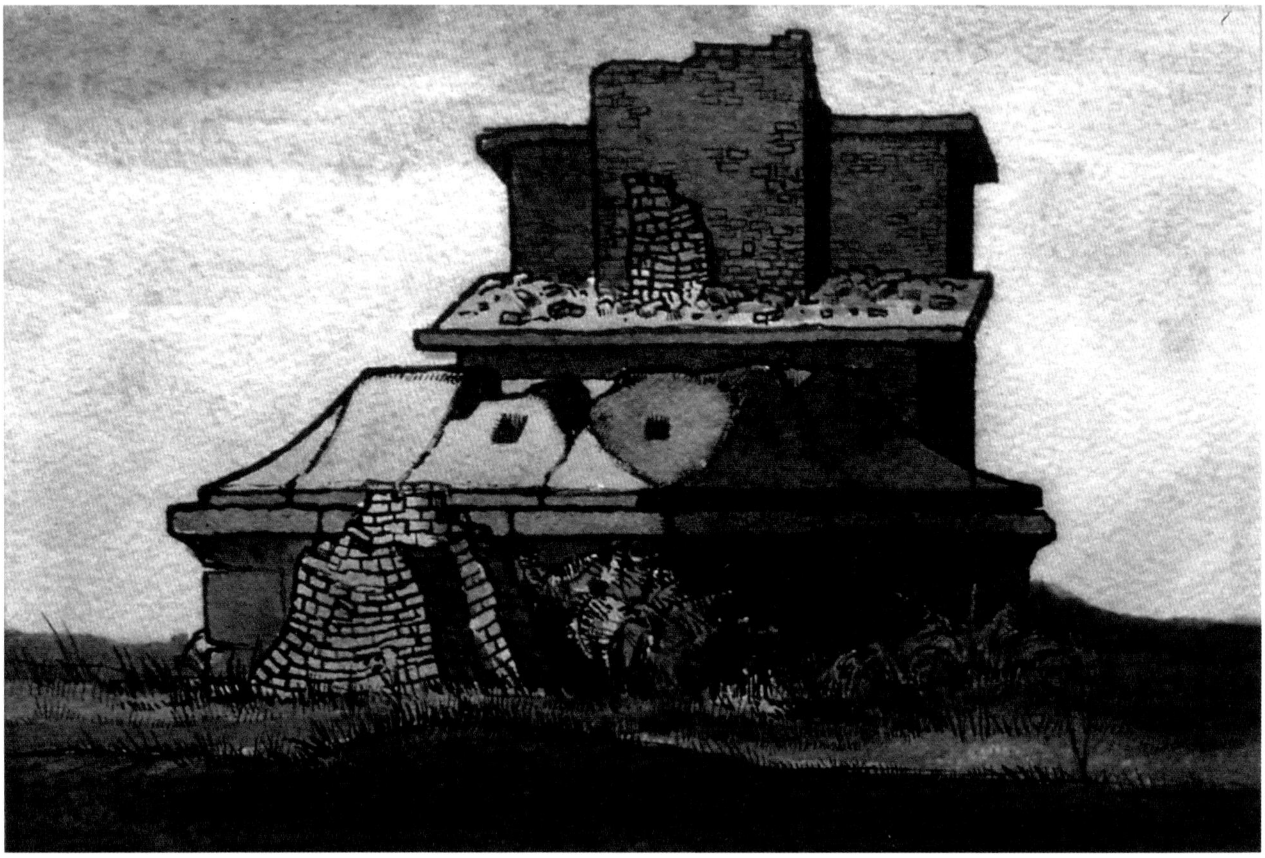

Old Mine Workings, Cleveland
200 x 140 mm, pen and wash

Frankland is now in his seventies. He is trim, of medium height, balding, active and intellectually vigorous, always on the go. He lives with his wife Dorothy. They have known one another since they were in their teens and been married for more than fifty years. Spending time with them over the months in preparation for this book and over the years I have been friends with the couple it is evident how completely they know and rely on one another.

Our conversations took place over several visits between November 2007 and the spring of 2008. I caught the train from north London to Clapham Junction and then the bus up to their house off St John's Hill in Battersea. (I was invariably late.) We began our days with coffee and Jaffa cakes in the sitting room. The room, which is also Trevor's library, is painted black although the black walls have an unexpectedly greenish tinge. The sofa and chairs and tables are also black. The Venetian blinds on the windows are always partially drawn to filter out the cold white light. Yet the room is unexpectedly warm and welcoming. Colour comes from the rugs on the floor, the cushions and the book covers – floor to ceiling, the books are about art, artists and their associates, and the esoteric. The items in the rooms have been collected on the couple's extensive travels or bought in sale rooms – Japanese cloisonné pots, Iranian and Oriental bronzes and ceramics, a Chinese incense burner in the shape of a dog from Christie's. A copper tray from Cliveden House in Buckinghamshire stands on top of a bookcase and a nineteenth-century bronze Japanese lantern hangs from the ceiling. On one wall hangs a drawing of the antique room at the Royal Academy Schools which won a prize when he was still a student and was exhibited in the 1955 R.A. Summer Exhibition. Conversation continued in the studio next door and in the other rooms around the house, talking about memories, pictures, opinions, and on one cold January afternoon we did a tour of the garden. Everything in both the house and garden is meticulously planned and has its logical place. We have a break for lunch (Trevor has been a vegetarian nearly all his life) and then we have another session before afternoon tea with Dorothy after which we call it a day.

I was able to ask whatever I liked. Whether or not I missed anything, I don't know. Occasionally he used to say, 'I don't want that in – don't use that.' His manner in telling stories is always eager and enthusiastic, wanting to explain. I saw Trevor start to nod only once – he was trying to recall the dates of some of his pictures, a rather dull job. I coughed and we continued.

When asked what stimulates him, sets his mind working, what, in short, 'makes him tick', Frankland replies that for him art is a way of life.

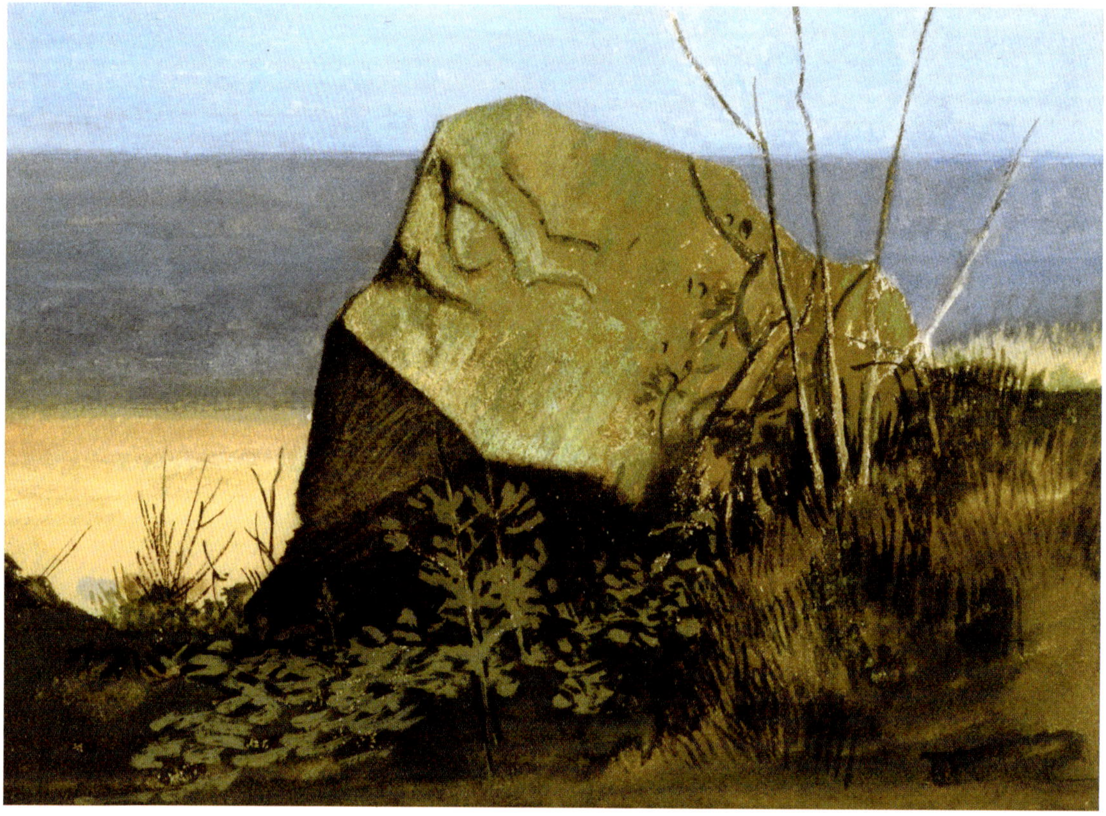

Indeed for him art is his way of life. Everything is related, your most intimate relationships in your interior world have a bearing on your exterior reality and on how you conduct your business with the outer world so that it becomes part of its fabric. For William Blake it was seeing 'a World in a grain of sand, and a Heaven in a wild flower'. This notion that everything is connected is also a principle of Zen, a philosophy which has influenced and moved Frankland greatly. I asked Dorothy the same question, 'what makes Trevor tick?' She says that he is always thinking about art and using his judgement. Immensely energetic, 'he rolls on and rolls on.'

A typical Frankland picture is calm, intellectually clear-sighted, neither sentimental nor aggressive. This is also true of the man. All art is autobiographical. What follows is an account of how Frankland's thoughts and experiences have been turned into his art.

Beach Rock, Saltwick Bay
240 x 180 mm, gouache

2

Eric Trevor Frankland was born in Middlesbrough on 7 July 1931. According to family legend his ancestors owned a large tract of land at Thirkelby near Thirsk in North Yorkshire in the mid-seventeenth century but because of the laws of primogeniture his forefathers lost out. His grandfather told him that when a young man his own grandfather used frequently to say, 'we should be riding around in a coach and four and not farming these Farndale acres.' A Thomas Frankland had a large building at Thirkelby pulled down in the late 1700s and had it replaced with a new house by the architects James and Samuel Wyatt. This in turn was dismantled in 1927 but the stables, clock tower and gate house remain. The local church has many memorial plaques relating to the Frankland family.

Frankland's great-grandfather lived at Bee Stone Farm in Farndale near Danby in the Yorkshire Dales where his family had been since 1800. However, by the end of the century there was not enough work on the farm to support all the family members so his grandfather went down into Middlesbrough to look for better employment. During such depressed time the railway and iron and steel companies offered the only work to be had in the town so he took a job with the railway company. Arthur Frankland, Trevor's father, was born in Middlesbrough. He grew to be a strong, muscular, practical man who did physical training. In his teens his parents paid for him to have art lessons and for his brother to learn the violin. He was also interested in archaeology – an interest which had started when visiting a relative's farm near Pickering where flint implements could be found on the land. Fascinated by the arts and crafts of the past, he encouraged his son to draw and paint and showed him how to harden and temper steel and how to fire small clay figurines in the ashes of a fire. He would always say that if you wanted to achieve anything in life it meant hard work. Arthur's own taste in art was for the Dutch school, particularly for the landscape artists such as Hobbema and van der Neer who had been favourites in Victorian England. Later in life he became a keen amateur photographer and for some years was Honorary Treasurer of the Middlesbrough Photographic Society.

The household consisted of Arthur and his wife Florrie and their four children (Trevor was the eldest). The family was considered 'artistic' and there were always pictures and books on art in the house as well as some little silver items which had come from a relation on his mother's side, a Birmingham silversmith called Lever. Florrie was well known for her ability to create cake decorations for special occasions, and sometimes it seemed as if they were taking over every flat surface in the house. Neighbours used to come and admire a fleet of sailing ships showing the influence of art deco which Arthur had painted in the space between the picture rail and the ceiling. They also came to look at the early railway carriage standing in the backyard where it had been turned into a shed. It still retained a door with a window which could be raised and lowered by a leather strap.

Trevor's desire and inclination to be an artist were clear from a young age – he had an accurate eye and could therefore draw without measuring. Many years later a love of geometry found a deeper expression in his involvement with freemasonry. Unfortunately Middlesbrough Technical School which he attended offered no art teaching whatsoever and he had to pursue an art education as best he could by becoming a member of the Cleveland Sketching Club and using the local library. He had joined the library as a child but had been mortified by finding that any books on art in the children's section were trivial and infantile so he asked to use the adult library. There, in a series of books by a writer on art called Bradshaw, he discovered Peter De Wint and J.M.W. Turner. He also first heard of the Royal Academy Schools (he remembers thinking it would be splendid to go there), the Royal Society of Painters in Water-Colours and of Suffolk Street, the home of the Royal Society of British Artists. Over the course of time all were to become part of his life. When he was fourteen he saved up and bought copies of Turner's *Liber Studiorum* for thirty shillings, only to be disappointed by their small – if accurate – size and the discovery that these were merely facsimiles and not the genuine article.

At the age of sixteen Frankland left the Technical School and in order to earn money he became an apprentice shipyard draughtsman at Smith's Dock Co Ltd at Southbank on Tees. An uncle suggested that he should work towards becoming a naval architect and he would provide some financial assistance. Frankland, however, hated the work and had set his mind on becoming an artist although he was uncertain how this was to be achieved.

Much of his free time he spent drawing and painting as well as reading about the history of British artists. In his early teens he was a member of the Middlesbrough Junior Water-polo team which became Northumberland and Durham County Champions earning him a county medal. The training was intensive and took up too much time however and he gave it up in 1950. Although the work at Smith's Dock gave him no pleasure it left him with a legacy which has lasted

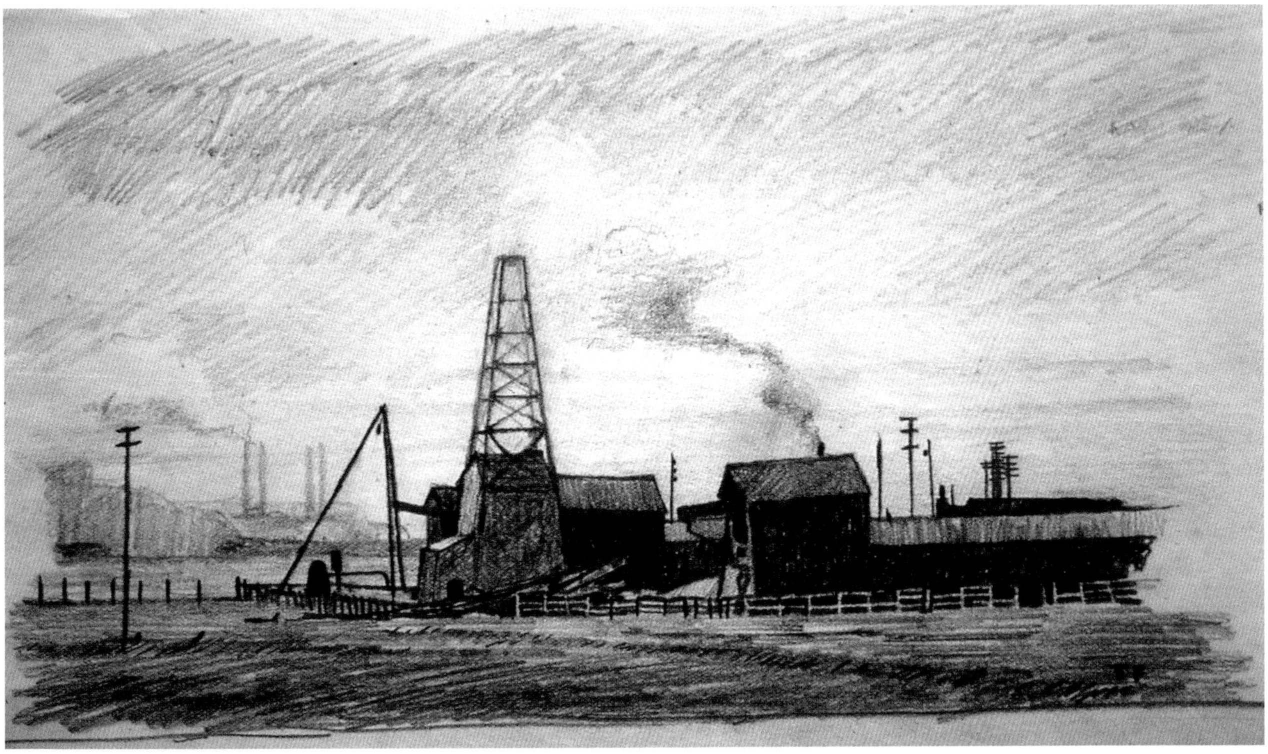

Salt-workings, Durham
260 x 150 mm, graphite

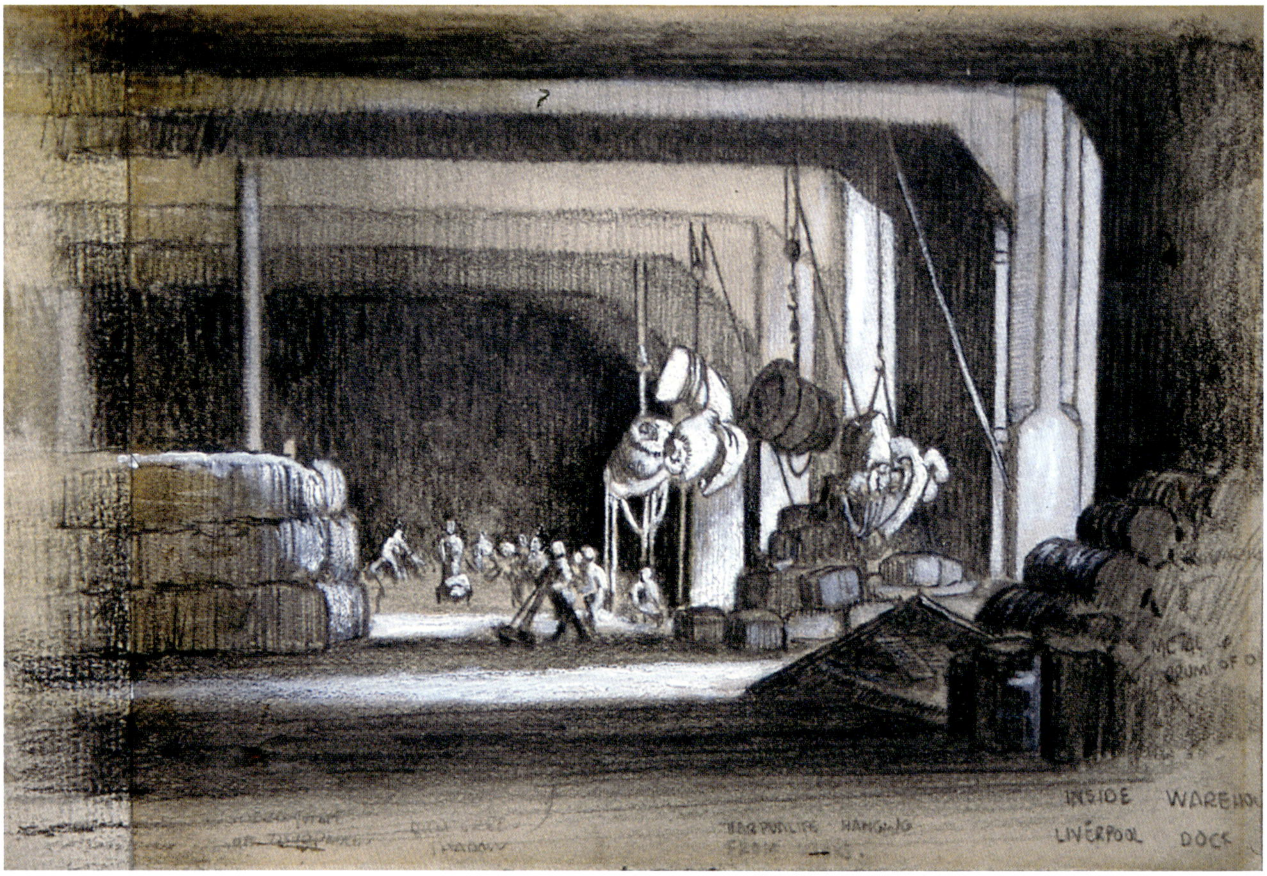

Liverpool Docks
190 x 130 mm, graphite and white gouache

since those early days: his idiosyncratic handwriting. Instead of a cursive hand he prints everything in capitals and he can do so at the same pace as any standard writing.

In about 1950 (neither is certain of the year) he met Dorothy Southern. Trevor had seen her riding her bicycle around the town but did not know where she lived and then his uncle, a local builder, met her when he went to her house to see about some work. Dorothy, he discovered, was also a would-be artist so he told his nephew, who lived only a few streets away, to go around and introduce himself. He told her he liked her work and soon they realised they had common interests which they could develop together. Her father was an engineer who, in his spare time, repaired clocks and watches and played the piano in working men's clubs. She gave up her cycling – she had been a keen cyclist for Middlesbrough, although industrial, was on the edge of the countryside and she and her friends had grown up free to go anywhere. Drawing and painting, they went walking on the North Yorkshire moors and spent the night in youth hostels. In the Cleveland Sketching Club they met Fred Lawson, the father of Sonia Lawson who in time was to become both a Royal Academician and a member of the Royal Watercolour Society. One day one of the members of the club, a topographical draughtsman called Alec Wright, invited them back to his cottage. They each recognised that as a creative artist he had his own distinctive style of living, and they saw what an art education could bring – it was a goal towards which they could both work, one which would eventually mean leaving behind the people and the town where they had been brought up. Dorothy and Trevor have been together ever since. It is curious, he once remarked to me, how some people succeed in finding their partners in life and some do not. He seemed puzzled – indeed amazed – by the role of chance in affairs.

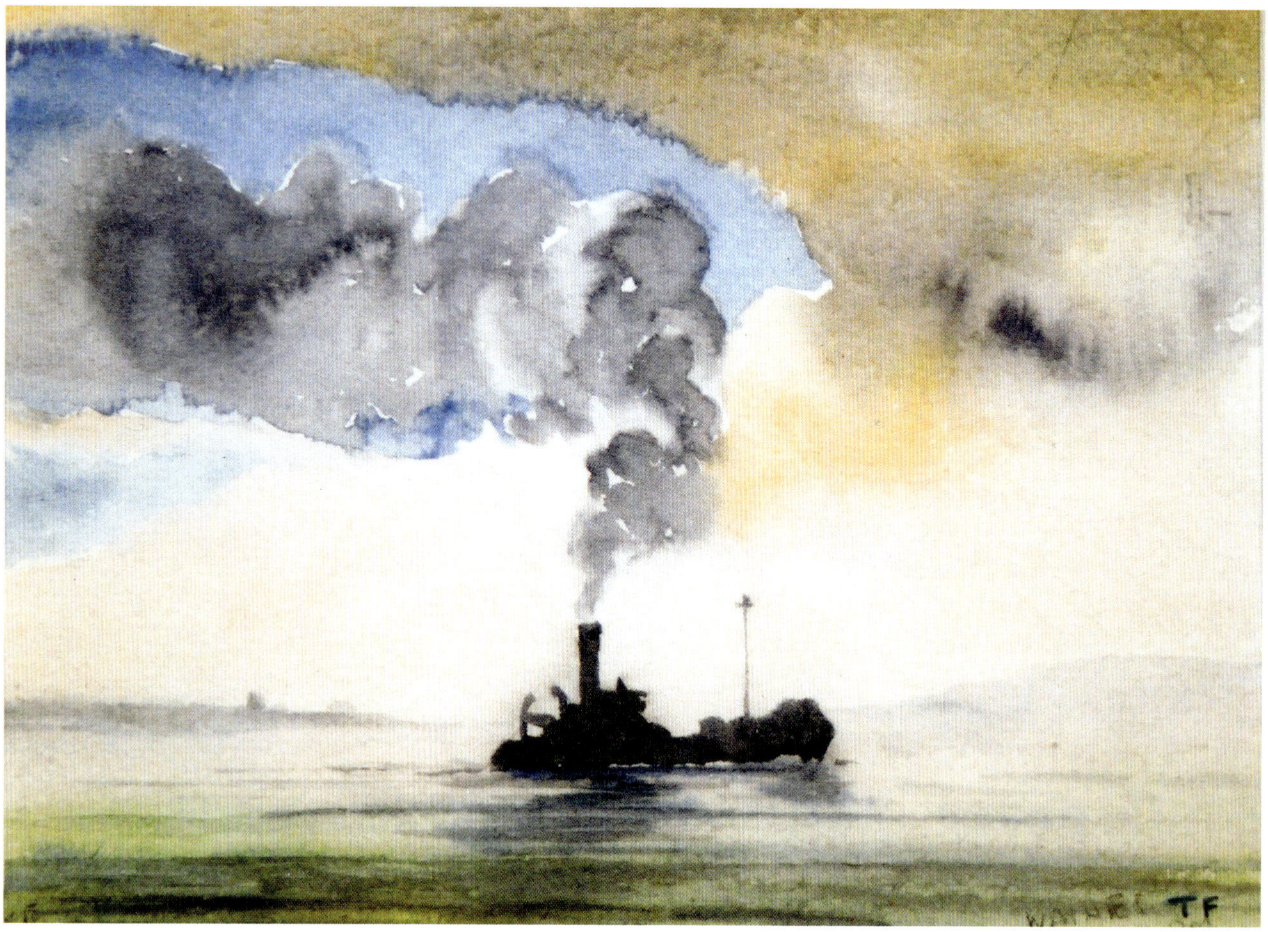

Tugboat, River Mersey
170 x 130 mm, watercolour

3

For Frankland leaving Middlesbrough meant, first of all, being called up for National Service and he joined the Royal Air Force to be trained as a pilot or a navigator. Needless to say – as with so many – this was not a career option of his own choosing but he managed to turn this enforced period of his life to his own benefit. He requested an educational posting only to be told that as this was not compatible with his training to be a pilot or navigator he would have to make a choice, and so he chose an educational posting which meant going to an auxiliary aerodrome. Here, through luck and divergent thinking, Frankland was able to attend the Laird School of Art at Birkenhead to study for the Intermediate Examination in art. He was in fact signing up for a full-time course.

At the aerodrome he was placed in air traffic control until the education officer, who had arranged for him to attend the art school, asked if he would do an audit of the camp's library. He then reorganised the whole library adding new chairs and a large powerful radio receiver recovered from the depths of a disused cupboard. However, his absence from the camp and his library activities meant that he avoided all the parades and led a number of his contemporaries to say that this was 'Frankland's Air Force'. On one occasion he and five others who never attended parades were obliged to form a guard of honour for the visiting Air Commodore. They drilled rigorously and the Commodore, having been told the circumstances, said they were the smartest group he had ever seen and gave them the rest of the day off while all the other camp members had to spend the rest of their day on the parade ground. But he was kept, fed and watered while he worked towards passing his intermediate examination and preparing himself for what really mattered: a future in art.

Towards the end of 1952 Frankland had started on the Intermediate Course at the Laird School of Art. The Principal, Harry Hoodless, had seen his work and said, 'Three days and four evenings plus outdoor drawing. You can begin next week.' Hoodless himself painted pictures of shipyards inspired by the artist Edward Wadsworth. The school gave a thorough grounding in the fundamentals and got students through their Intermediate and National Diploma in Design examinations. He found the opportunity to study exciting, utterly different and liberating after the dreariness of the draughtsman's office. Liverpool and its bookshops were another novelty and there were visits to London to see exhibitions. The emphasis on examinations meant that although original ideas were not promoted reading was encouraged. The library had very few books on the modern movement, however. When he asked for information on Picasso he was told that at this stage he did not need to know anything about him. Instead he should concentrate on the Intermediate Examination. In retrospect Frankland thinks that at the time they were probably correct. Instead he was encouraged to paint and sketch what he saw about him – the Mersey tugboats and the bombed Birkenhead docks, the ruined ironstone mines on the North Yorkshire moors, the seawall at Hartlepool, monochrome studies of industrial landscapes.

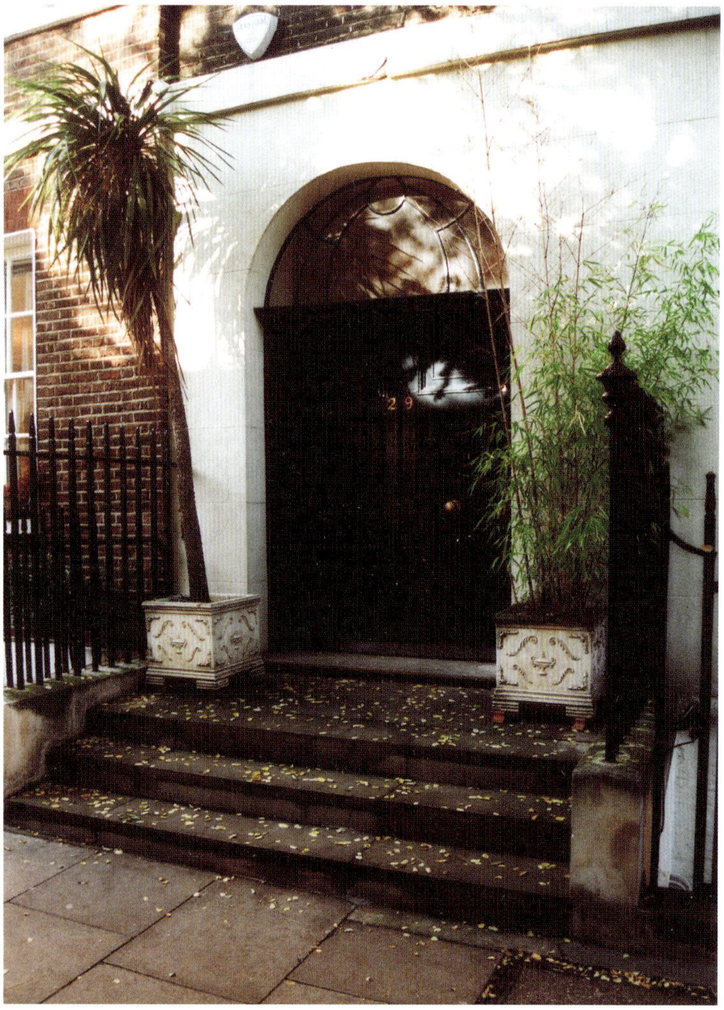

While he was still at Birkenhead, a fellow student happened to say that he had been accepted to continue his studies at the Royal Academy Schools in London. The remark changed Frankland's life. It gave him the idea that he might fulfil his childhood notion by applying himself. In 1954 he was accepted and a grant from Middlesbrough Education Committee allowed him to take up his place at the Schools without needing to finish his National Diploma beforehand (he eventually took the final exams at Camberwell School of Art instead).

Arriving in London Frankland found lodgings in Percy Street. The street runs directly westwards from the Tottenham Court Road into a part of London – stretching north from Oxford Street to the Euston Road – that had long been inhabited by an artistic community. In the mid-nineteenth century the watercolour painter John Joseph Jenkins attended the artists' school in Clipstone Street near where the Post Ofice Tower now stands. Jenkins lived with his brother, a solicitor, in Newman Street and then in Upper Charlotte Street; he was also the Secretary and, in a sense, the first archivist of the Royal Watercolour Society. But by the 1940s and 1950s the area was generally

29 Percy Street W1

known as 'Fitzrovia' after the Fitzroy Tavern which stood on the corner of Percy Street and Charlotte Street. It had a louche reputation. *The Times Literary Supplement* of January 1958 described the neighbourhood as 'a world of outsiders, down-and-outs, drunks, sensualists, homosexualists and eccentrics'. And Tambimuttu, the editor of *Poetry London,* wrote of the danger of catching 'Sohoitis' in Fitzrovia. 'If you get Sohoitis you will stay there always day and night and get no work done ever. You have been warned.'[1]

No 29 Percy Street was a large Georgian townhouse directly opposite Rowney's art shop. The house had its original York stone staircase and many other original features still in place. The leaseholder was a middle-aged woman called Eileen Davies, a former commercial artist with a love of the arts. She was married to a stockbroker but her interests bored him and their marriage was not a success. However she enjoyed the company of young people and so, instead of her husband, she often took Trevor to the theatre. He remembers going with her to Ninette de Valois's ballet *Checkmate* and its striking black-and-white sets designed by Picasso made a deep impression on him.

One day while looking around the extensive basement of the house where he kept his bicycle Frankland heard the sound of rustling paper; he called out to ask if anyone was there. His call was returned and in the darkness he discovered a bearded man living like a mole in an unlit room piled high with rubbish and old papers in a state of utter squalor. When he asked his landlady about this improbable encounter with the stranger she told him the man was a chemist who had kept a shop on a corner of Charlotte Street until it was hit by a bomb during the war. She had been an air-raid patrol warden and the chemist had saved her life. However his mind had been damaged by the bombing – a post-traumatic stress disorder – and now he was incapable of perceiving the state in which he lived. Out of gratitude Mrs Davies provided the chemist with somewhere to live – but she sent in professional cleaners once a month to clean his room.

She was less well-disposed to another of her tenants, Nina, a kennel-maid, when she discovered that she had placed an advertisement in a local shop window offering 'personal services' at the Percy Street address. Eileen Davies employed kennel maids for her business, breeding toy poodles. She had a client list of rich and famous people whom Trevor sometimes encountered in the entrance hall. The litters of puppies were kept in spare rooms where inevitably they fouled the furniture (the fact that this annoyed her husband was a matter of indifference, or perhaps even satisfaction, to her).

1 Quotations from Stephen Inwood, *Historic London, An Explorer's Companion,* Macmillan 2008 page 228

As well as visits to the theatre, Frankland's landlady also took him to see Alice Bomberg, the artist David Bomberg's first wife, in her first-floor flat off Charlotte Street. Mrs Bomberg showed him a large number of drawings which in 1917 her husband had been commissioned to make for the Canadian War Memorial Fund. She asked him what they might be worth (he advised her to ask a dealer). When he left she gave him Bomberg's coffee pot and the walking stick studded with metal badges which the artist had taken with him to Jerusalem in the 1920s. To his lasting regret Frankland forgot to collect them when he left Percy Street and moved elsewhere.

He lived in Percy Street for two years. (When he left Mrs Davies gave him a Japanese print from his room; it now hangs opposite his studio door.) The house was within easy walking distance of the Royal Academy Schools and the attractions of central London. He felt that he had arrived in a world he had hitherto known only from books: Bohemia.

The Royal Academy with its library and galleries and its aura of history and tradition also came as a revelation. Contemporaries included John Hoyland, Brian Kneale, John Copnall, Paul Huxley, Brian Organ and Eric Hebborn. Anthony Caro had left the previous year. Some students such as John Hoyland showed a predilection for American abstract expressionists, whereas Frankland's inclination – for the time-being at least – was for European art. After a compulsory first term in the drawing school where students drew from life, they were expected to get on with what they had already learnt in their previous training. The policy of the School was to give the help of appropriate teachers to students of every inclination, whether abstract or figurative. Teaching at the Academy generally consisted of leaving the students alone, offering specific advice only if called upon to do so, and concentrating instead on methods and materials and giving general advice.

Teachers – Visitors as they were called – included the portrait painter Bernard Fleetwood-Walker, a stout man who invariably wore a big spotted bow-tie. He made interesting comments, and always looked at students' palettes. Warm colours must not be combined with cool, he said, and if the palette was dirty and ill-mixed he did not even bother to look at the pictures, commenting that the palette indicated the state of the painting.

Peter Greenham was another portrait painter. He lectured on the history of pigments and gave practical demonstrations, such as how sunlight affected the mixture of rose madder with white oil paint;

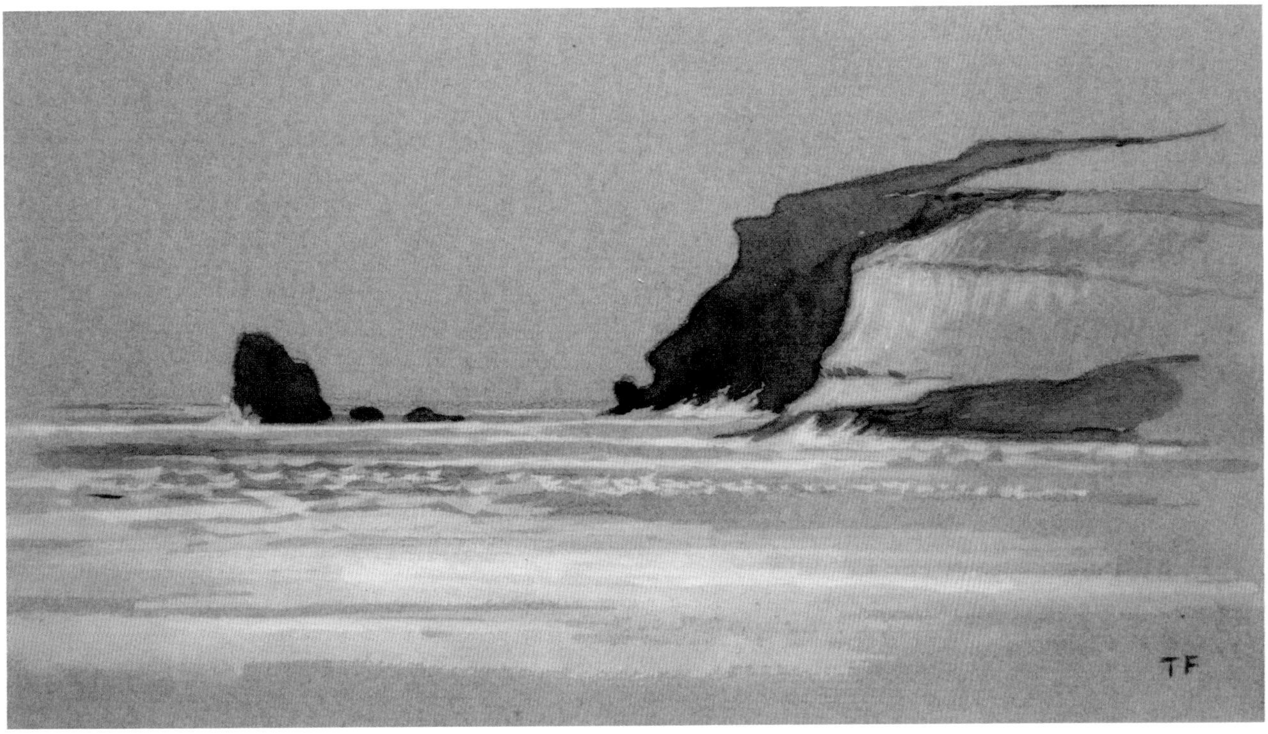

North East Coast
190 x 110 mm, watercolour and gouache on toned paper

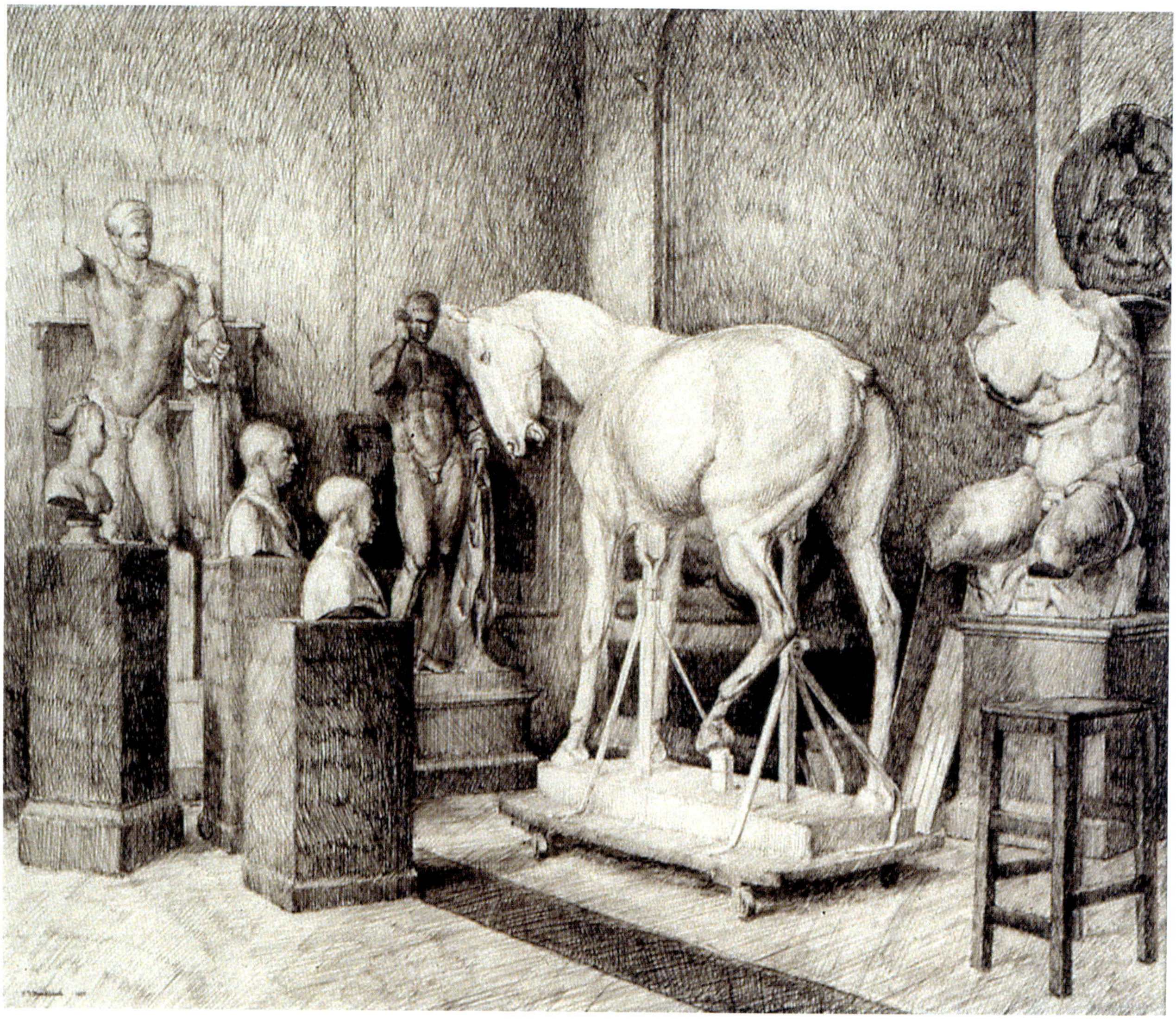

The Antique Room, Royal Academy Schools
560 x 480 mm, pen and sepia ink

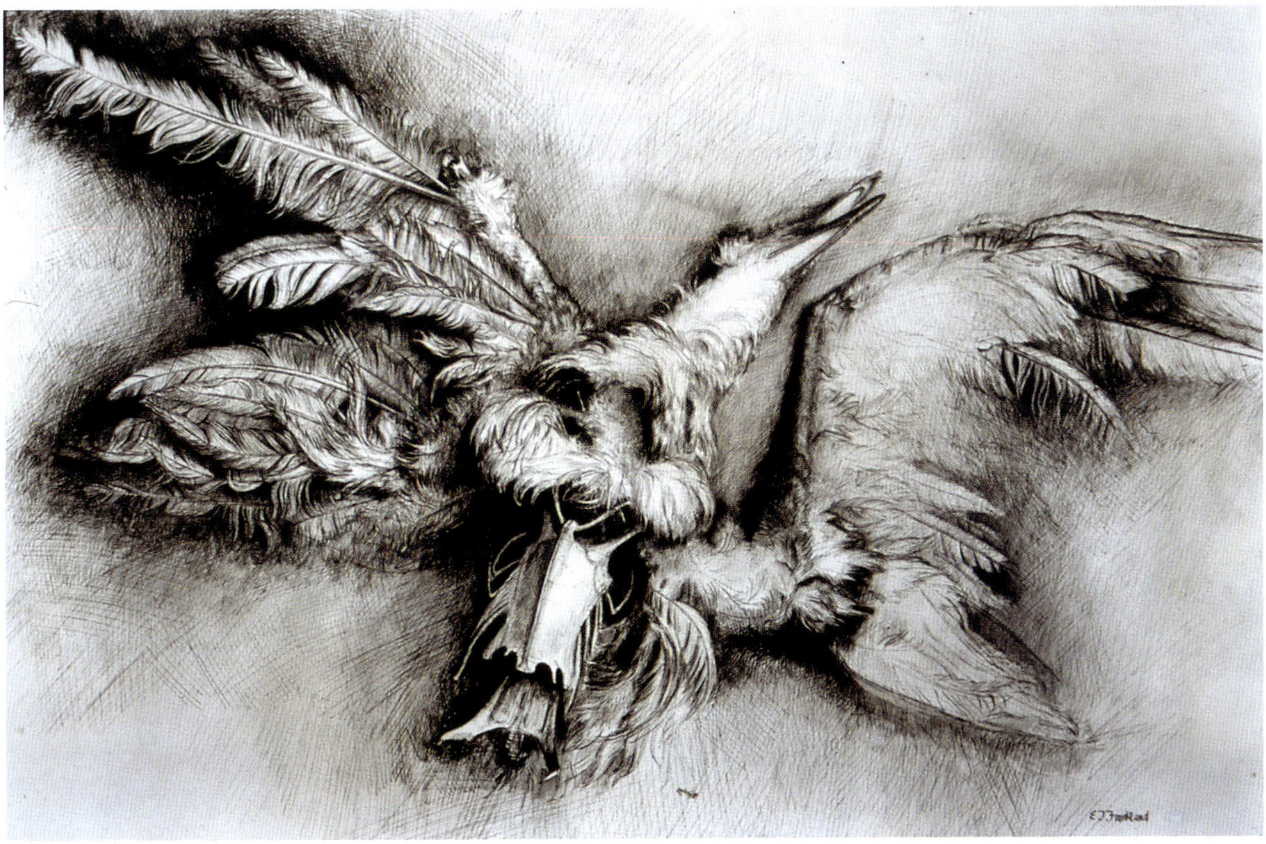

Drawing of Dead Seagull
750 x 520 mm, pen and sepia ink
Purchased by the Royal Academy (Annie Hugill Fund)

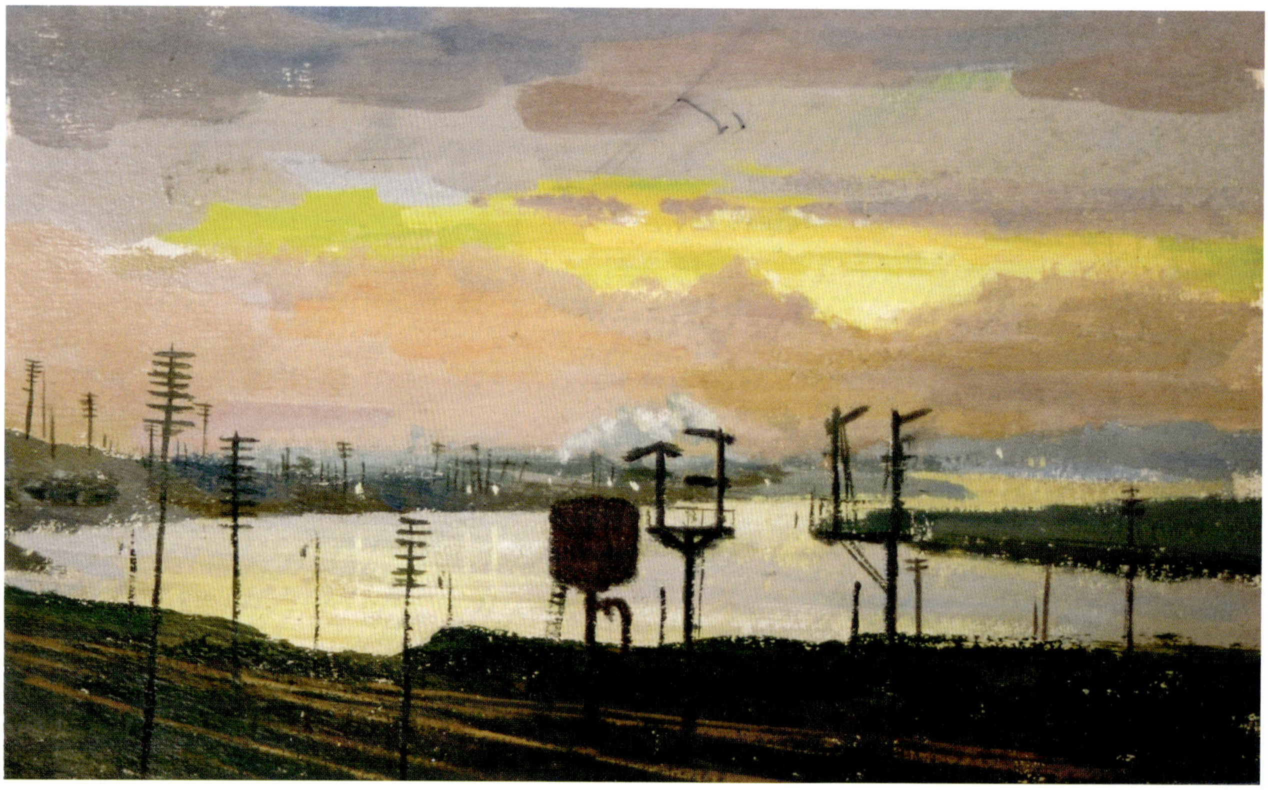

River Tees, Evening
170 x 110 mm, gouache

although creating wonderful pinks they soon turned to grey. He also emphasised the importance of cleaning brushes after use. In later years Peter Greenham's recipe for sepia ink made from oak galls was used by Eric Hebborn in his forgeries. In his autobiography *Drawn to Trouble, the Forging of an Artist,* Hebborn remembered Greenham as an avuncular figure, the visiting Academician students saw most frequently. He always wore a rather crumpled grey suit and was seldom seen without a cigarette dangling from his bottom lip which left a trail of ash in constant descent as he toured the studios. Although a portrait painter, Greenham never tried to impress a client by looking like a business man. He told Hebborn 'that one could tell an artist whose work had deteriorated by the smart clothes he would be wearing. If true, it was clear from his old grey suit of crease and crumple, ash and splash that his own talent was yet intact'. To Frankland his manner seemed at times apologetic. If he made critical comments about a piece of work he would often make a drawing to make clear what he had said (Frankland still has a pen and ink drawing from that time). Greenham once invited Trevor and Dorothy round to dinner and served the meal on a distinctive 'tablecloth' which consisted of layers of impacted newspapers piled up on top of one another.

The Keeper of the Academy and the Head of the Schools was Sir Henry Rushbury, a topographical painter and etcher. An immensely kind man, short, white-haired and ruddy-faced, Rushbury was always ready to encourage and help find work for students – like Frankland – who were hard-up and needed every penny they could earn in order to stretch out their grants and allowances as far as possible.

The architect and historian Sir Albert Richardson was also President of the Royal Academy. He was knighted in January 1956 and was now in his seventies. His lectures on architecture were vigorous and delivered without notes but with the aid of hand-drawn slides and a long pole. His great love was the architecture of the Italian Renaissance, and he taught the all but lost art of sciagraphy which demonstrates how shadows are cast and the way cornices overhang to produce shade in strong sunlight (an effect rather wasted in northern climates). His lectures were given in the lecture room within the architecture school. The walls of the room were covered with dust-laden casts from the antique which created an atmosphere of mystery. The school itself was closed and only the few painting students who had moved in and the lectures brought life into the space.

Professor Richardson had his own particular style of presenting a lecture and when he wanted the projectionist to change the large hand-drawn glass slides he had made to provide illustrations he used

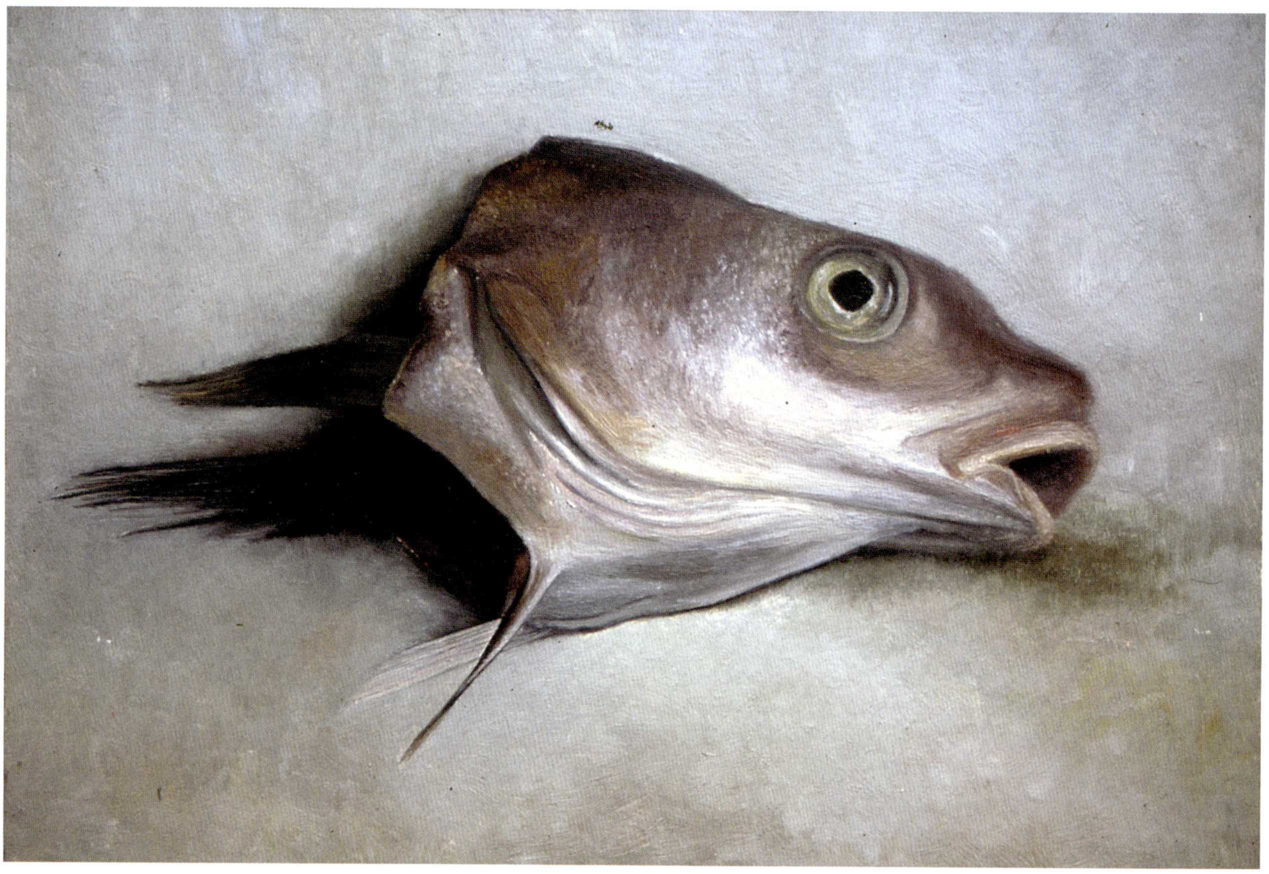

Fish Head
340 x 245 mm, oil on plywood panel

to bang the floor rapidly with a pole twice in succession. He frequently delivered his lectures wearing eighteenth-century period costume, acting the part of an English Georgian gentleman of fashion. This habit was not confined to the lecture room. His own large Georgian house at Ampthill was filled with a collection of period paintings, sculpture and furniture as vast as it was extraordinary. The house was lit with candles and oil lamps as he abhorred electric lighting which he considered removed all the mystery and romance that traditional lighting could create. The telephone was an invasion of modernity into the era he was trying to create so it was banished to his office.

One of Richardson's first acts as President was to revive for one year only the tradition of presenting each probationer (first year student) with a large ivory disc engraved with his or her name and the year of admittance. This originally granted the students free entry to the Royal Academy exhibitions, but had, in recent times, been discontinued in favour of a card. The presentation was followed by a grand dinner which was also paid for out of Richardson's own pocket.

During his years at the Royal Academy Schools, from 1954 to 1958, Frankland won many awards and prizes including several David Murray Studentships, a Landseer Scholarship and a Landseer Prize for a drawing from the antique (a large sketch showing a corner of the studio with a plaster horse, busts and torsos), as well as prizes from the Duff Greet Fund. His drawing of a dead seabird, its feathered wings pinioned and out-spread, won him the Royal Academy Silver Medal for Drawing and was purchased by the Royal Academy at the 1957 Summer Exhibition under the terms of the Annie Hugill Fund. Frankland's sketch of a fish head dates from this time. The studio at times stank of the carcasses of dead animals which the students sometimes painted. Finally, a £200 grant from the Leverhulme Fund paid in quarterly instalments enabled Frankland to stay at the Schools for a fifth year and study printmaking. He recalls how – in less safety-conscious times – he used to breathe in the noxious brown fumes created when etching zinc plates with nitric acid. The exposure affected the thin membranes of his nose and caused nose bleeds.

In 1957 while still students Dorothy and Trevor had a modest wedding in Middlesbrough Registry Office. Dorothy had stayed at Middlesbrough School of Art to complete her studies for the National Diploma in Art and Design, while he continued his studies at the Royal Academy Schools. (Trevor's brother Allan also studied at Middlesbrough School of Art and eventually became Head of the Art and Design Department in a large comprehensive school near Newcastle upon Tyne) Once she had received her teaching diploma she was able to join

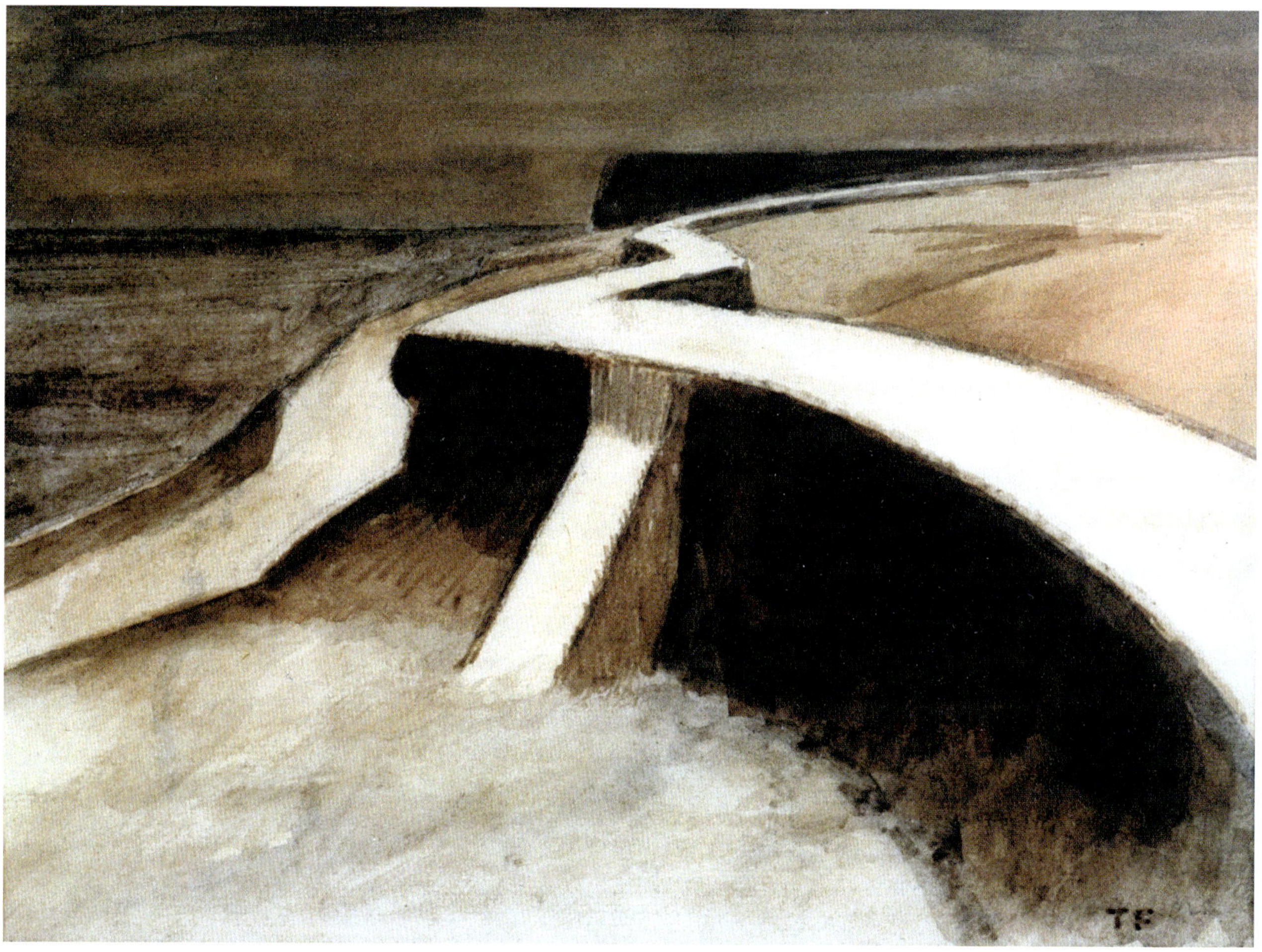

Hartlepool Breakwater
230 x 180 mm, watercolour

Trevor in London, taking a job in a girls' school; it later became a mixed comprehensive where Dorothy was head of the art department. For four years they lived in a one-room flat overlooking Wandsworth Common with a little kitchen which Frankland built for them in one corner.

Having completed his post-graduate studies Trevor was hoping to obtain a position as a part-time lecturer at an art school within the London area. In *The Times Educational Supplement* he saw an advertisement for such a post at Medway College of Arts at Eastgate in Rochester: 'applications are [also] invited for Part-time TEACHERS in DRAWING, GRAPHIC DESIGN & TYPOGRAPHIC DESIGN with A.R.C.A., A.T.C. or N.D.D. qualifications'. He was subsequently appointed to teach drawing and composition. Although Frankland enjoyed the discipline of teaching – imparting knowledge and getting the best out of students – throughout his career he has believed in the importance of staying away from a full-time job. Always anxious for money, he was now paid £20 a day, a heady increase on his past job; he was still grateful for the extra work the Principal Stanley Hayes found for him such as the £200 he received for drawing parts of industrial machines.

To make ends meet he took whatever work was available to help them survive, even if this meant painting a sign for a hot-potato bar. He did some book illustration for the publishers Chatto and Windus and A & C Black. On Fridays and Saturday mornings he worked with the picture restorers Freeman & Son of Albemarle Street who had a Royal warrant. There he was taught how to make minor repairs and remove damage by 'spotting' – the filling in of small points on a canvas where flakes had come off. He also made a visit to Windsor Castle with Clifford Freeman to help surface clean two large pictures *in situ*. However, when Frankland complained about being paid only thirty shillings for a day and a half's work he was told 'you're learning a craft.' Shortly afterwards he left them. Meanwhile there was London life to be lived fully. On free days and in the evenings there were exhibitions to attend and plays to see. Dorothy had a friend who was able to provide cheap tickets and they often went to see plays by Samuel Beckett and others at the Royal Court Theatre.

In 1964 they found a semi-detached Victorian house off St John's Hill in Battersea which they liked. The owner – a greengrocer with a tame field-mouse – took a liking to the couple and was happy to sell to them. Having seen the house on the Monday, Dorothy came home from work on the following Monday to find that Trevor had opened a book like a pitched roof on top of another flat book placed on the kitchen table: he had had news that they had been accepted for a mortgage. They could now afford to buy a place of their own.

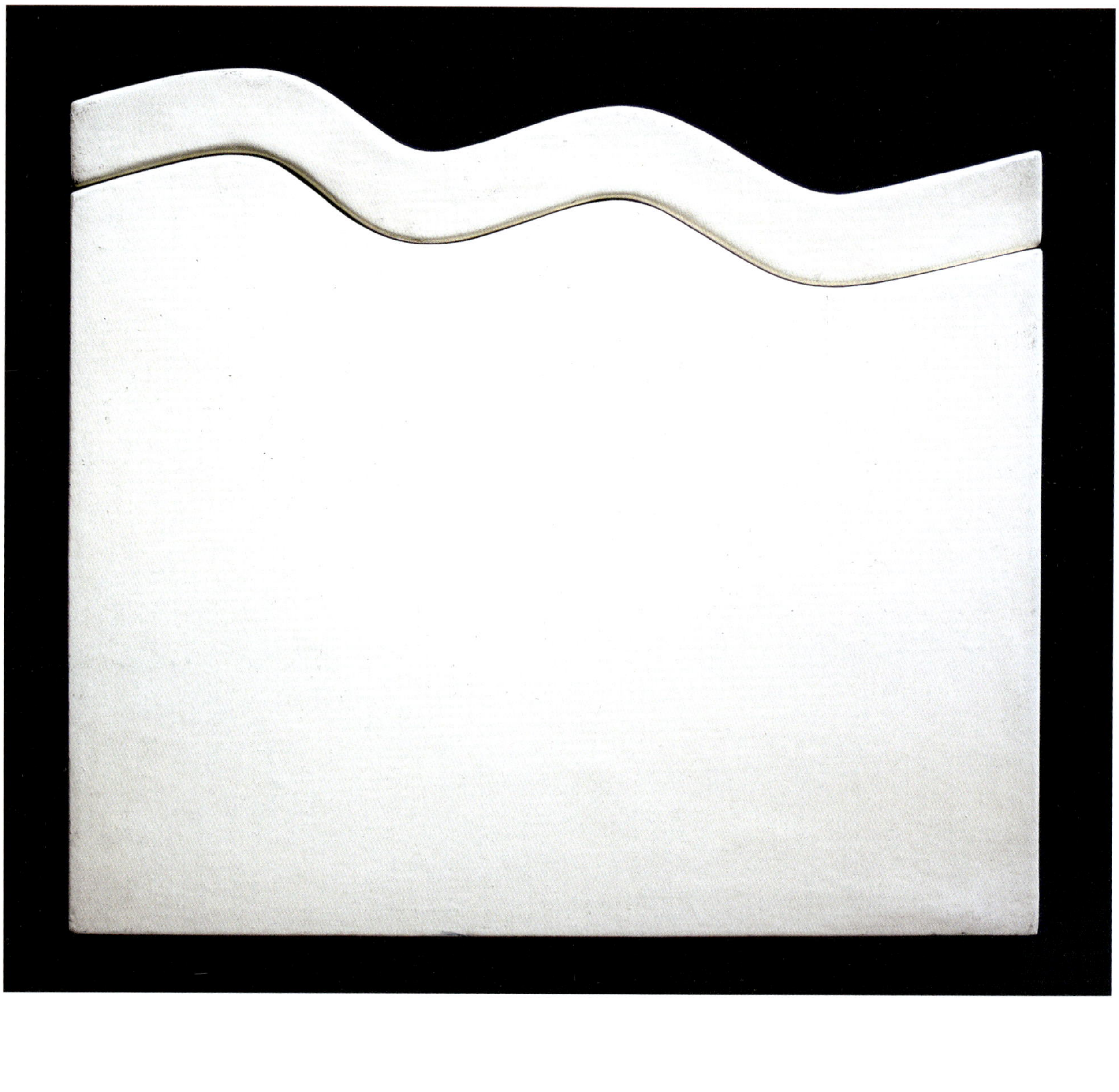

Beach
290 x 260 mm, 3D painted chipboard

4

In the wake of the Coldstream Report setting up a new system of art and design studies, Ian Simpson, one of Frankland's colleagues, moved from Medway College to Hornsey College of Art in London to be head of Visual Research Studies. Simpson in turn employed people he already knew and trusted, including Trevor Frankland. According to the 1965/1966 College prospectus, the aim of the Hornsey course was to enable the student 'to acquire a visual vocabulary and the analytical mind to make use of it.' The training was common to all students following the diploma courses and, as students with different specialist subjects were grouped together, it was supposed to provide an opportunity for the exchange of ideas and experiences. 'The course is based on a progressive and systematic study of visual appearances,' the prospectus continues. 'It presents for examination elements of the visual world, and this is done by providing, in the main, a constantly changing series of physical situations which are closely studied and analysed. These constantly changing situations, and the appearance of objects in unusual environments, help towards ending "habitual" seeing, and the breakdown of visual perceptions.'

The end result of this theory was the expansion of creative thinking in the applied arts. Frankland taught for two and later three days a week and as student numbers increased an extra tutor was appointed to the group. The purpose of Frankland's teaching was to encourage divergent thinking through projects which involved three as well as two-dimensional work. The ideas activated by Visual Research Studies were eventually to bring about a profound change in his own work but his time at Hornsey College was to become famous – or infamous – for its student sit-in which led to its closure for six months.

The College, which was founded in 1880, was situated just below Highgate, on the leafy top of Crouch End Hill, among prosperous and leafy Victorian houses 'like a last outpost of necessity' and had a number of annexes spread over north London. 1968 was a year of student revolt all over the world – political action was in the air. At Hornsey events began with a row over the control of Student Union funds which had been frozen by the Bursar. Encouraged by staff within the warren of offices of the General Studies Department where there were many foreign students, this developed into major political activity. A Students Action Committee (S.A.C.) was set up and on 28 May 1968 took over the building and over the course of six weeks filled with radical spirit they held their meetings in 'a fug of Gauloises and

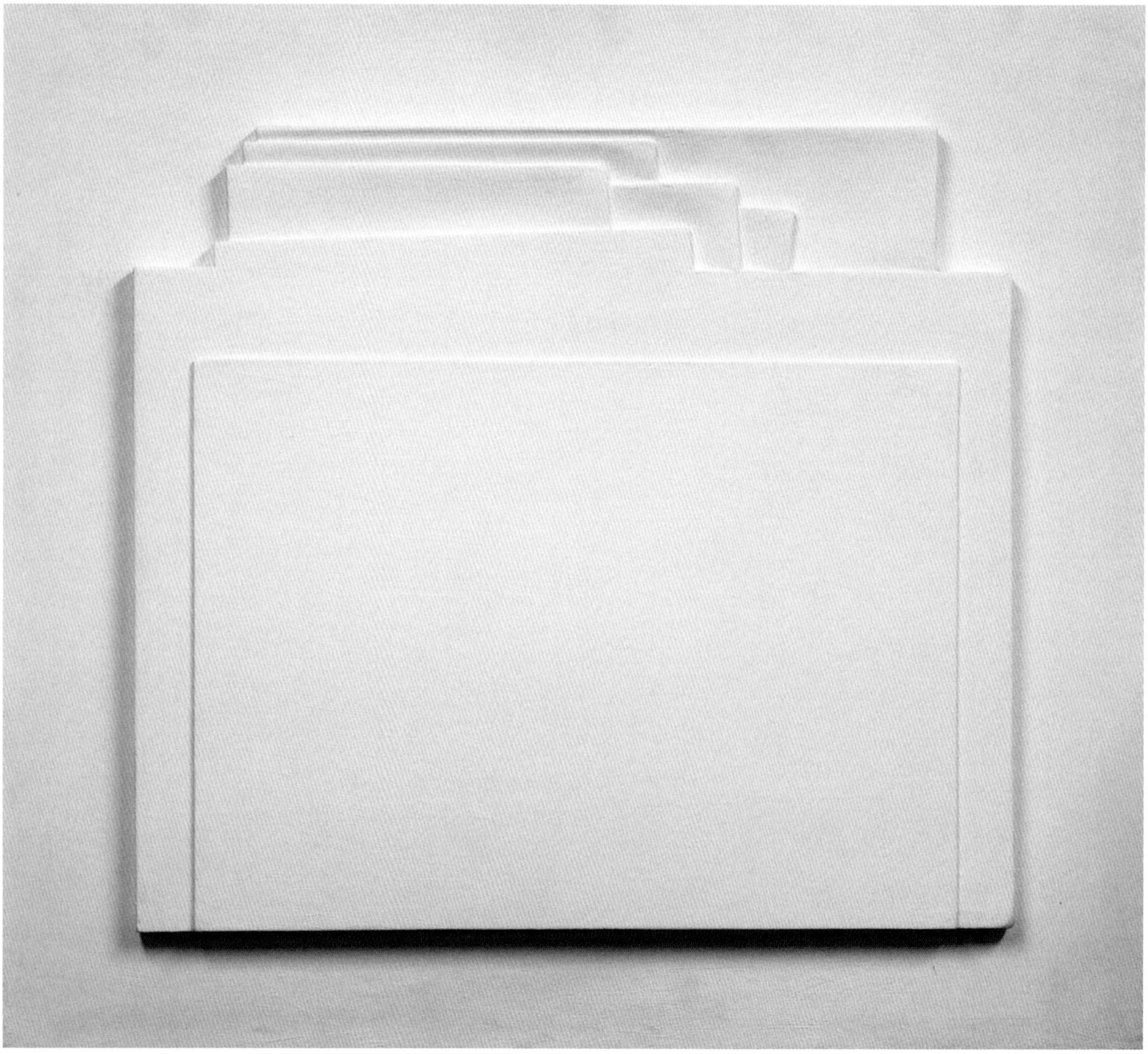

Coast
670 x 620 x 70 mm, painted wood construction

blasphemy'. The Committee also produced a number of documents on a Gestetner duplicator as well as revolutionary posters, a number of which Frankland preserved. The Principal of Hornsey College was Harold Shelton. The S.A.C. produced a poster portraying him as a rapacious capitalist monster. Frankland says that he always thought him a reasonable man to work with; he found money for projects and looked after staff members.

One of the sheets from the documents Frankland saved proclaims:

> Shelton must resign now. During the sit-in it was felt that this man was of no significance and was best ignored. Now, however, the situation has changed. Because of the actions of a few unprincipled men, led by Shelton, the participation and reforms offered to the staff and students have been rendered meaningless. Selective victimisation of both staff and students, in the most shabby and disgraceful manner, has taken place. Once again administrative lies are being passed off as answers. Perhaps the saddest thing of all is the way in which a small number of selfish, egoistic men have been allowed to behave in a savage and repressive manner, exhibiting a flagrant disregard for morality and the basics of human dignity. Shelton and the rest of his gang of administrative hooligans must go.

The same paper adds a quotation from Herbert Marcuse:

> The total mobilisation of Society against the ultimate liberation of the individual, which constitutes the historical content of the present period, indicates how real is the possibility of this liberation.

Inevitably such lofty aspirations and the many aims and demands of the sit-in went unrealised. Term ended, Shelton barricaded the building with bars, the sit-in was quashed and on Monday night 8 July everyone left the Main College. When Hornsey re-opened to students six weeks late on 4 November, 'Normality returned with a heavy stench of carbolic acid,' as one of the staff later wrote. The corridors were blank, and scrubbed, and all the posters and notices had been torn down and consigned to dustbins. Several students were excluded. The offices of the General Studies Department had been turned into a caretaker's flat, and most of its part-time staff were dismissed and the remainder consigned to a distant annexe. However, Lord Longford later remarked in a report 'that in certain ways Hornsey College of

Art was run worse than any whelk-stall he knew of.' Many of the intentions of the Coldstream plans were thwarted and Shelton's own ambitions to become Head of the Royal College of Art were dashed. As Lisa Tickner has written recently on the fortieth anniversary of the sit-in, it was like any historical event 'a different experience for different people.... There were those who were for or against the arguments, or for the arguments but against the methods. There were those caught up in the excitement of "a real, lasting, valuable, indelible, active, transforming, future-orientated, inspiring adult education", and those who thought it was "revolt for revolt's sake", those who lent conditional support, and those who waited it out at home.'

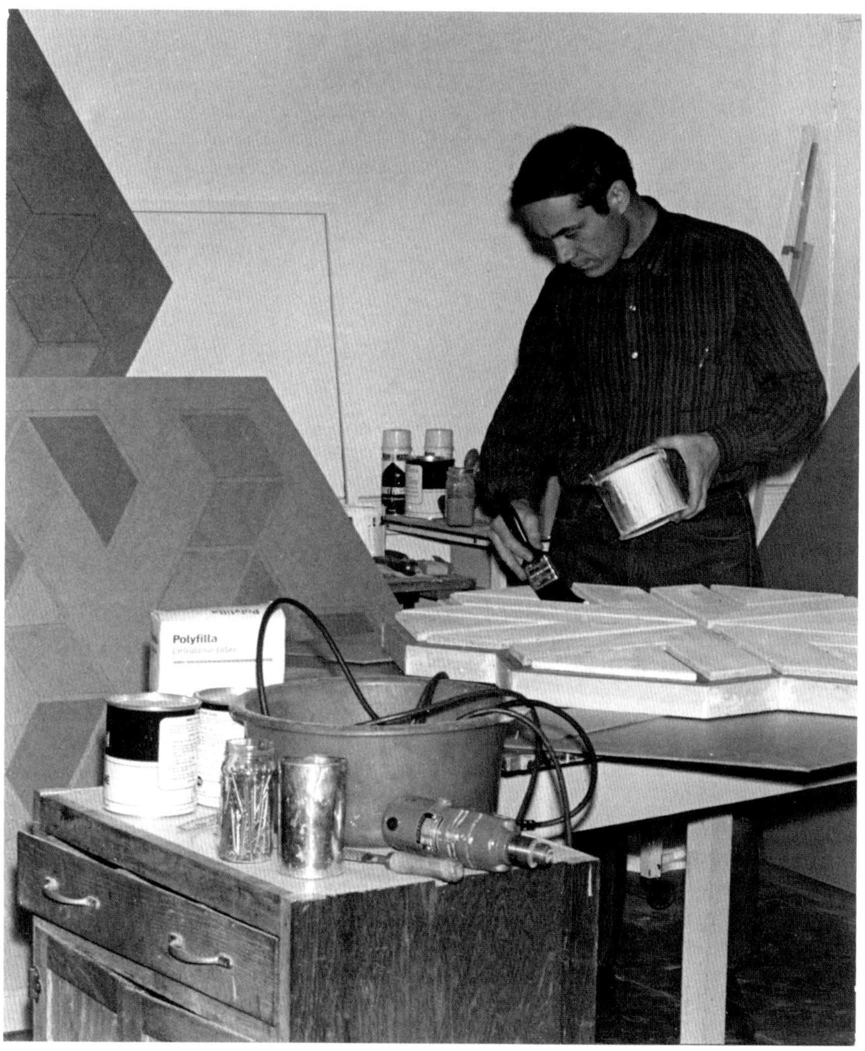

Making a 3D relief structure

5

Frankland had not sympathised with the students' demands. Ironically, however, he found the six months of protest very liberating, presenting him with a kind of unexpected sabbatical. Part-time staff were obliged only to sign in for a day's work, then they could go home and spend the rest of the day as they wished. Frankland spent this leave on his own creative work in his studio.

The college library had a number of books the staff had been asked to read for background information and it was the intellectual and theoretical, rather than political, *zeitgeist* which captured his imagination. Among the books he read was James Gibson's *The Perception of the Visual World*. It was to provide a significant stimulus for changes in the development of his work, turning away from the realistic and representational into the abstract and conceptual. Gibson's book dealt with the visual field and the visual world which he regarded as an amalgam of what we know and what we *think* we see. Frankland began to find such ideas intoxicating. American painting had hit London in the fifties and continued to influence many artists well into the future. Another writer had pointed out how at Hans Hofmann's School in New York there were two distinct opposing groups. One faction blended Hofmann's teachings with Wassily Kandinsky's doctrines of transcendent symbol and spontaneous expression. They were the 'romantic Hoffmanites'. The other group achieved a reputation of being a 'clique of geometers'. They regarded Mondrian as their mentor and saw his straight lines and hard edges as the true way forward. Frankland instinctively aligned himself with the latter. He was also encouraged by reading a book on *The Poetics of Music* by Igor Stravinsky: 'The more constraints one imposes, the more one frees oneself of the chains that shackle the spirit'. Although some artists saw the whole approach of optical or 'systems' art, linked with geometrical construction, as too limiting, Frankland decided that if he had to choose between the followers of Dionysius or Apollo, then he was decidedly an Apollonian – rational rather than instinctive – in spirit.

His work developed rapidly and he began a series of large three-dimensional biscuit-shaped structures made from wood and hardboard which were then covered in five layers of polyeurathane finish. The gloss of these new works made them look as if they had been manufactured from ceramic. In 1969, encouraged by Dorothy, he struggled to the College with one of these large constructions onto the Underground across London for a viewing organised by Harold Shel-

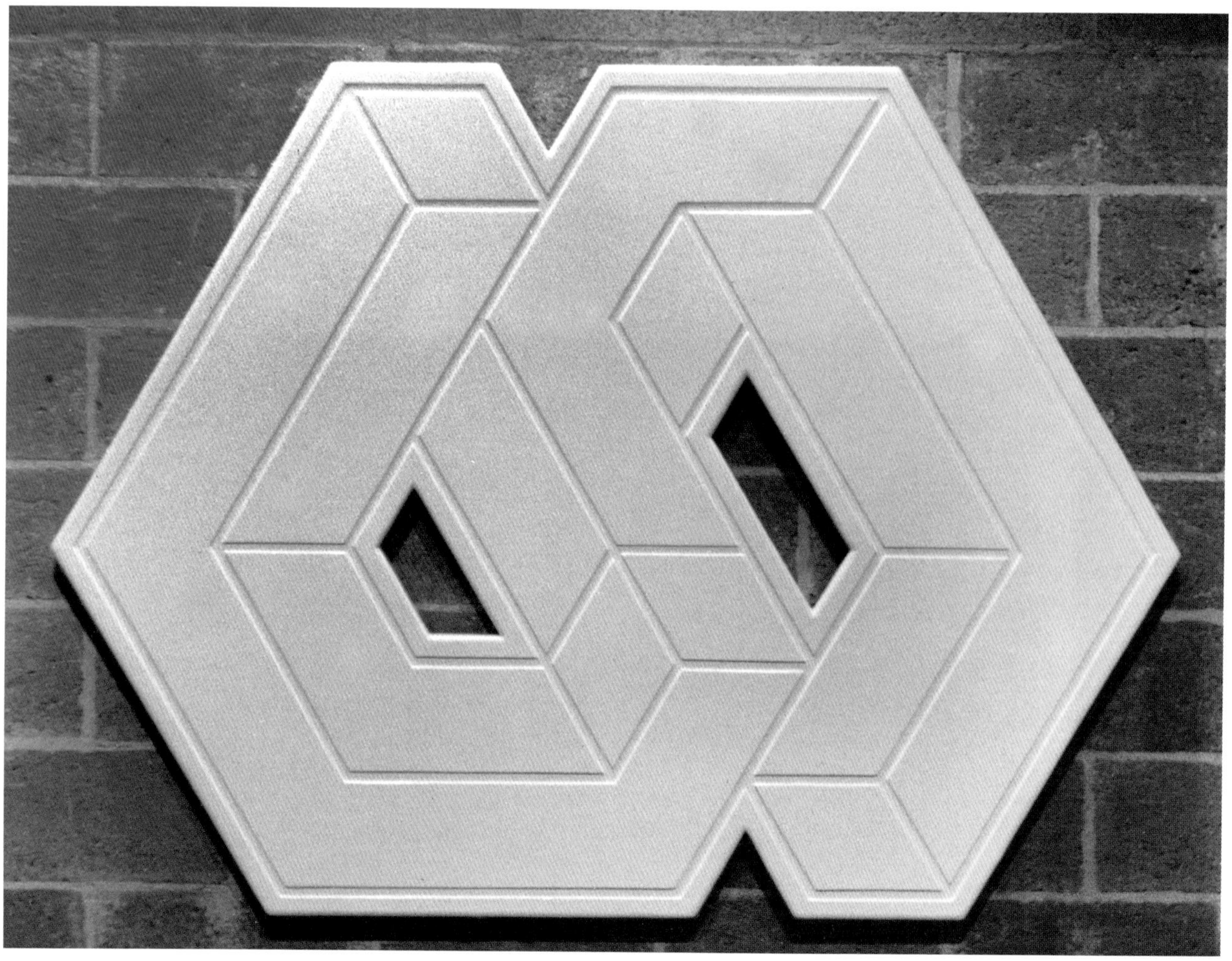

Sway Through
1600 x 1220 mm, painted wood and hardboard relief

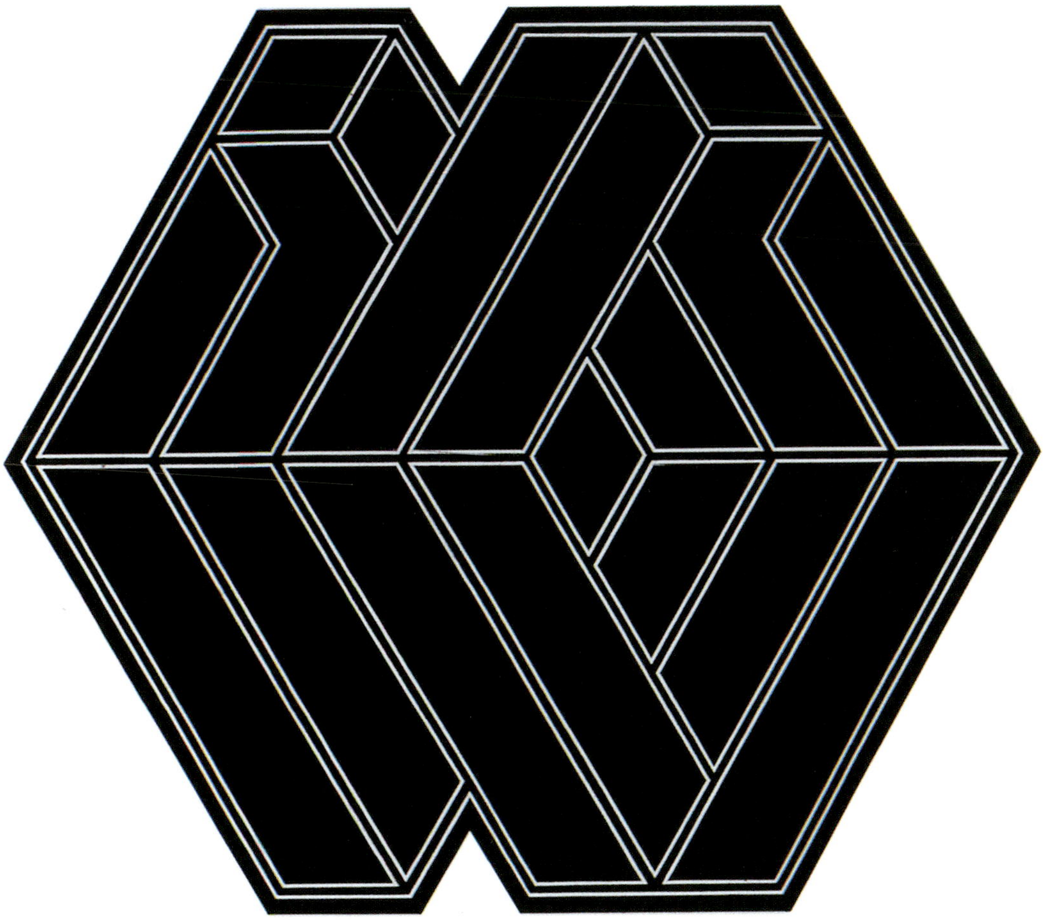

Janus 2
1320 x 1220 mm, painted 3D structure

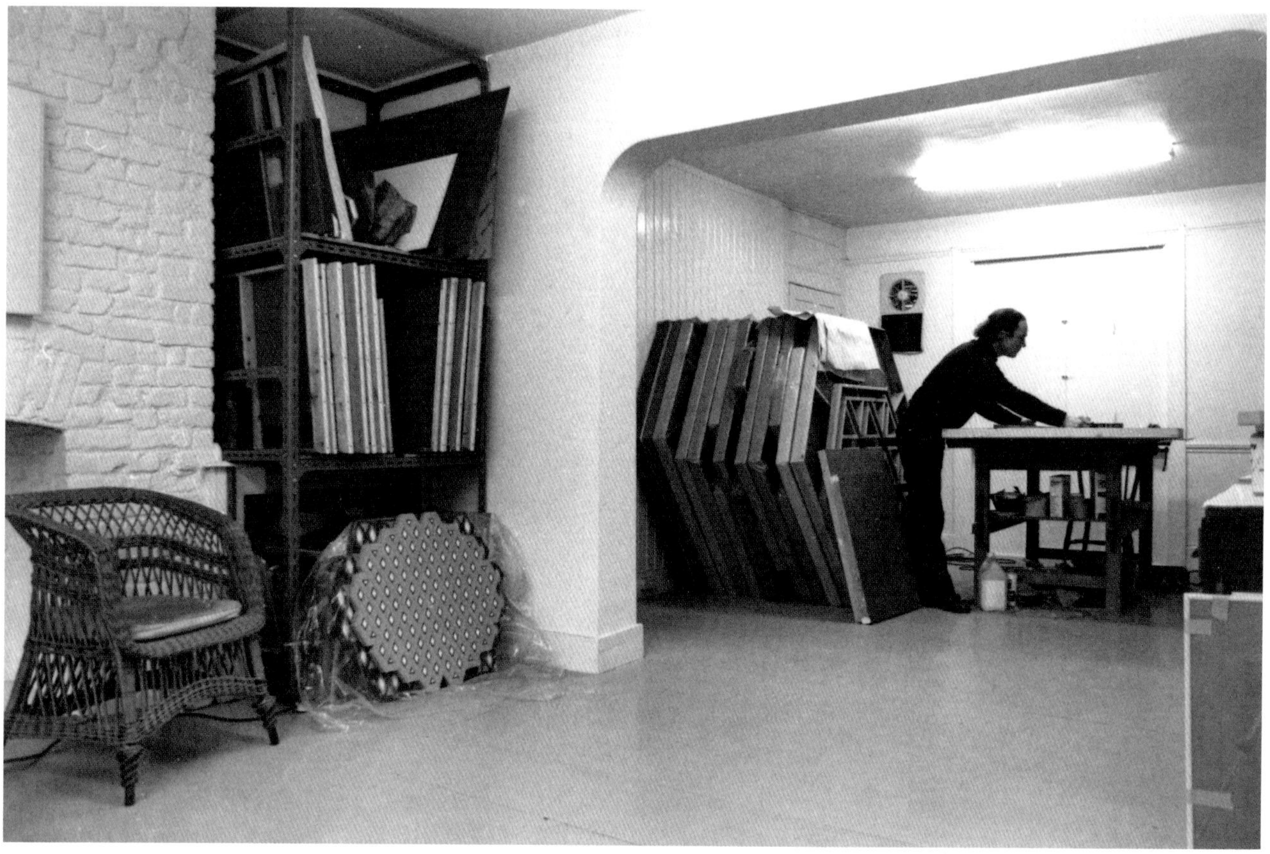

Studio Conversion 4.6 x 9.85 metres
(32 x 15 feet)

ton which involved a number of staff members. To Frankland's great surprise and pleasure the piece was bought by Rank Xerox for 100 guineas – his first sale of a new work. The structure, entitled *Euryalus* because it echoed the illusory design of a supposedly impregnable castle in Sicily of that name, built on principles of Archimedes. It was to hang on the walls of the Rank Xerox executive dining room.

In May the following year Geoff Watson, the Head of Teesside Galleries, Museums and Recreational Facilities, who had seen Frankland's work on one of his buying trips to London, arranged for him to have his first one-man exhibition opened at Billingham Art Gallery. Transport, catalogue and the reception were all paid for by the gallery. Some fifty paintings, reliefs and drawings were shown and the exhibition was enthusiastically reviewed – the local papers taking pride in a local boy who had made good in London and come home. W.E. Johnson's Art Notes in *The Northern Echo* of May 29 1970 bore the subheading 'Frankland's 15 years of growing up':

> It is, as he just reminded me in a letter from his London home, some 15 years since I first became excited by the work of Middlesbrough-born Trevor Frankland. He was then a student at the Royal Academy Schools, having graduated from being a draughtsman at Smith's Dock, South Bank, and the Laird School of Art, Birkenhead. He was showing work in the old Municipal Art Gallery in an upper room on the site where the police headquarters now stand in Dunning Street. Then as his alma mater suggests, he was much interested in the more academic aspects of art. Now, as visiting lecturer at Hornsey – and from evidence of the work on view at Billingham Art Gallery until June 13 – he has joined, as it were, the enemy camp. Perhaps the link between the two modes and manners is to be found in some of the analytical drawings he did, in the years in between, of the underside of a bird's wing. Now, as then, he is still interested in structure. For the present exhibition, impeccably presented in predominantly black and white, he presents large, six sided 'individual place mats' covered in what appear at first sight as flat geometric open patterns.

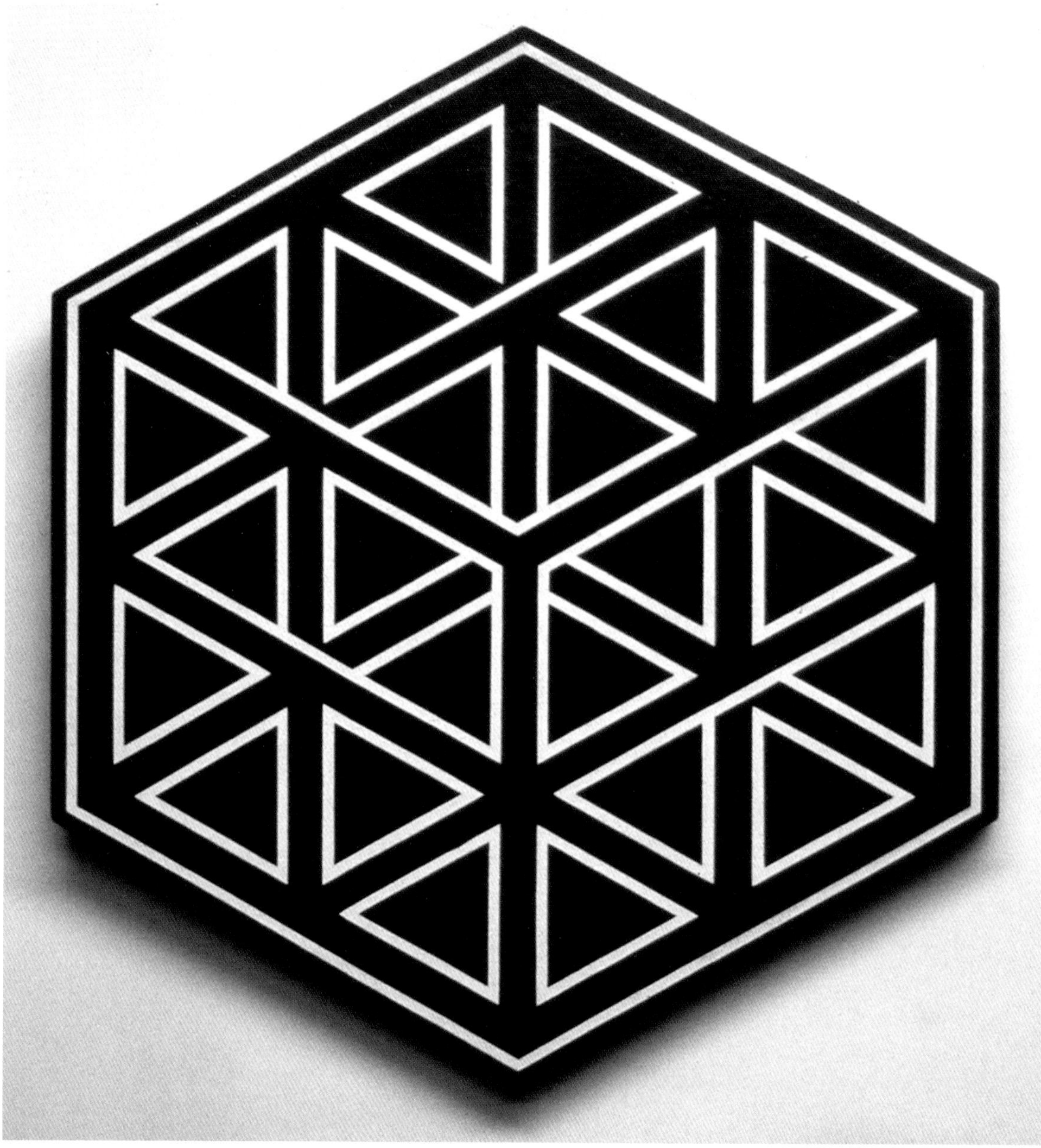

Euryalus no 2
1220 x 1320 mm, painted 3D wood relief

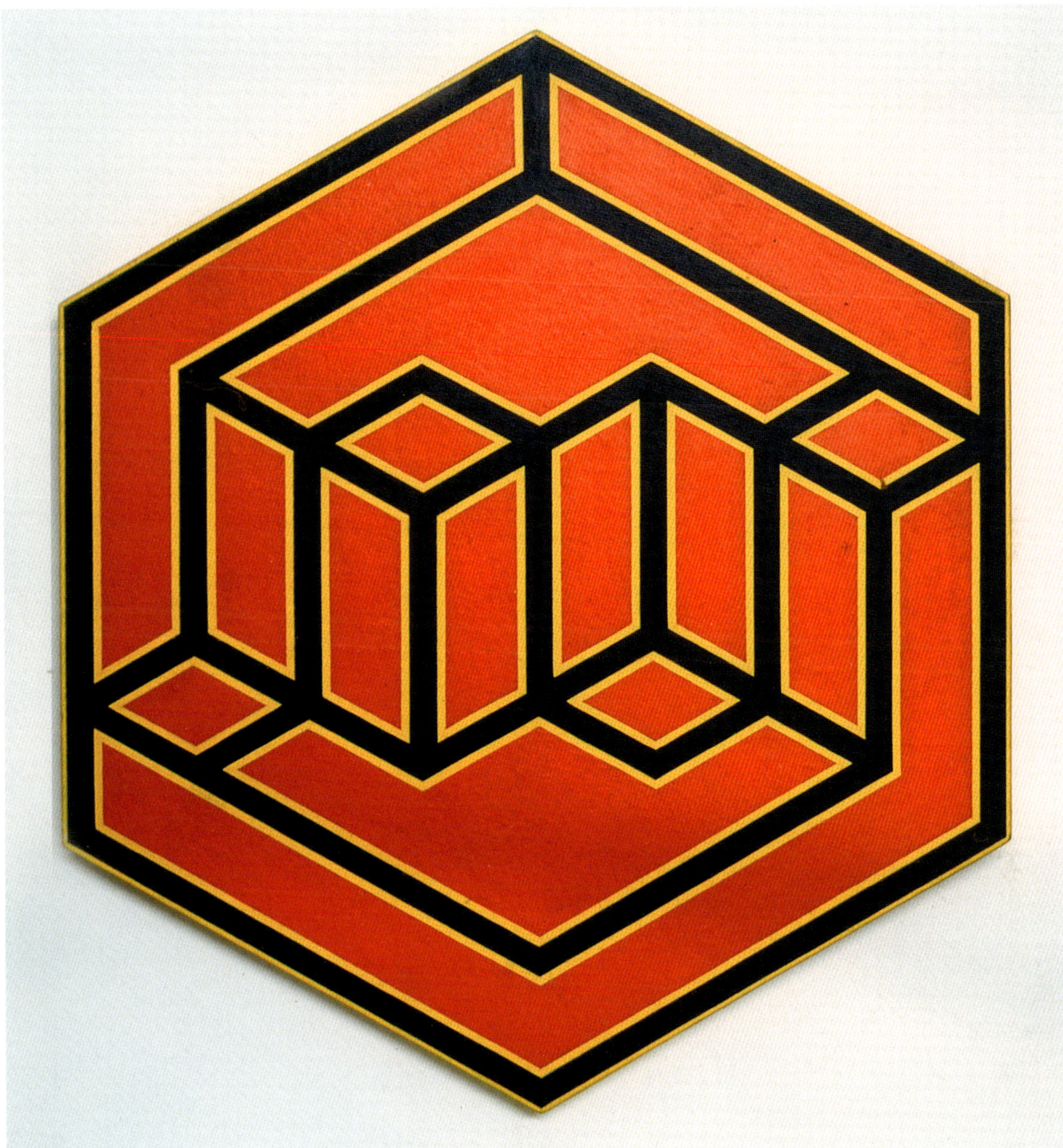

Regular Return
430 x 510 mm, painted wood relief

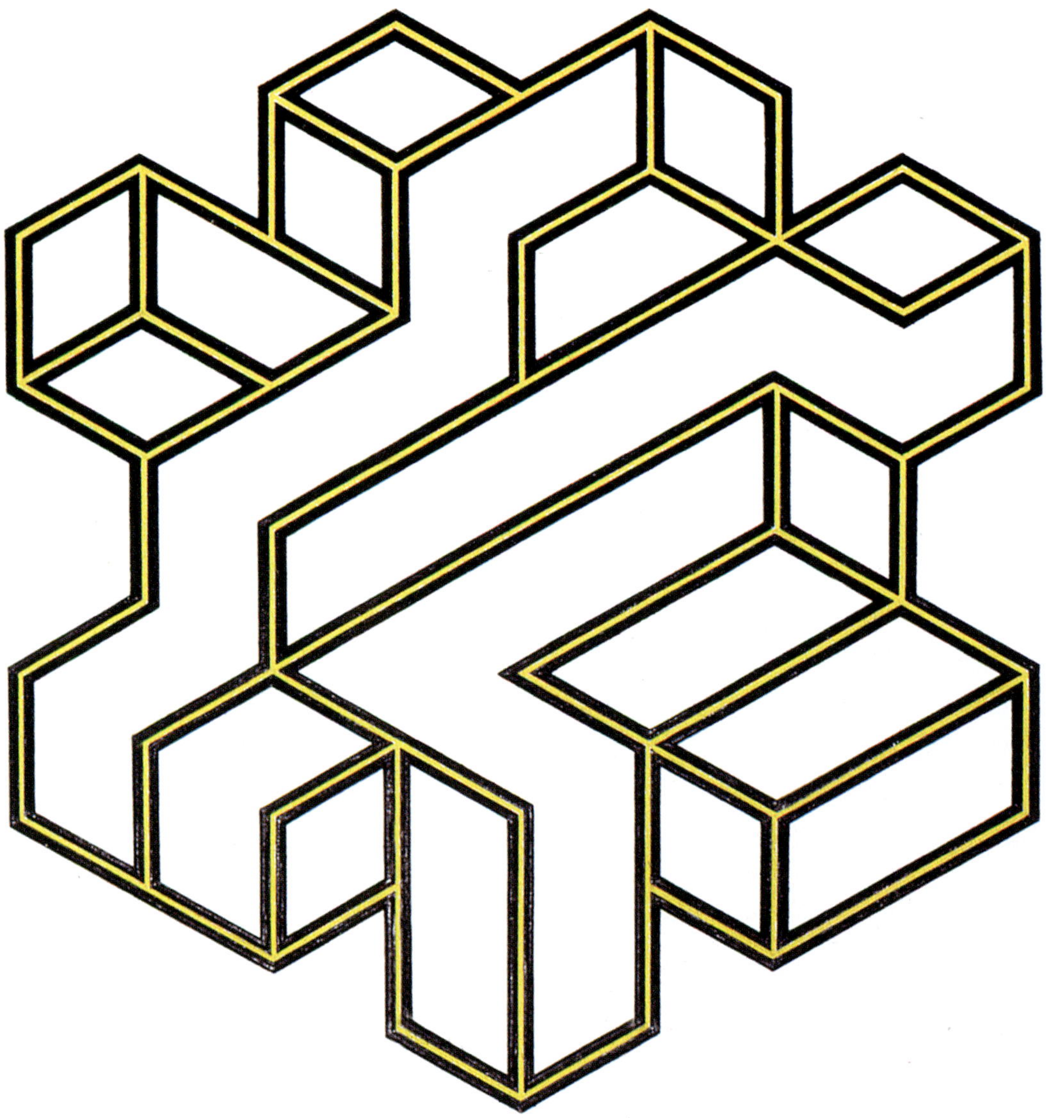

Under and Over
550 x 490 mm, pen and ink on paper

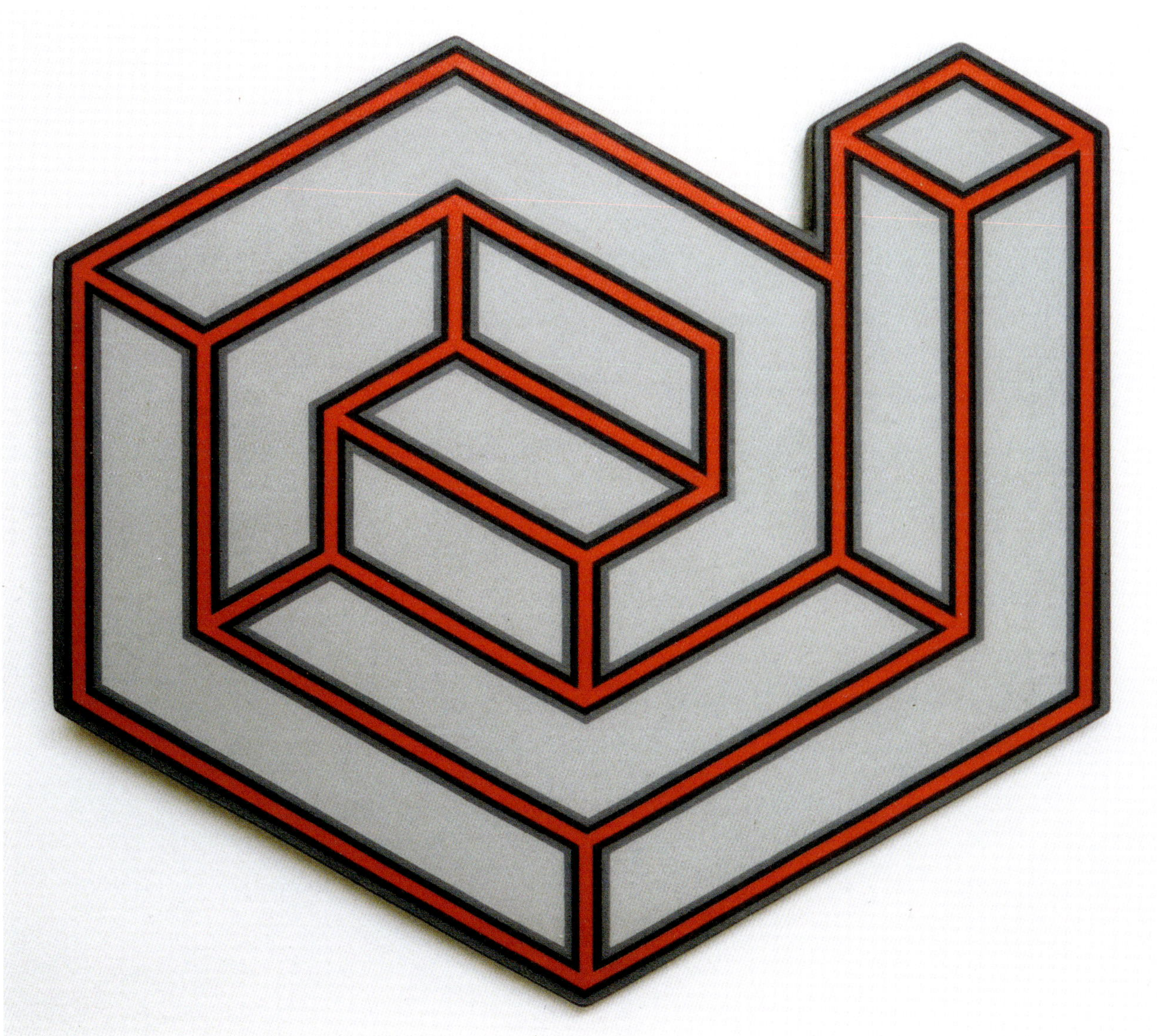

Space Double Up
420 x 450 mm, painted wood relief

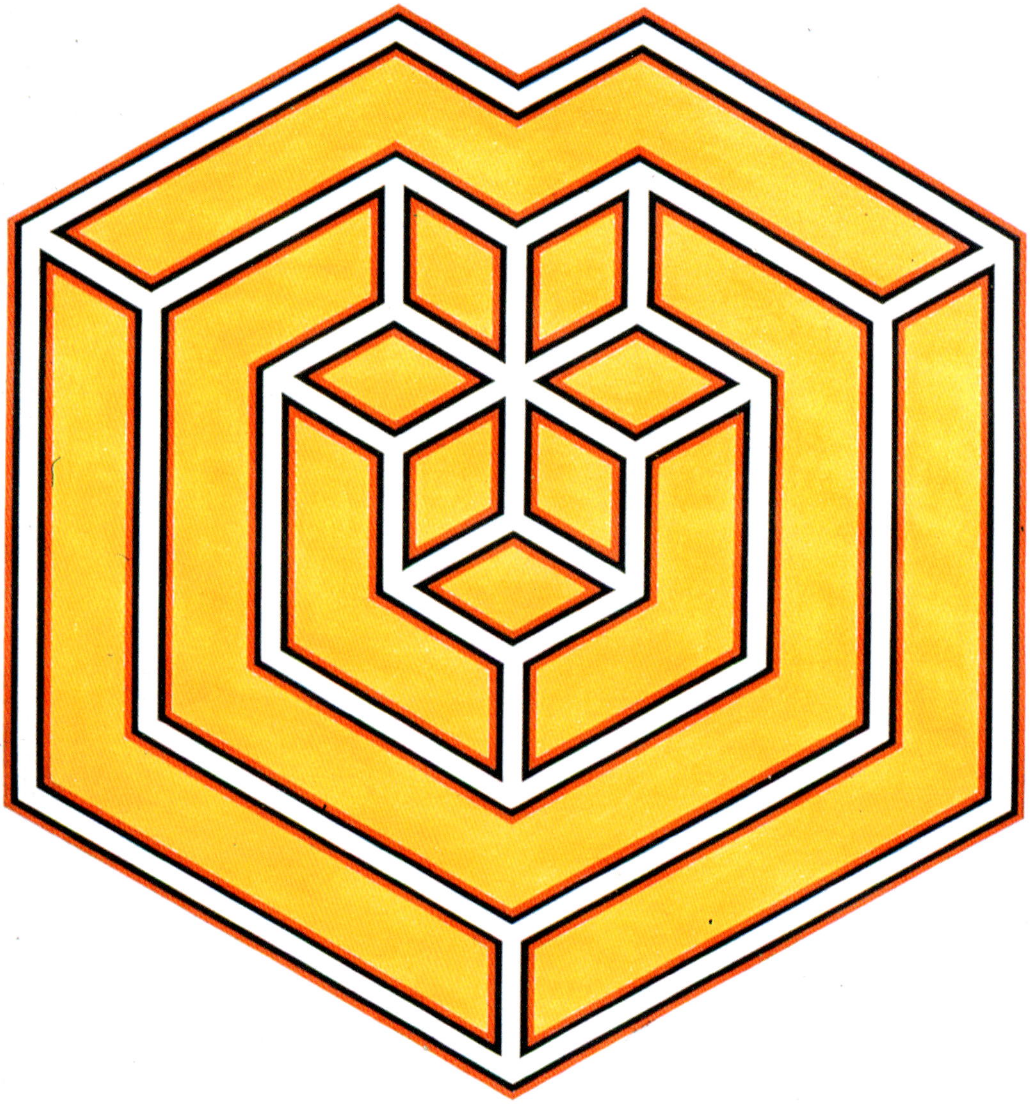

Timgad
610 x 630 mm, acrylic paint on paper

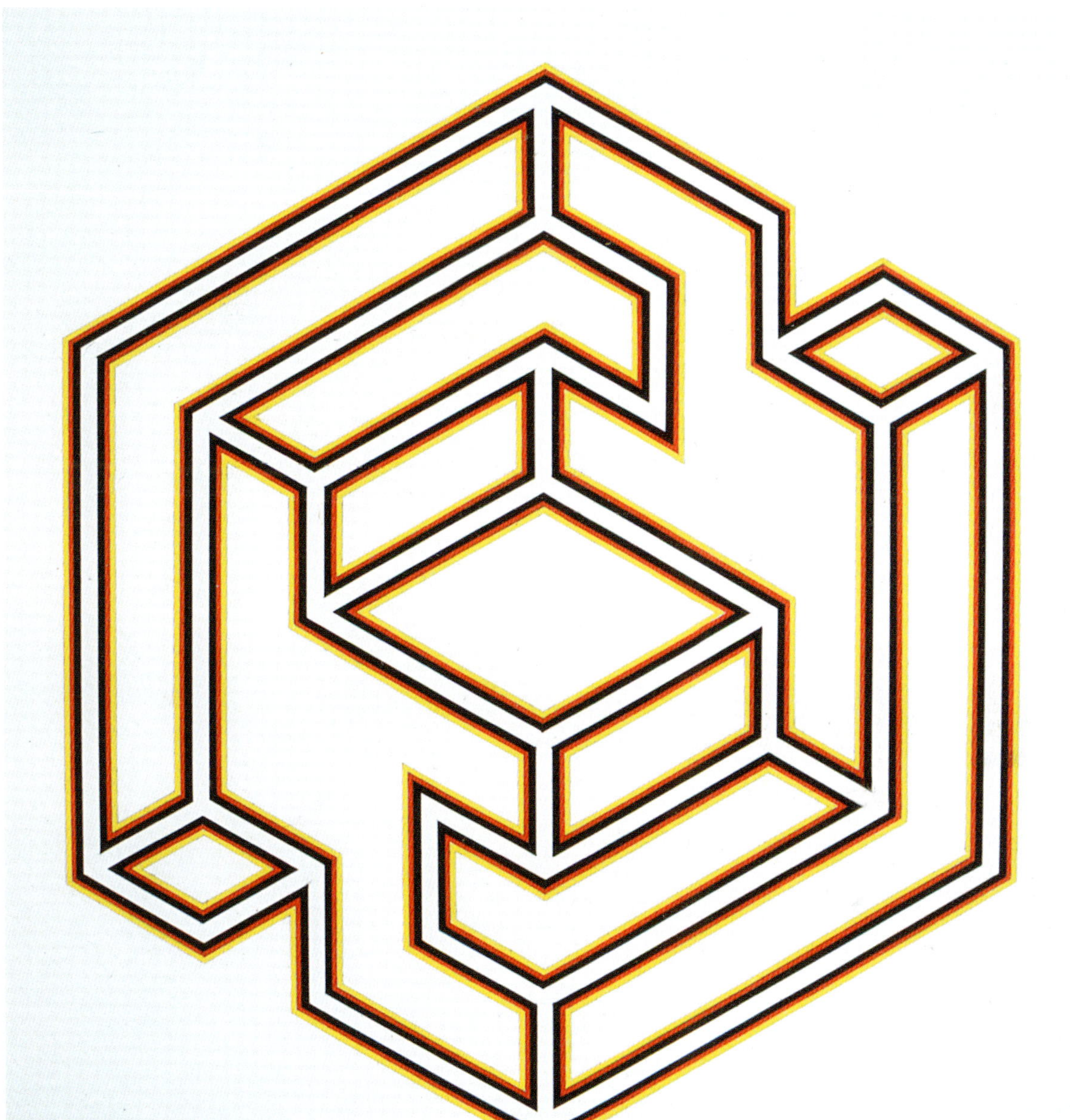

Regular Return no 2
610 x 630 mm, acrylic paint on paper

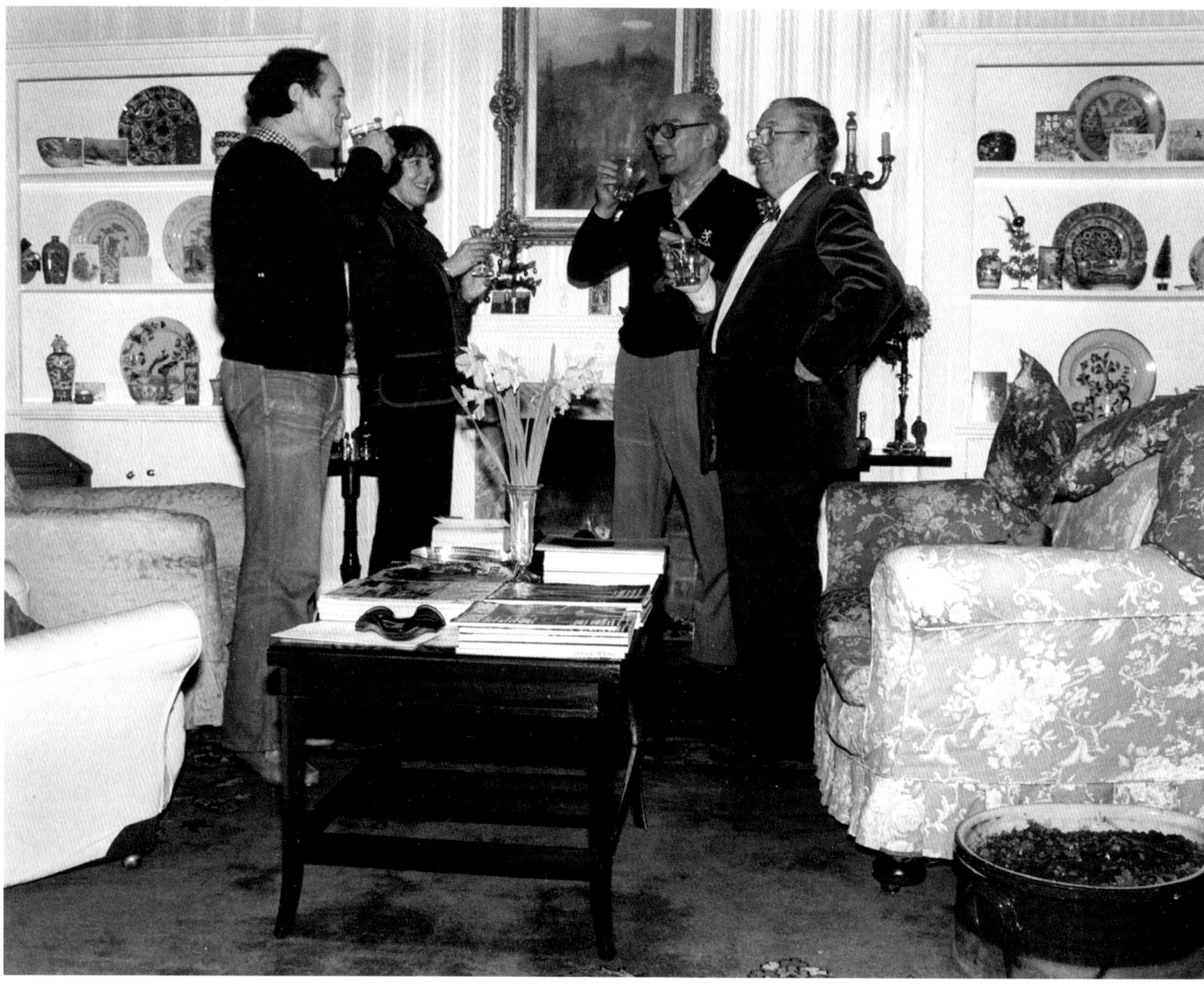

Larpool Hall, Whitby, home of Geoff Watson, Head of Teesside Galleries, Museums and Recreational Facilities
left to right: Trevor Frankland; Dorothy Frankland; Geoff Watson; Ken Cozens, Fine Arts Officer for Middlesbrough

Another reviewer, Margaret Hoggarth, remarked upon how 'Almost 20 years ago Frankland painted realistic Cleveland landscapes with an unflinching detachment. Today, living and working in London, his paintings, taken to far, far more specific limits, carry the same calm conviction. His own development and that of the stylish new Billingham Art Gallery are strangely intertwined and it must be very gratifying to all concerned – and indeed of considerable credit to Teesside – to show such a finely produced and presented exhibition.'

Watson persuaded William Varley of *The Guardian* to see the exhibition and Varley went so far as to write of Frankland in terms of Leonardo da Vinci who

> was splendidly prejudiced about illusionism in art. Sculptors, he thought, were merely rude mechanicals because they simply made artefacts in three dimensions whereas painters, much cleverer beings, created the illusion of solid form on a plane surface. Had Leonardo lived on, one wonders what he would make of Trevor Frankland's work. Frankland almost deserves a supplementary chapter to himself in Professor Gombrich's "Art and Illusion" for many of his drawings and reliefs resemble the diagrams of experimental psychology and in fact provoke similar sensations.

Most of his work is composed within hexagons, a shape which lends itself to endless permutations of geometrical division, by quadrilaterals, diagonals, equiangular triangles and so on. Lines cross and overlap, and illusions of space, solid volume and elaborate fore-shortenings are created. At times the reliefs resemble architecture and in imagination we can we walk along this plane, climb up that and then stop, for we are presented with contradictions. For although they are non-representational these reliefs inhabit the same ambiguous world as Escher where perspectival and perceptual 'laws' have been subverted and rivers flow uphill.

Middlesbrough Art Gallery bought a relief and associated drawing for their collection from the exhibition. Geoff Watson also acquired pieces for his own home at Larpool Hall, an eighteenth-century mansion at Whitby in North Yorkshire.

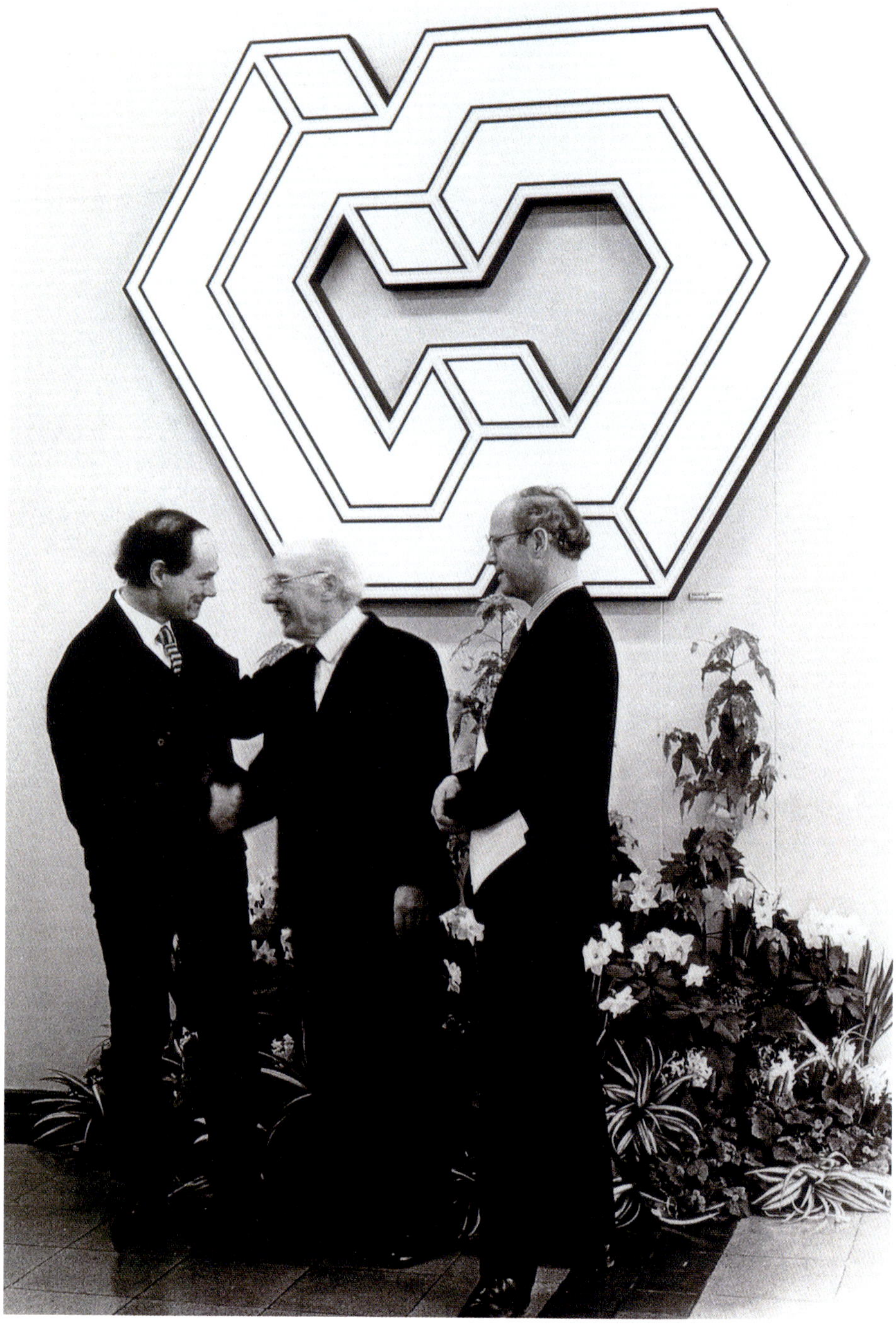

Shirvan
painting (one of three) presentation to Middlesex Polytechnic (now University), 20 March 1987
left to right: Trevor Frankland, Governing Body Chairman, Councillor Jack Lucas, Professor Penning Rowsell, Dean of the Faculty of Social Science at Enfield

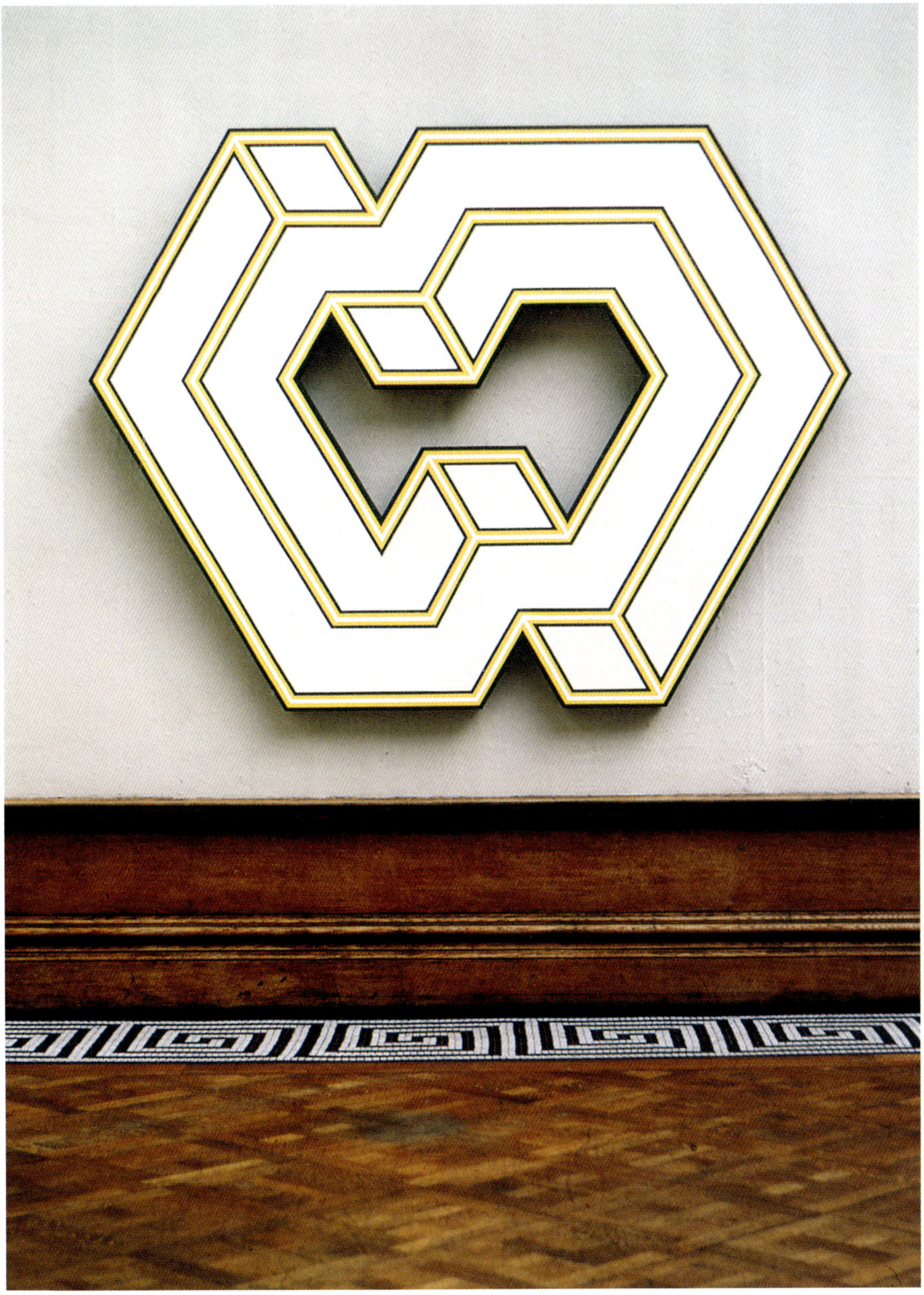

Shirvan
1640 x 1220 mm, painted wood construction

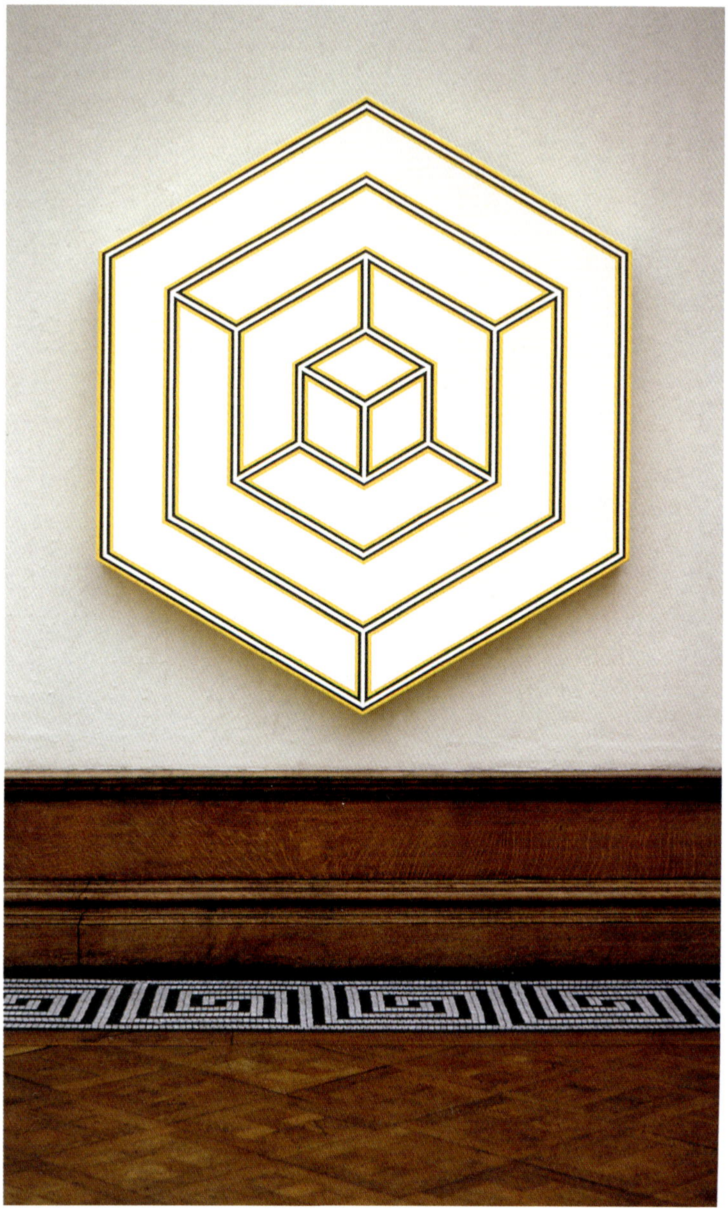

'Perfect Ashlar'

Information on the painting presented to the Library and Museum of the United Grand Lodge of England, October 1989 to commemorate the Centenary of Philbrick Lodge No 2255.

The composition is based on a grid of equilateral triangles which symbolise the sacred word. At the centre is the perfect ashlar, which has a dual nature being both positive and negative. As the image is ever changing it points out the paradoxical nature of time, space and existence and although changing it remains constant and changeless.

The GGOTU is its essence.

Yellow / Gold
- the symbol of the sun and constancy.

Black
- silence and secrecy.

White
- purity, truth, innocence and hope.

Exhibited at the Shipley Art Gallery, Gateshead, July 1972 in a one-man show of paintings.

Perfect Ashlar
1220 x 1320 mm, painted wood construction
(presented to the Library and Museum of the United Grand Lodge of England, October 1989)

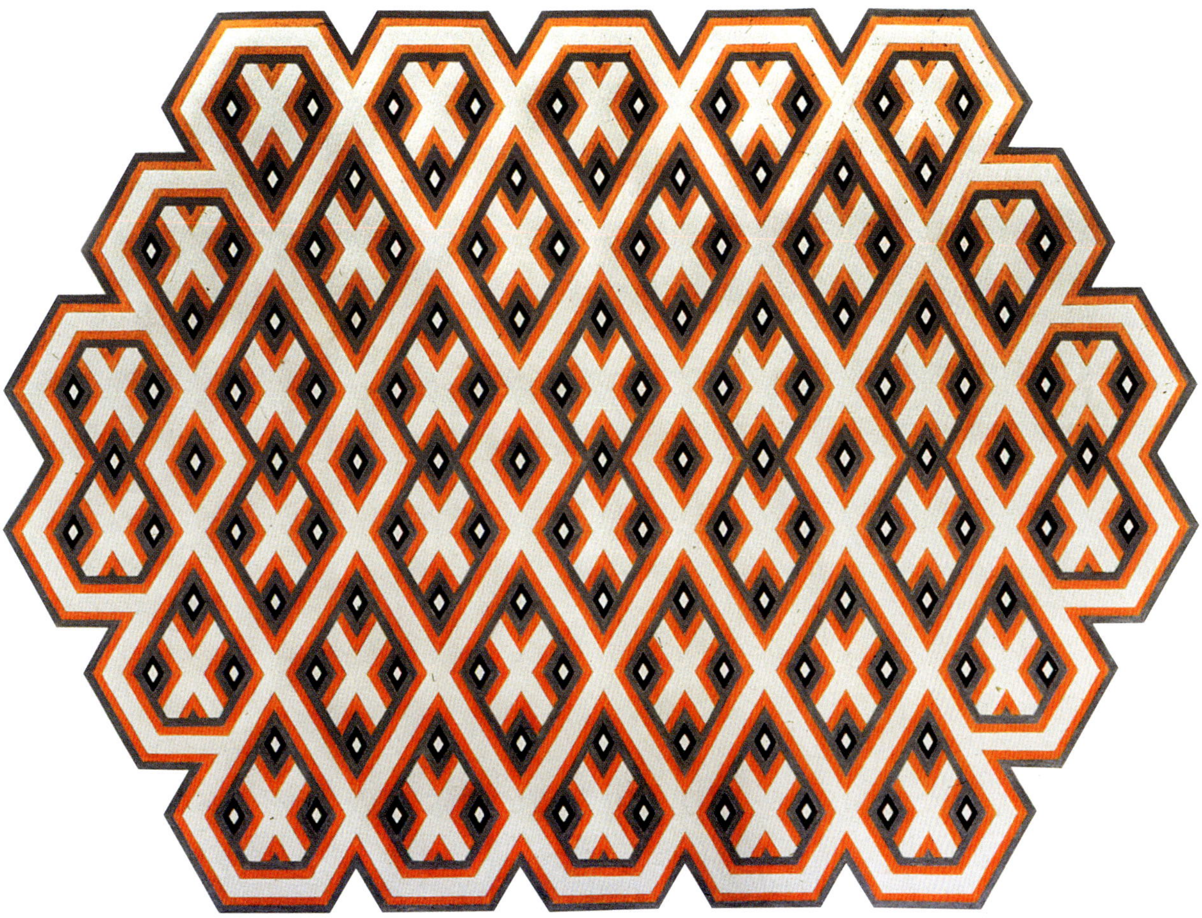

The Astrologer's Key
800 x 690 mm, acrylic paint on paper

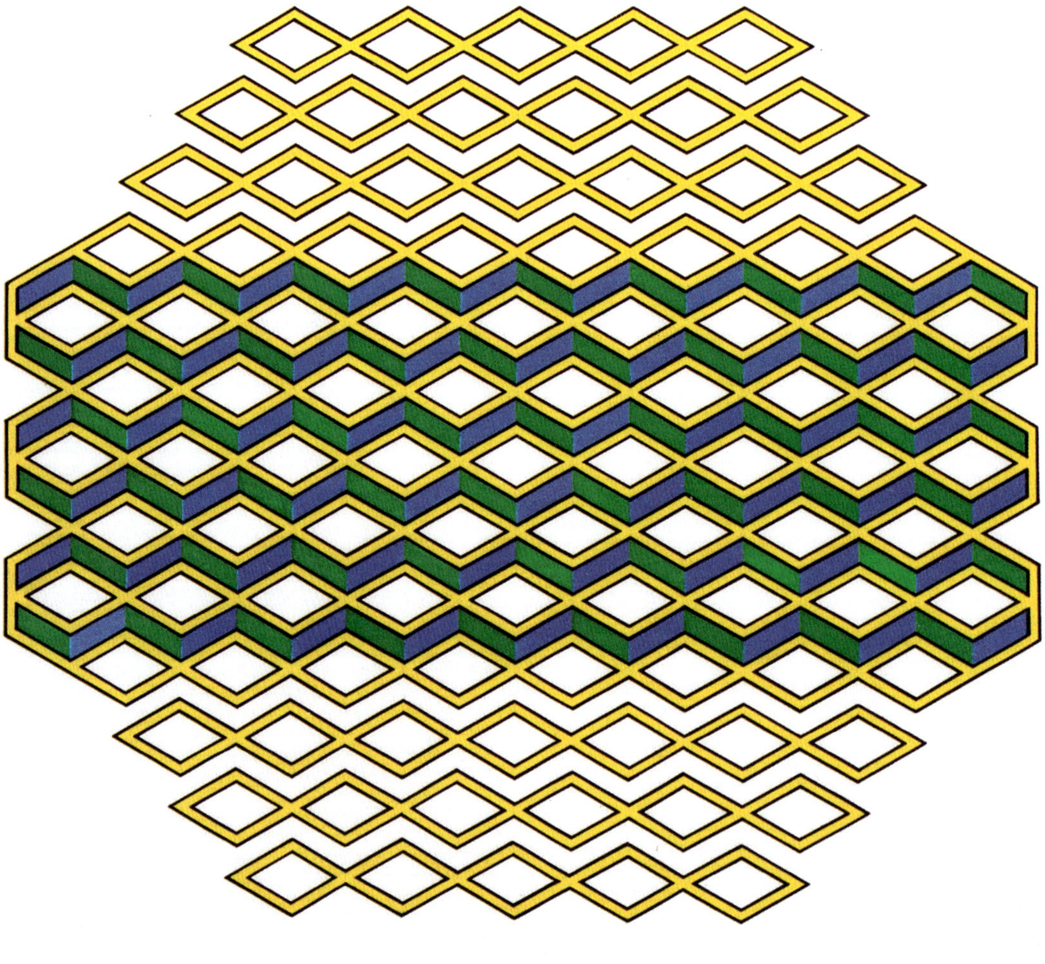

Sunny Beach
790 x 690 mm, acrylic paint on paper

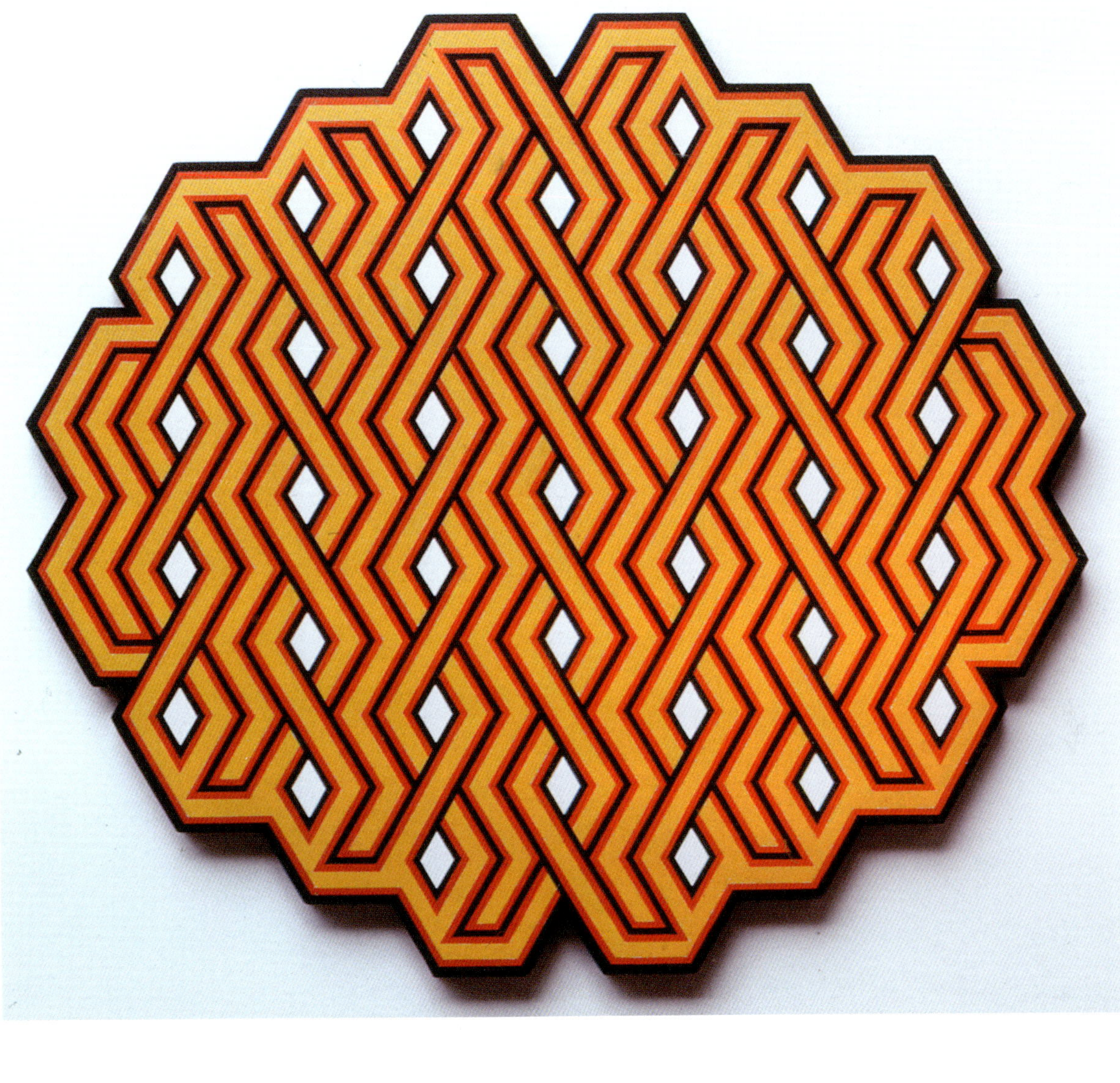

Sadalmelek
1000 x 920 mm, painted wood relief

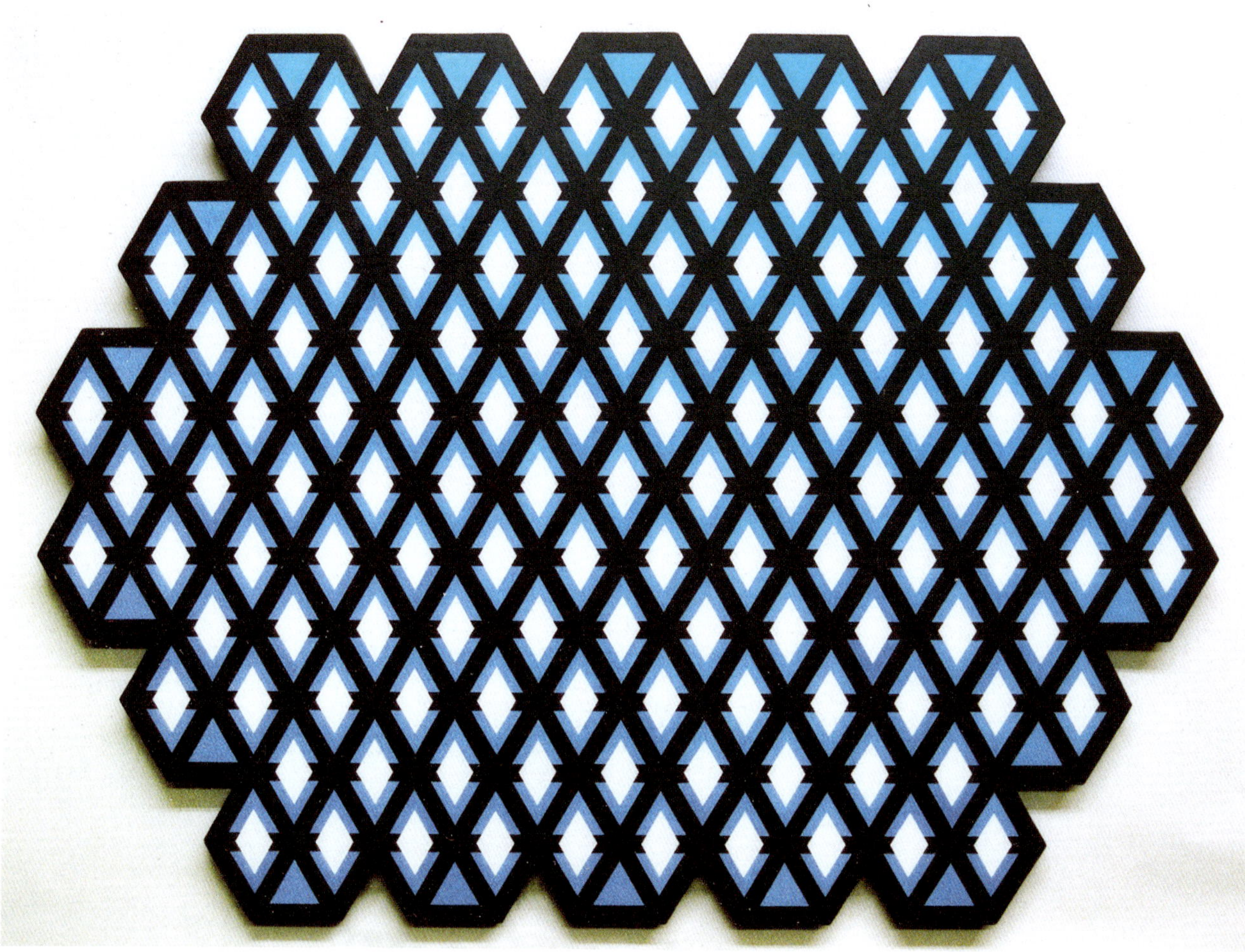

Circadian Rhythm
860 x 660 mm, painted wood relief

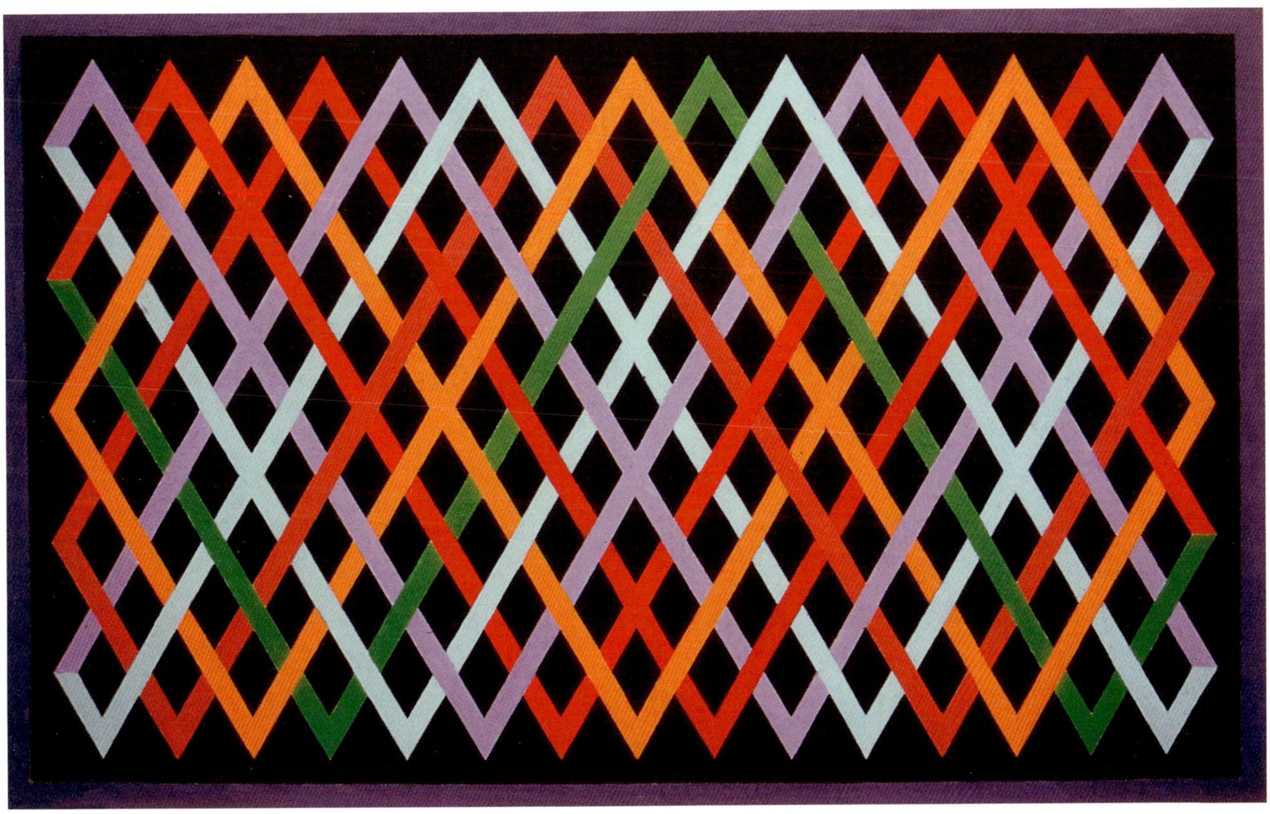

Regular Return
1950 x 1170 mm, acrylic painting

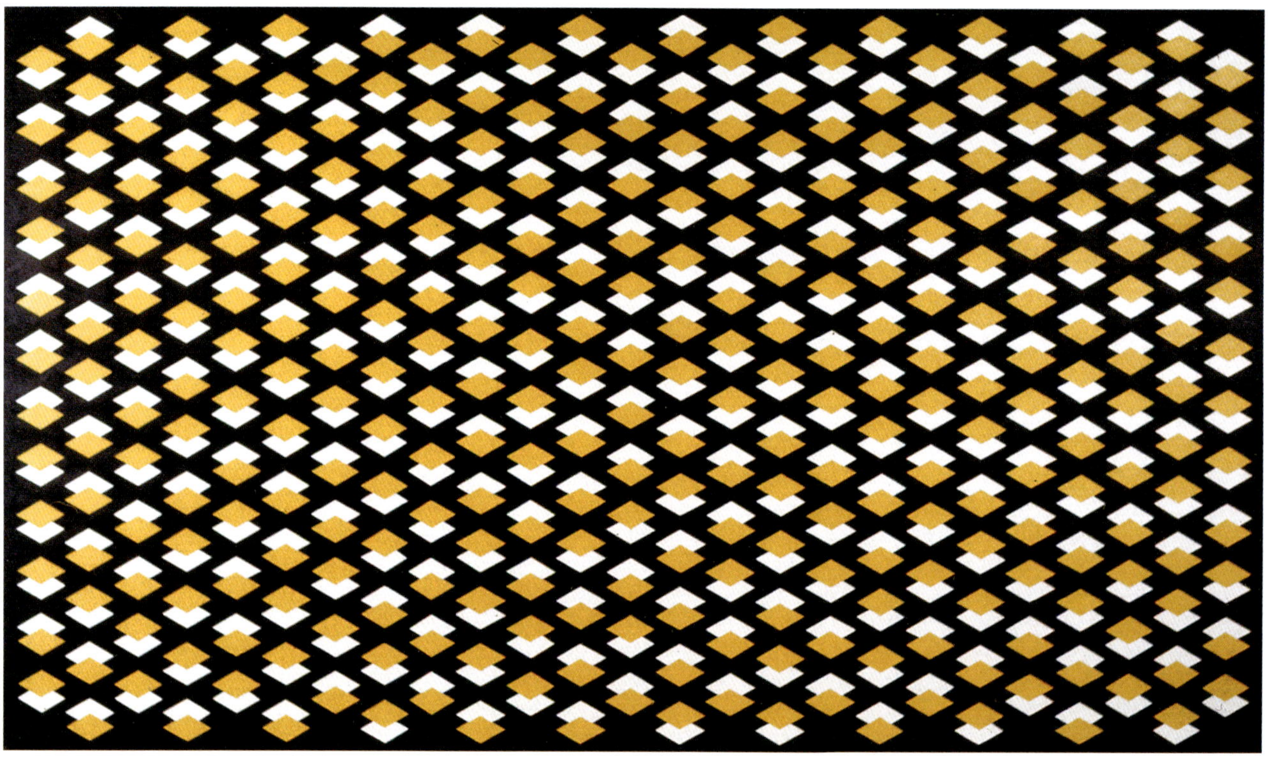

ABC Infinity
1950 x 1170 mm, acrylic painting

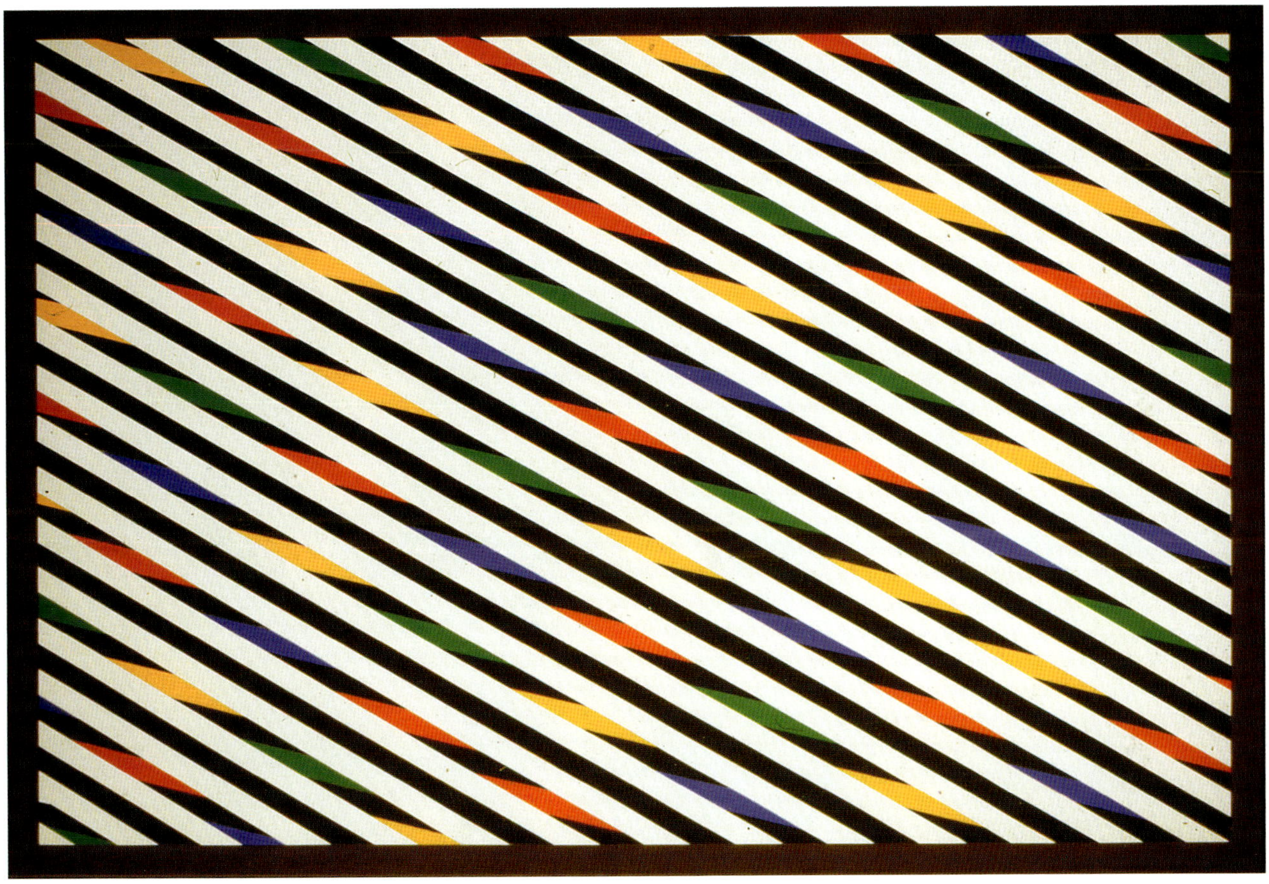

Shimmer
1750 x 1220 mm, acrylic painting

In 1969 Trevor and Dorothy, who had come across a brochure in the staff room at the school where she worked, went on a three-week trek to Morocco. This was the first of their many trips abroad. Despite a stay in a cockroach-ridden hotel in Marrakesh, it was the beginning of a succession of travels which over the years took them to the Middle East and North Africa – Turkey, Iraq, Jordan, Syria, Tunisia and Algeria, and beyond to Afghanistan and Iran, Pakistan and India. They felt drawn to wild and arid lands, and the dryness of remote deserts, barren save for scrub, bits of tree and outbreaks of rock, silent, but heavy with the spirit of the place.

At a time when his own work was wholly abstract the non-representational elements of Islamic art which he saw on his travels were deeply sympathetic to Frankland. The abstract rhythms and patterns made by the intensely coloured tiles on the Persian and Afghan mosques and monuments fascinated him. Observing the sometimes breathtaking way in which the grids, webs and designs on the Islamic buildings dissolved in light and space, he has written:

'The structuring of relationships is the subject of my work, it helps to give visual form to intuitions that, like myths, have a structure buried deep below surface detail.... When working with the grids it seems at times that structures appear and disappear out of and into the surface web of lines without any pre-planning.'

It seemed to him like the void of the quantum field out of which atomic particles are continuously coming into existence and vanishing again in unending motion. It is the mystery of how in a world of change there is included the underlying unity of all things. These are themes present both in a number of eastern philosophies and in current theoretical physics.

The layered grid systems and network structures, modular and serial orders became the basis for Frankland's own paintings and constructs – such Op-art illusion was also in fashion with the art of the time. On his meticulously constructed field paintings, using paper glued on chipboard with acid-free pva and stretched cotton duck over hardboard panels, he made his floating structures which change as you stare at them. By mathematical and geometrical calculation these scrupulous, punctilious constructions – they can scarcely be called pictures for they depict nothing precisely - have neither frame nor border. Even the edge echoes the interior *ad infinitum*. However rigorous and cerebral in approach, Frankland's work is not without feeling. This, after all, is how he responds and expresses himself. The discrepancy between what you see and what you know enthrals, and by use of what his wife calls his 'well-organised little grey cells' is turned by him into art.

Between 1972 and 1983 there were further one-man exhibitions at the Shipley Art Gallery in Gateshead, Middlesbrough Art Gallery, the Calouste Gulbenkian Gallery in Newcastle upon Tyne, the Williamson Art Gallery and Museum in Birkenhead, Northampton Central Museum and Art Gallery, the E.M. Flint Gallery in Walsall, Worcester City Art Gallery, Birmingham University in both 1980 and 1983 and at the New Gallery, Hornsey Library in London.

Frankland's sister Judy was married to an Italian businessman in Milan. In 1972 she arranged for him a one-man exhibition at La Darsena Galleria, which included forty pieces of his work. He also took part in several small group shows as part of 'Group One Seven' including one in 1973 at La Viscontea Galleria in Rho in Milan where he was awarded the 'Amici del Pomero' medal. The local weekly newspaper wrote of Frankland's 'works of fantasy but also of a reality which lives in us and which Frankland has discovered and brought out with apparent detachment suitable to his own temperament.' Judy and her husband also drove Trevor and Dorothy around Italy down into Sicily. This journey provided images which were used at a later date in the creation of quite different works.

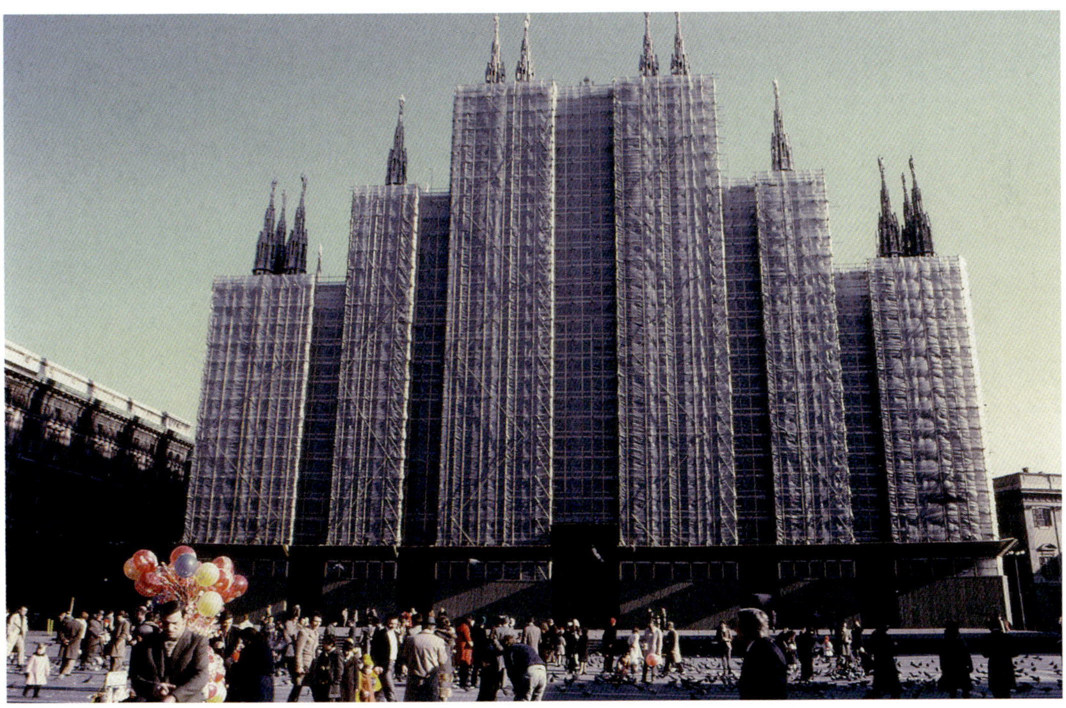

Milan Cathedral, Italy, during conservation 1972

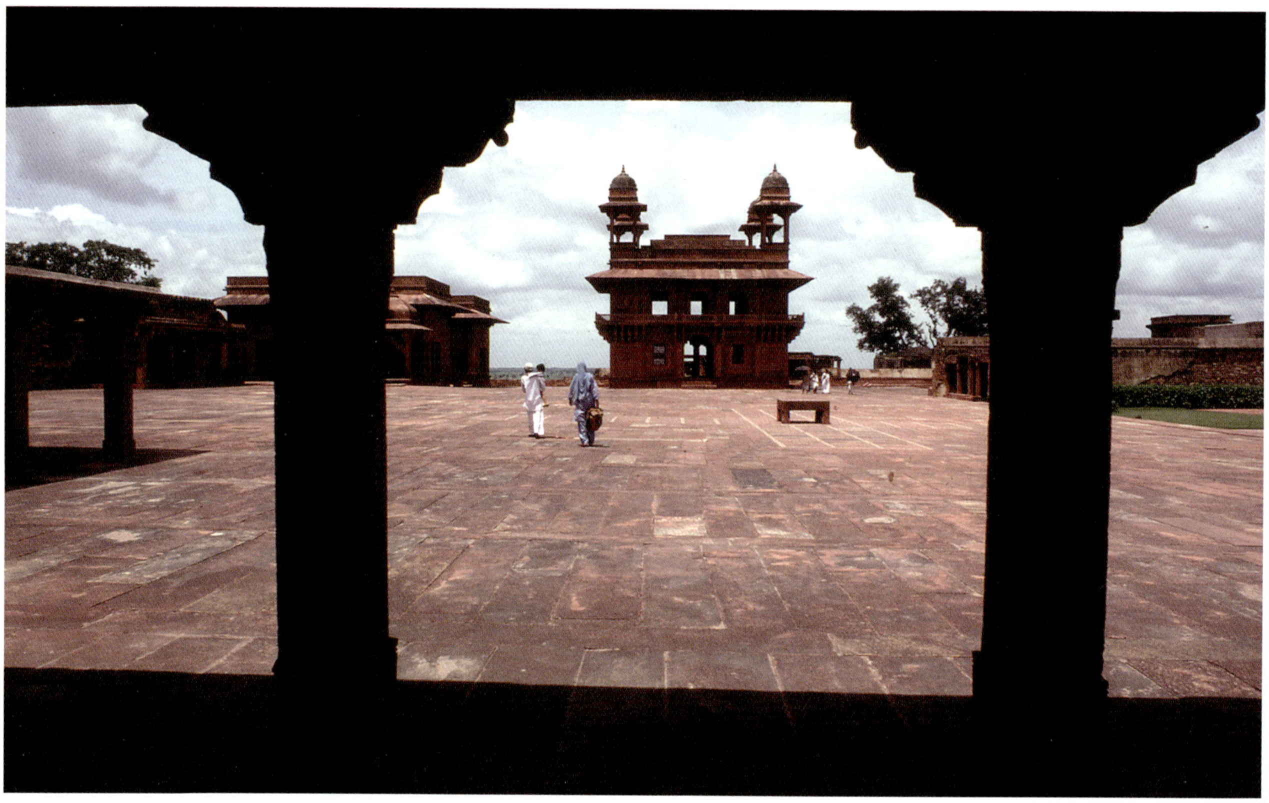

Fatehpur Sikri, India

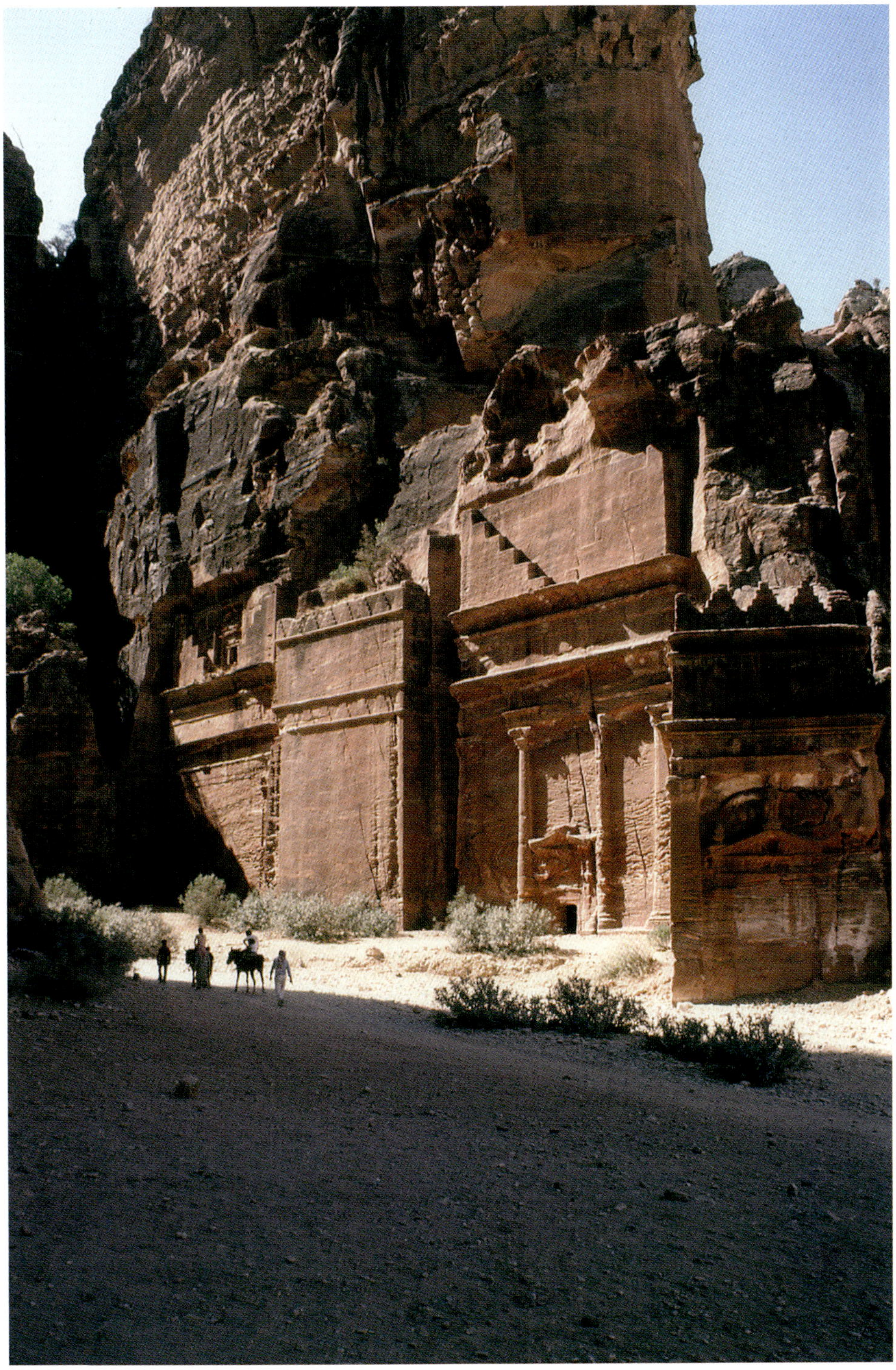

Petra, Jordan

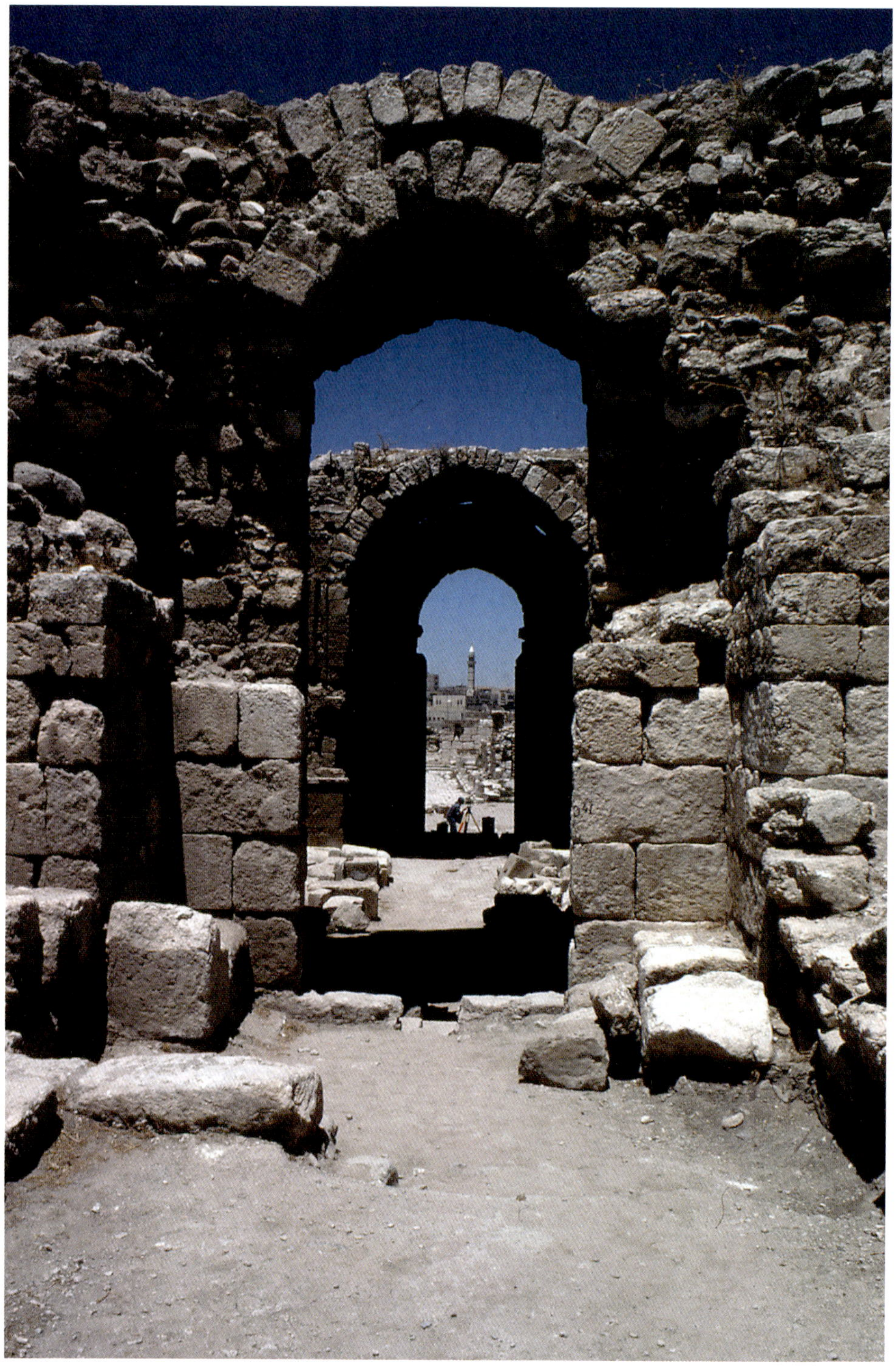

Amman, Jordan

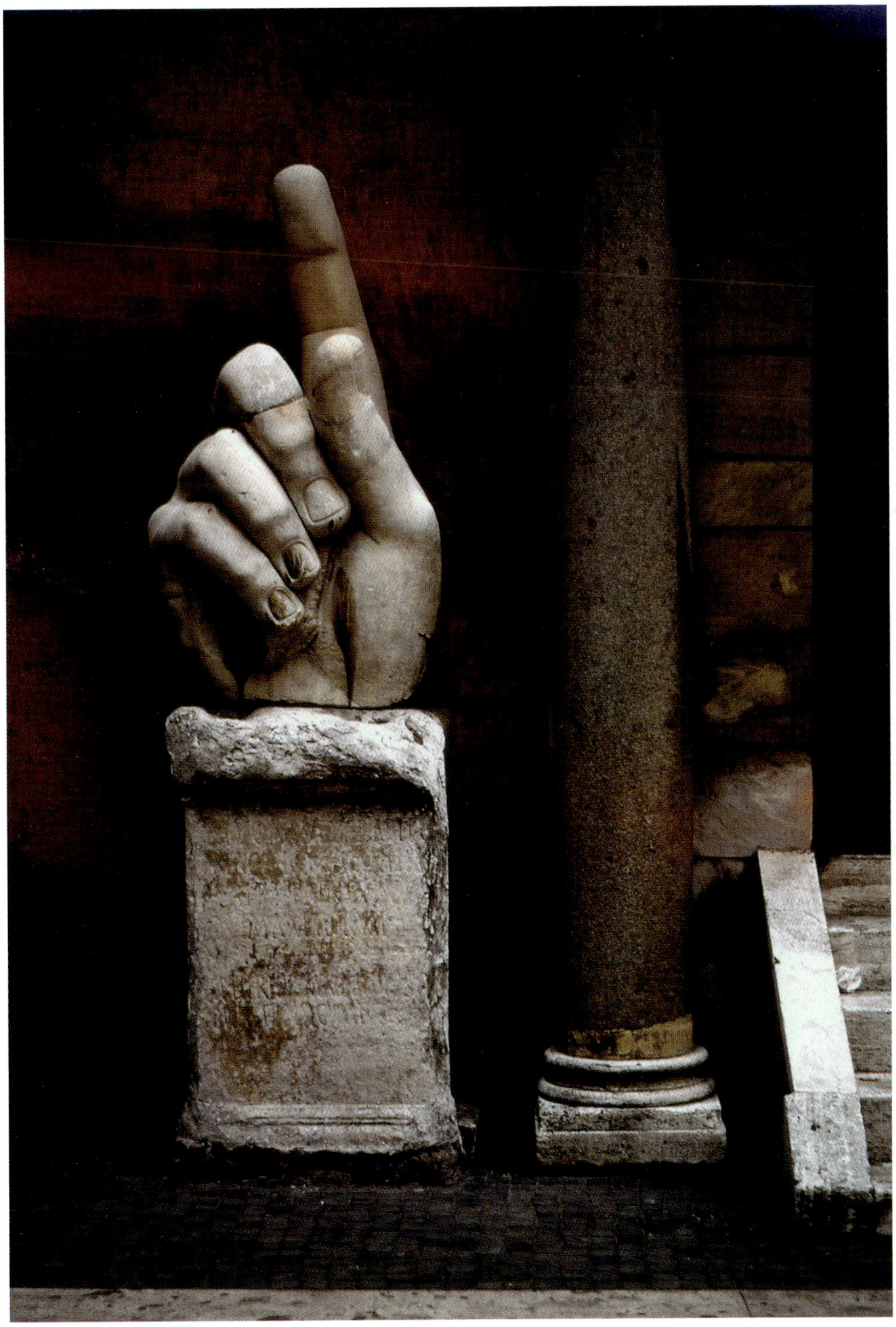

Rome

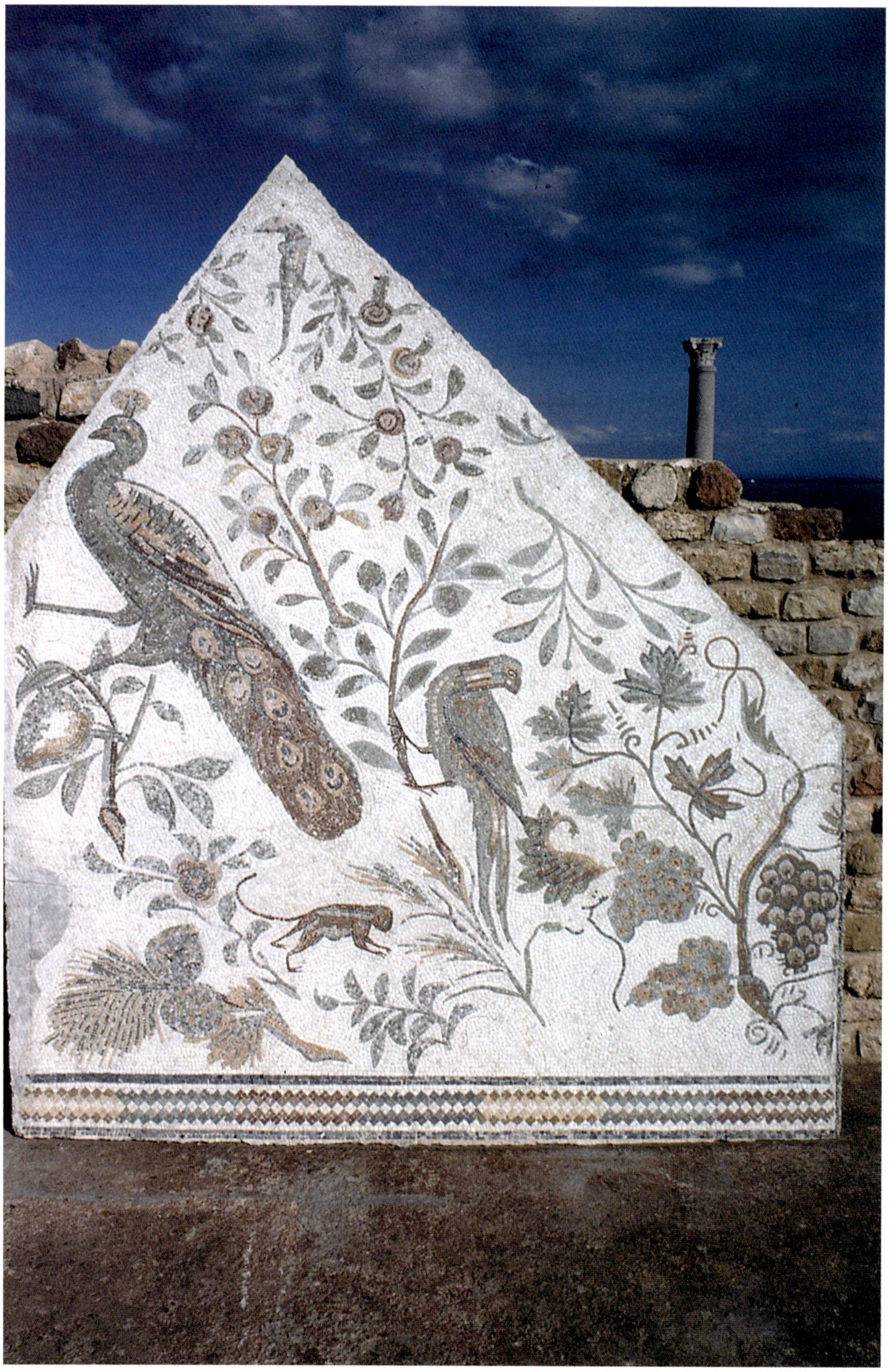

Mosaic from Carthage, Tunis, Tunisia

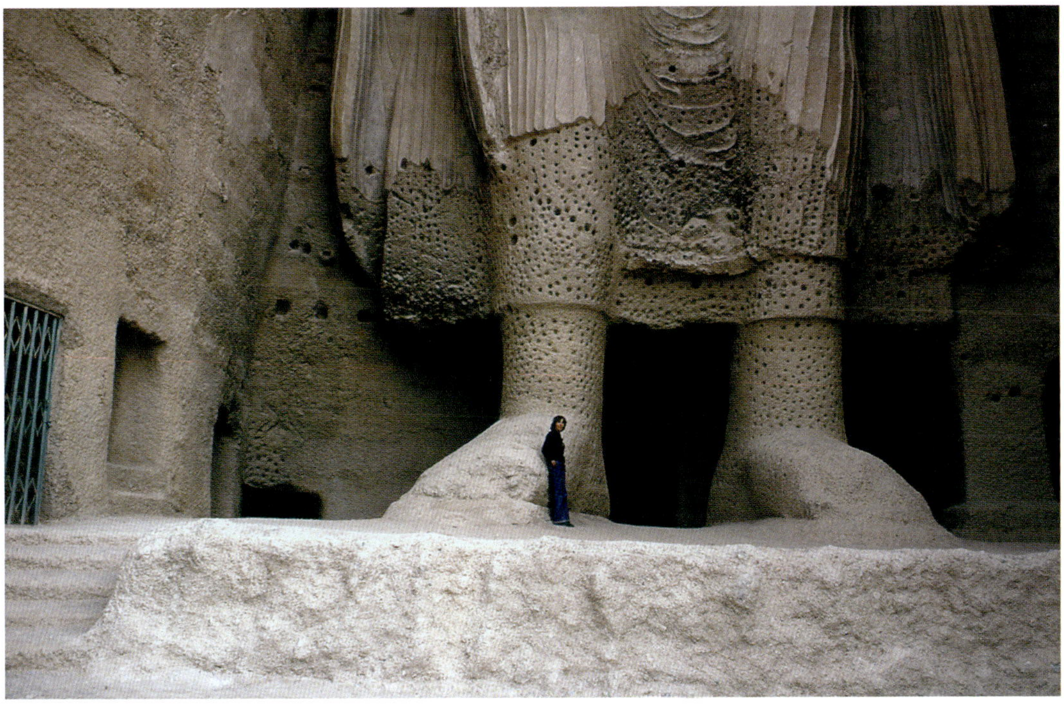

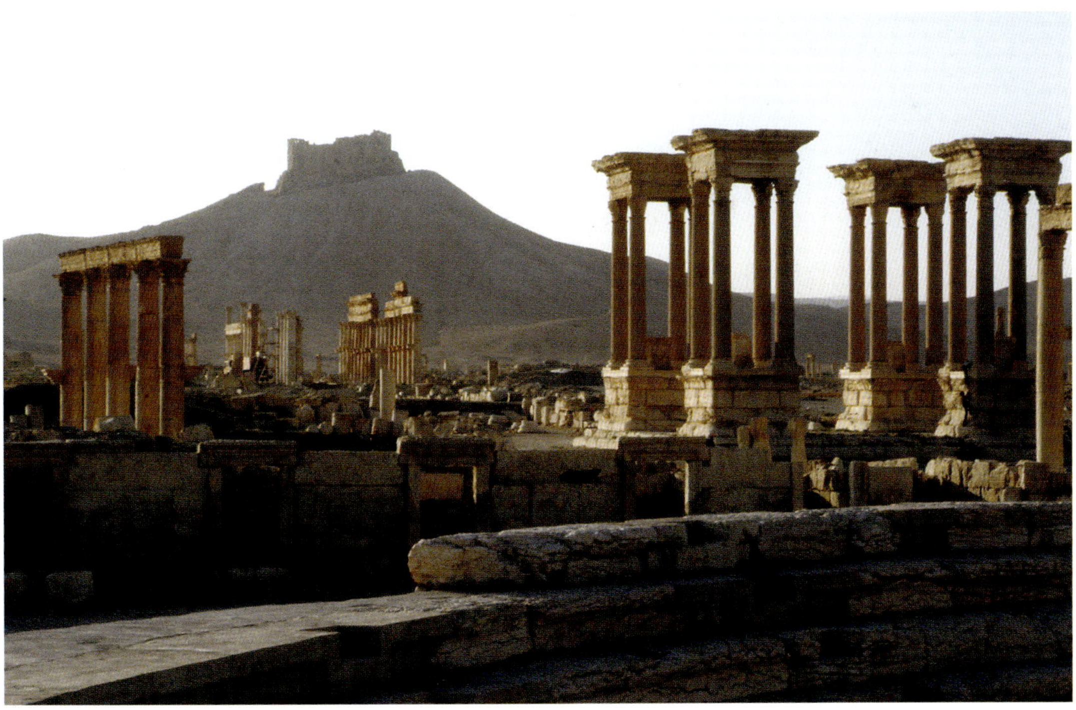

Giant Buddha, Bamiyan, Afghanistan (now destroyed by the Taliban)

Palmyra, Syria

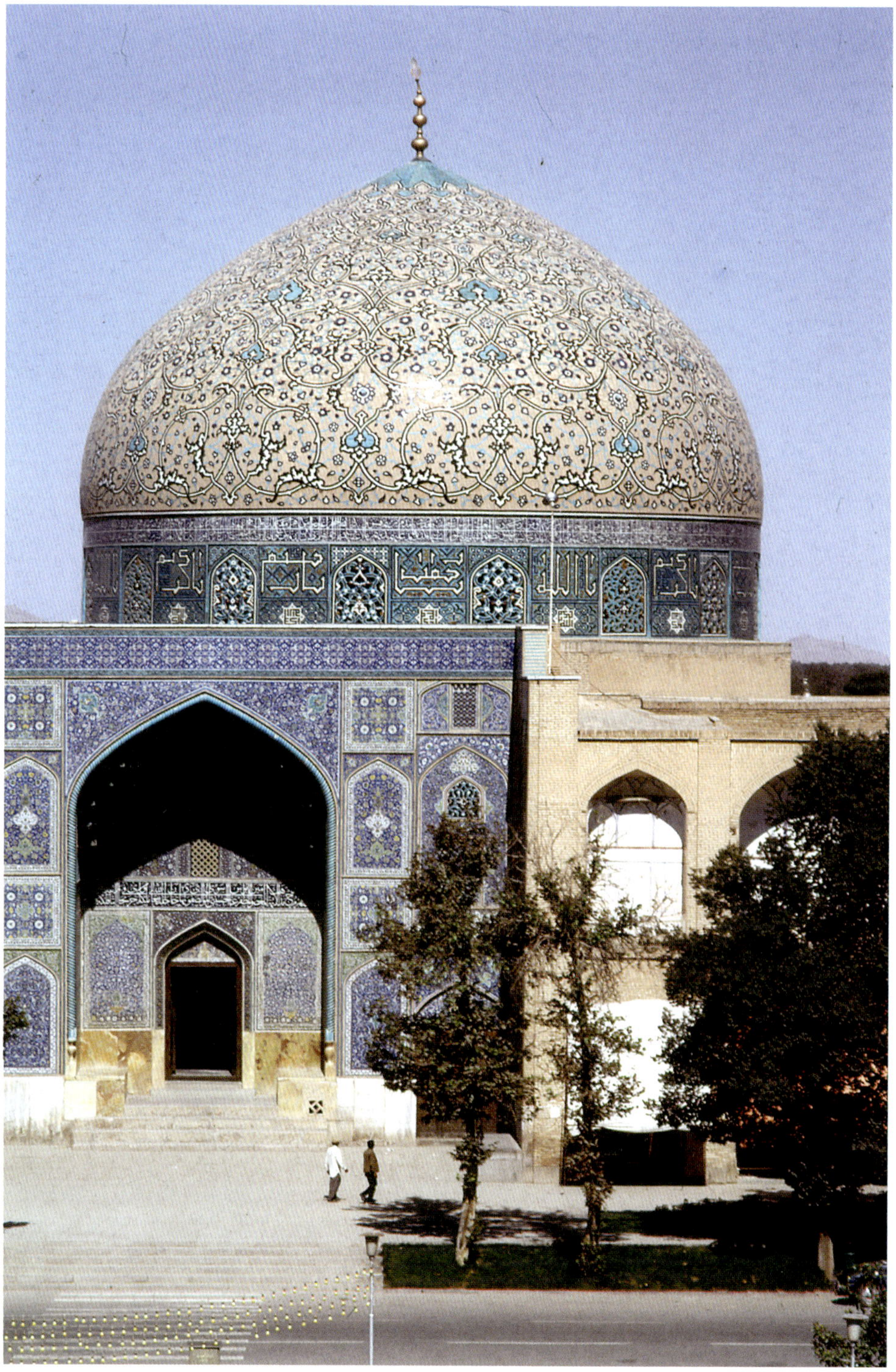

Esfahan, Iran

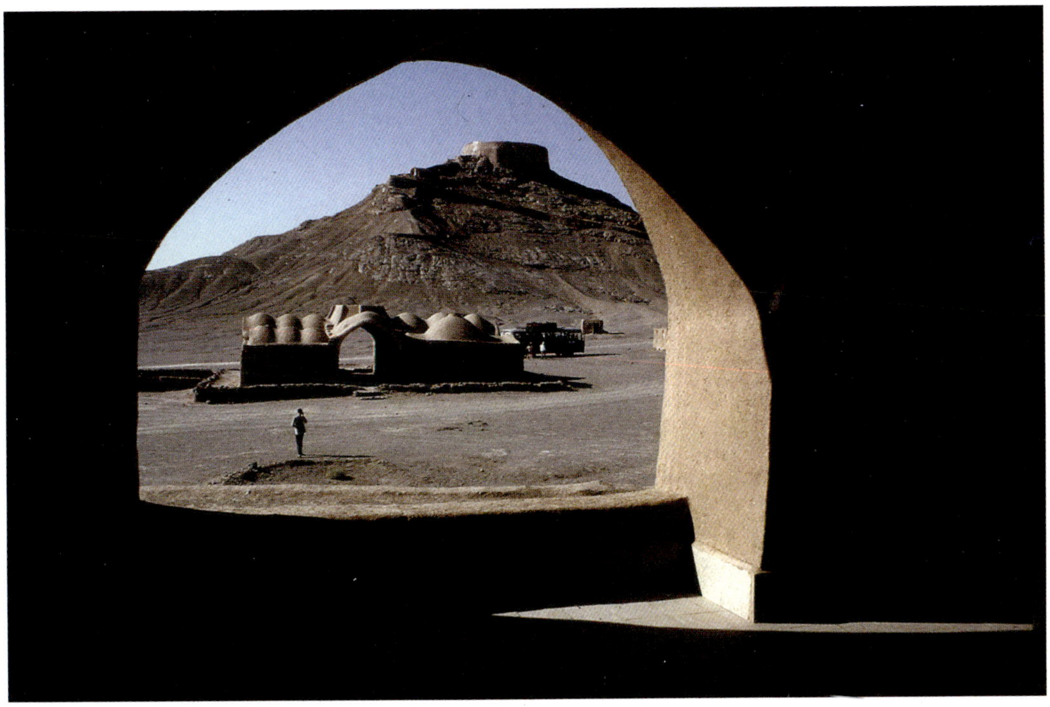

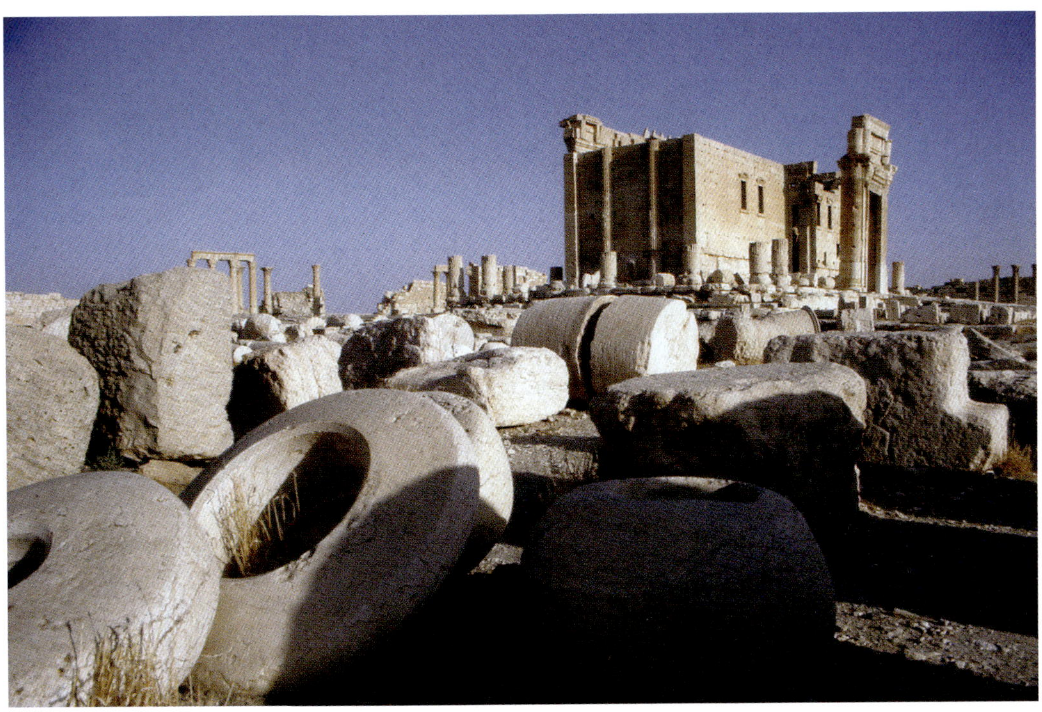

Yazd, a Zoroastrian religious complex, Iran

Palmyra, Syria

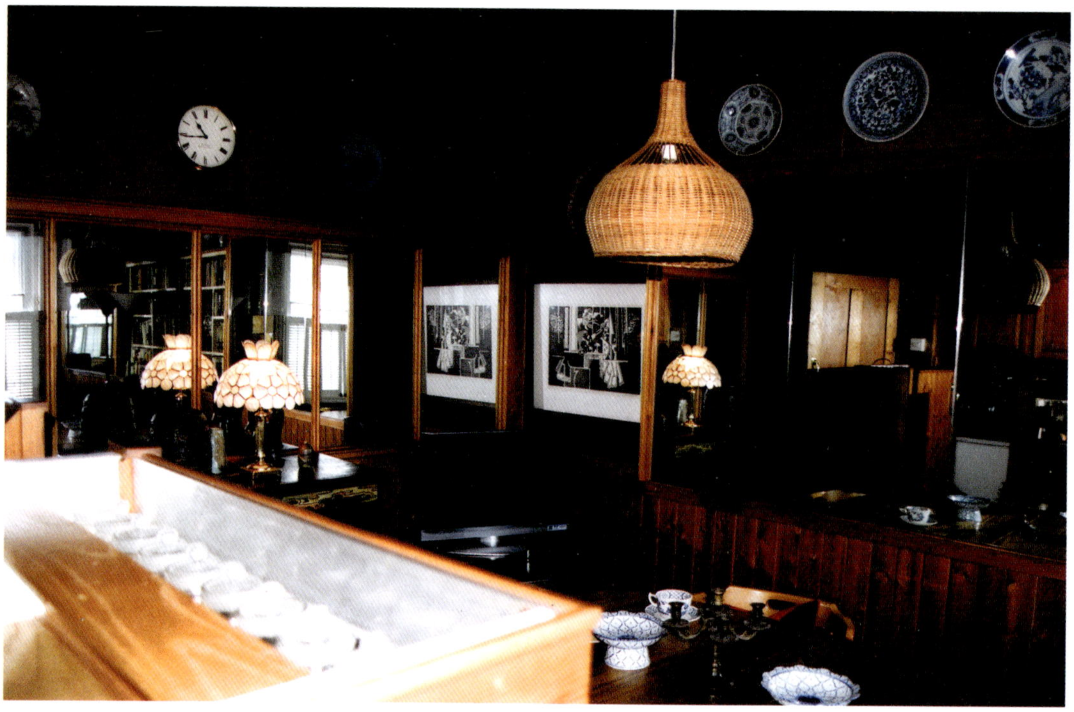

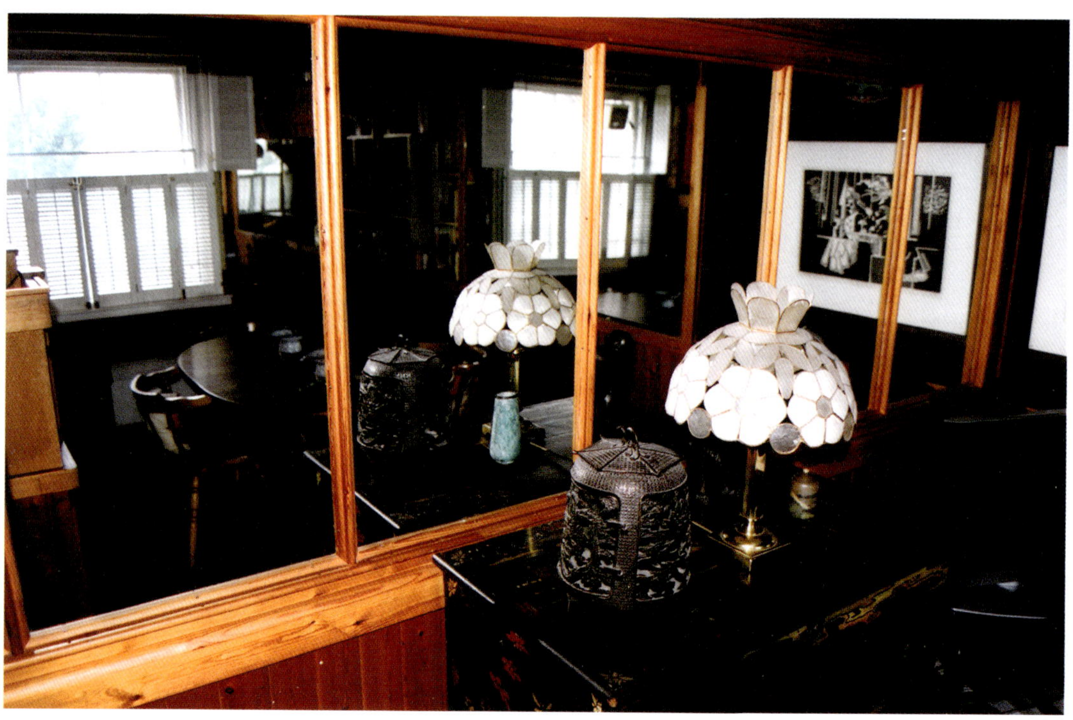

Kitchen interior showing reflections in mirrors

6

In the 1960s Frankland was working with a model posed in front of mirrors to demonstrate to his students how a figure could be viewed from different angles to create multiple images. Many years later this project gave him the idea of installing mirrors in his kitchen-dining room in order to create an illusion of extended space, and he bought ten large mirrors cheaply from a glazier in Hornsey Rise for his house. The room often accommodates a large number of people. Over the years Trevor and Dorothy have given many dinner parties around their long dining table which stands to one side, and every one of the parties is meticulously planned and recorded. In the tradition of the artist and diarist Joseph Farington R.A., who in the late eighteenth century had also attended the R.A. Schools, Frankland keeps detailed records of the seating arrangements and menu for each occasion. The use of mirrors to expand a confined area is a common interior decorator's trick but at the time they were put in place Frankland was reading Gaston Bachelard's *Poetics of Space* which added an extra dimension to his thinking. Bachelard had written about two forms of the imagination, the formal and the material, and how the emotional relationship we have with the world around us distorts what we think we see, suppresses some things, exaggerates others. There is an affinity with dreams (one thinks of Jean Cocteau's film *Orphée* or of Lewis Carroll's *Alice in Wonderland* and *Alice Through the Looking-Glass*), for although distortions in a sleeping state appear to hint at something significant, ambiguity prevents a logical interpretation; when we are awake we force logic onto what we encounter.

A well-worn seventeenth-century wainscot chair rescued from the Frankland farm stands in the dining room. Here on the first floor, the room looks out onto the garden and it was to the garden that he began in 1979 to turn his attention. The illusion of space created by mirrors in the kitchen inspired the initial idea for an illusion of extended space in the garden, although Frankland prefers to think of it as a 'domestic landscape', which has been influenced by dry stone or waterless Japanese Zen gardens. It has been featured on television several times and given a name: 'Summer River Bed Winter Flood Plain'. In essence it simulates the excavation of a winding river bed and the rock formations around it, as if in some far distant past flowing water had carved a history of its journey through the landscape and continued to show the influence of the past on the present.

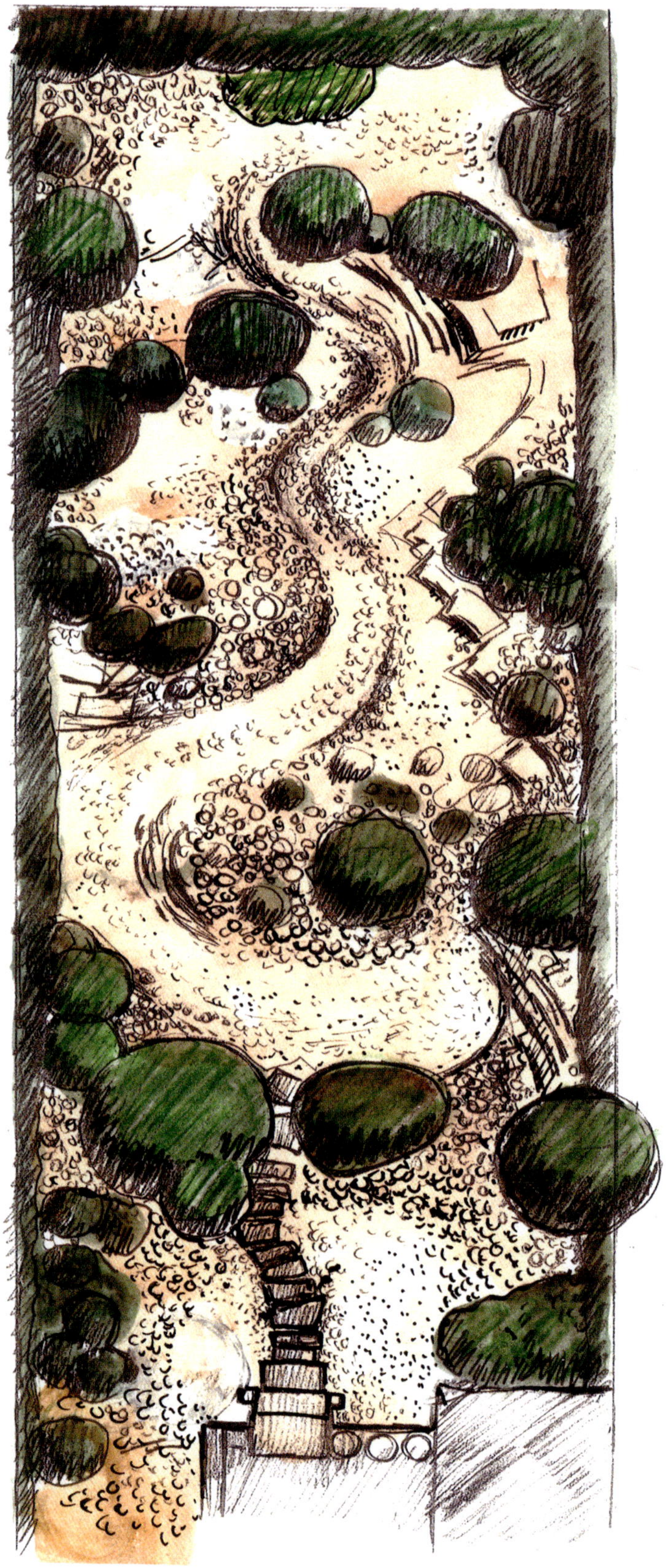

Summer River Bed, Winter Flood Plain,
a domestic landscape - plan of layout

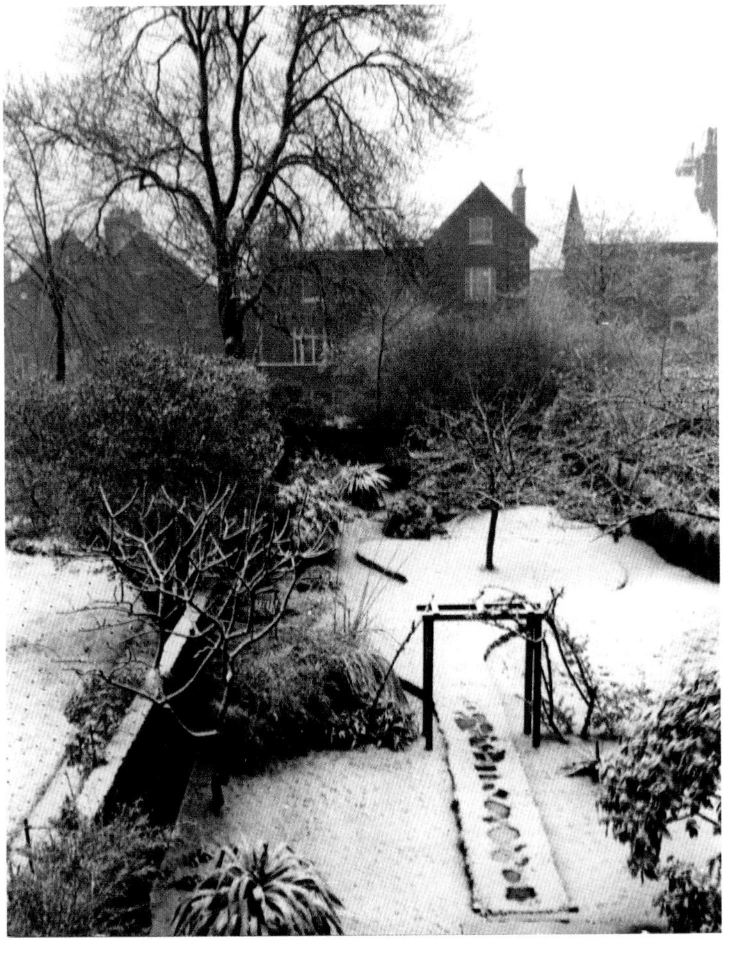

He began by cutting the lawn into sods and using them to mould the ground into a concave basin. He then created Plasticine landscape models as a guide and built outcrops of rock from council paving stones, breaking them up and covering them with a mixture of concrete and PVA before sculpting them into shape. As well as being more easy to handle and much cheaper than the real thing, paving stones have the advantage of giving sheer faces which is in keeping with some aspects of Japanese style. He encouraged moss to grow on the 'rocks' by using powdered milk and fertiliser. The ground was then covered by tons of cobbles and shingle along the banks of a meandering dry 'river'. To give the impression that the garden continues into the distance, the river winds round a corner of rock and out of sight. The boundaries themselves are entirely concealed by a row of leylandii at the back, ivy on the walls at the sides, and, higher up, foliage from the adjoining gardens. Frankland refers to his neighbours' trees as 'borrowed scenery' – or *shakkei* in Japanese. 'In Japan they would also call it *ikedori* – "to capture alive".'

A visitor might think on first impression that the garden lacks colour and is monochromatic but there is in fact every shade of green here from the smoky grey of a Japanese black pine to the cool blue of *Juniperus squamata*, and the muted palette increases rather than detracts from the sense of space. Grading the cobbles and shingle is also used as a distancing device, a textured gradient as he puts it. At the end of the garden full-sized trees have been planted to act as a backdrop against which the rest of the garden can be seen. He prunes the others severely to make them look like miniature versions of mature trees and indeed this whole garden is testament to what can be held in check with a mere pair of secateurs. As well as keeping them stunted the trees are thinned out so that the light gets in between the branches and the bottom branches are shaped to follow the curve of the ground or nearby rocks.

1976 Before the start of the construction

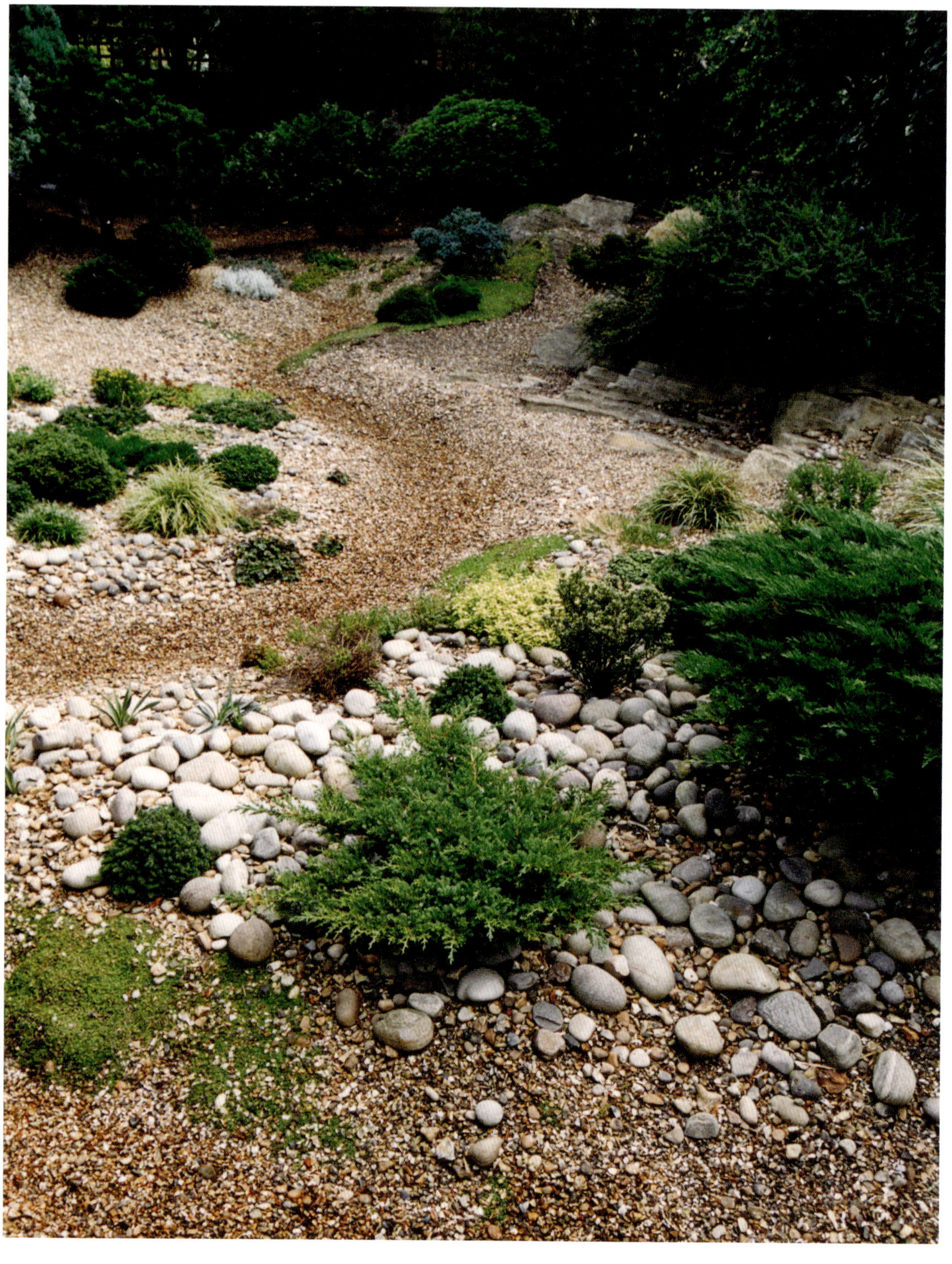

Looking towards the far end of the domestic landscape

Seen from the other end as one looks from the conservatory or walks from the back door the visitor passes from the large-scale plants packed close together to give a feeling of enclosure – laurels, healthily sprouting yuccas and a mature hardy palm – towards a more open area where everything is smaller-scale. In this part of the garden dwarf pines, spruces, conifers and acers are set in a scaled-down 'valley', giving the illusion of being viewed from a great distance. It is playing with perspective and the 27-metre garden suddenly seems like a sweeping vista surrounded by gentle sloping hills. It's a very convincing optical illusion.

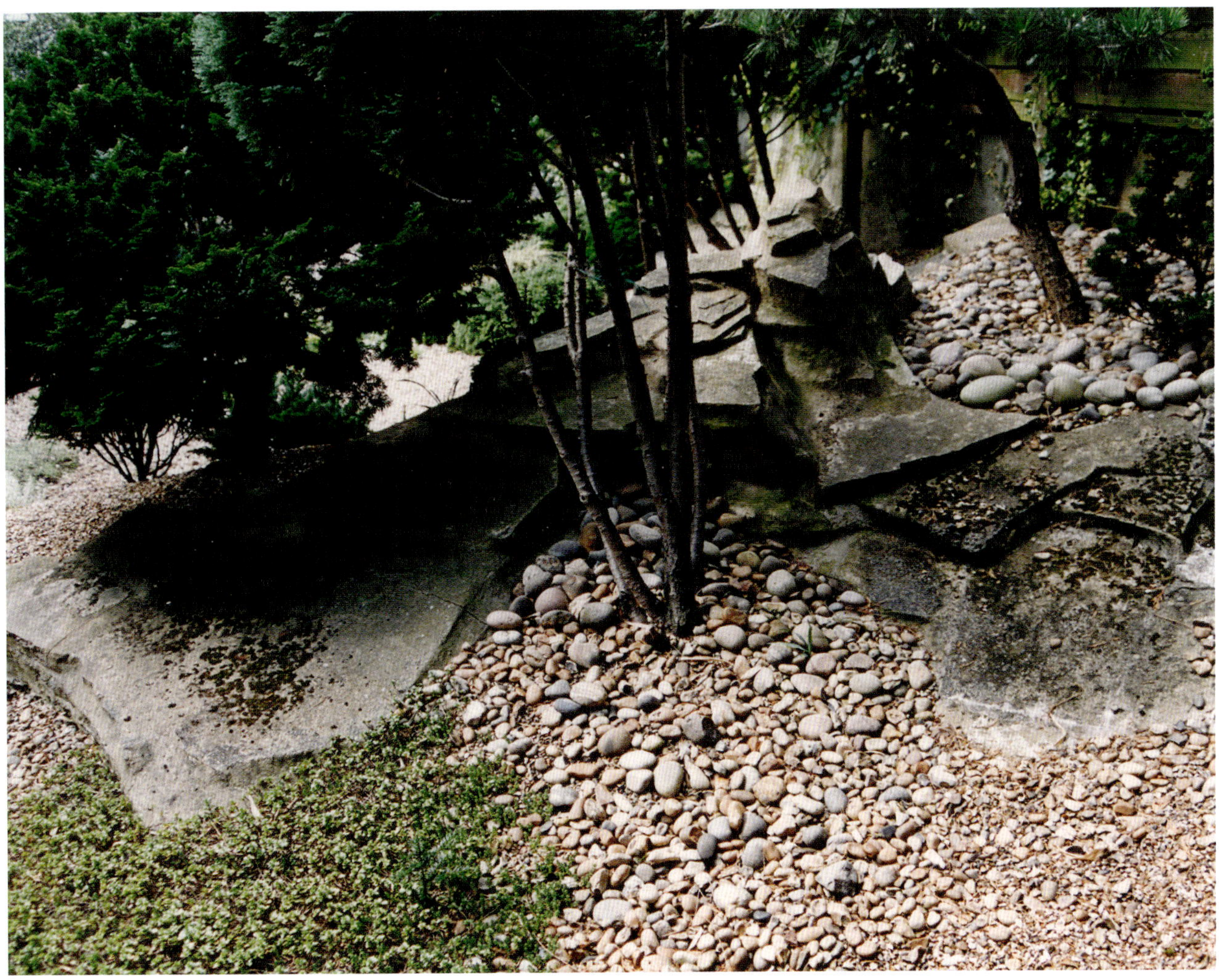

Rock structure, top end of domestic landscape

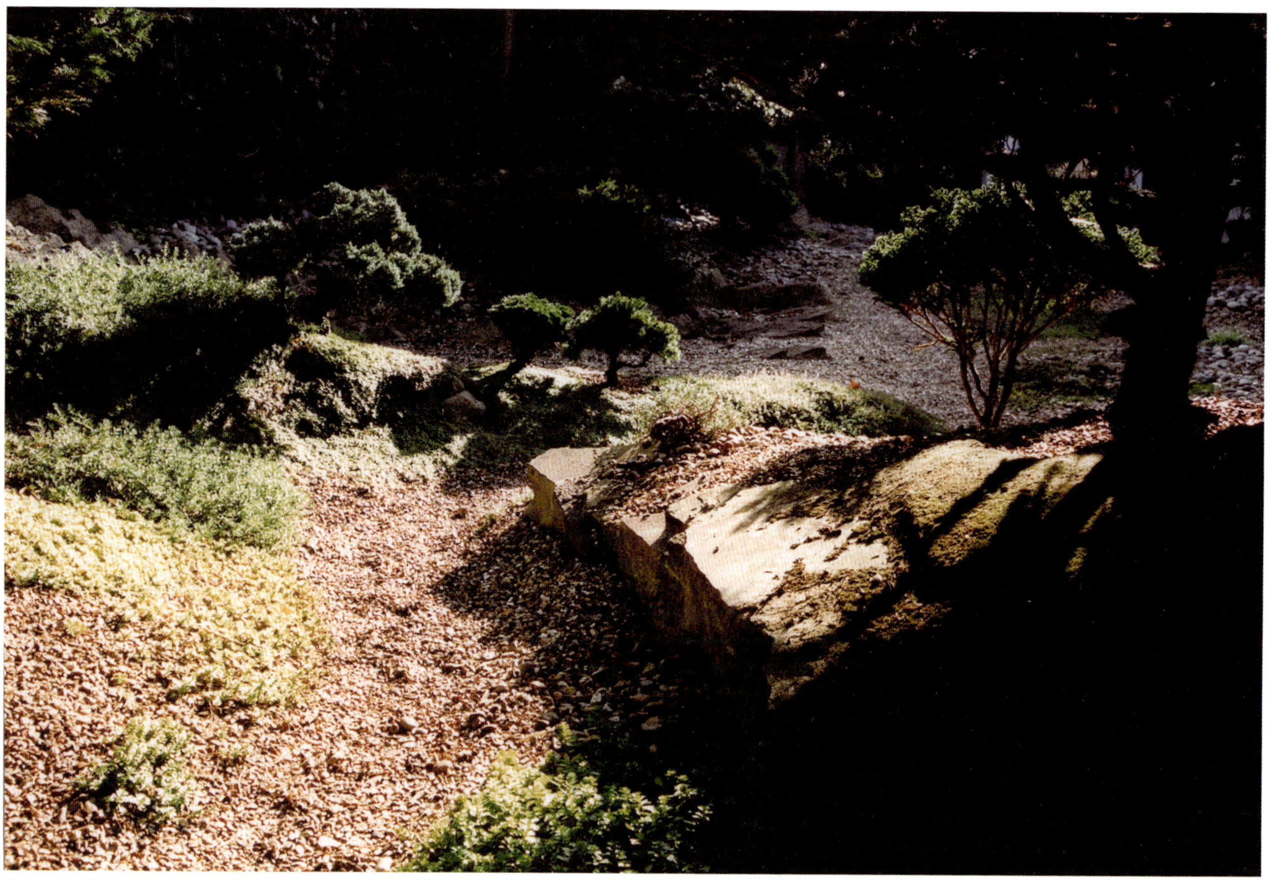

Looking back towards the house

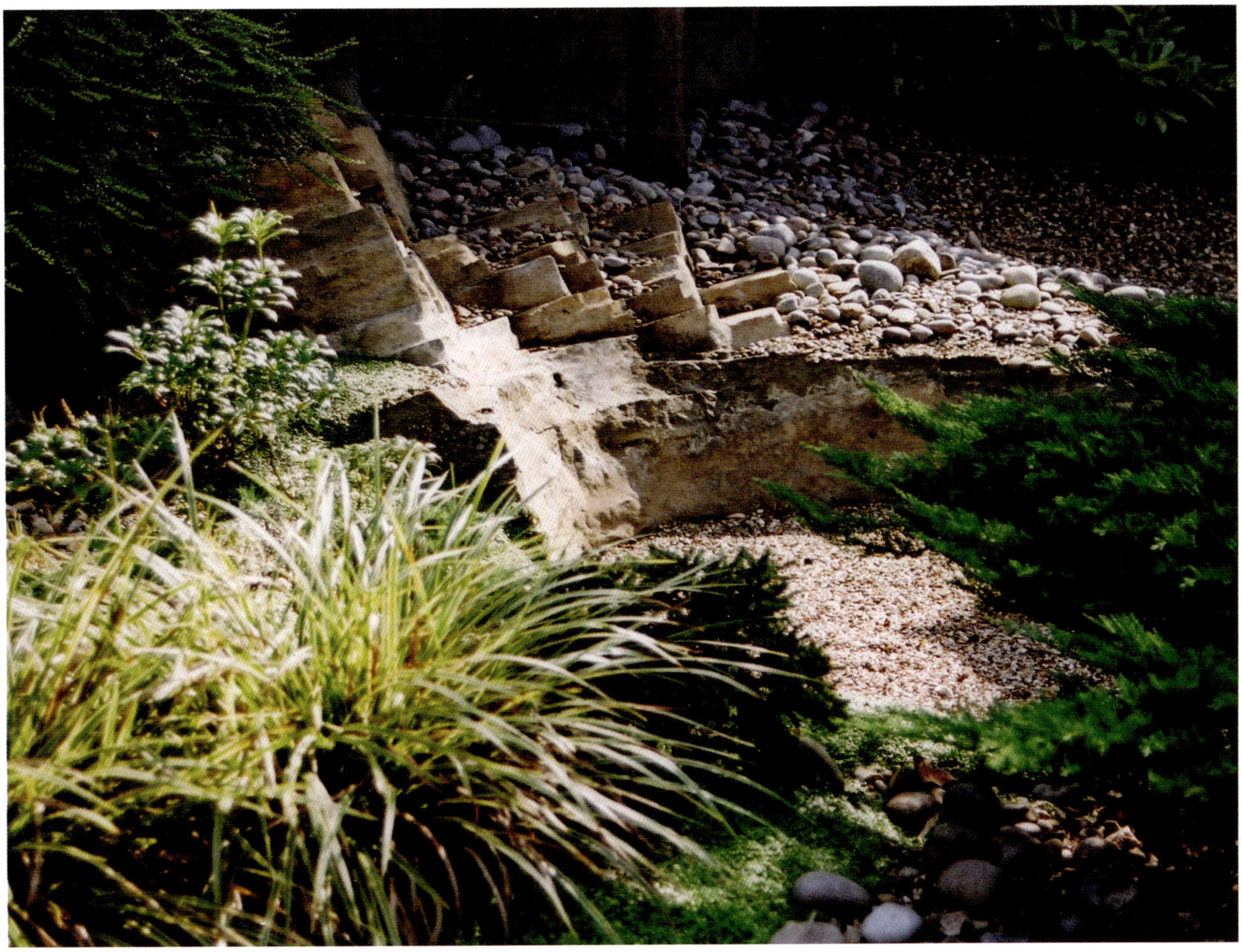

Rock structure left-hand side looking towards the house

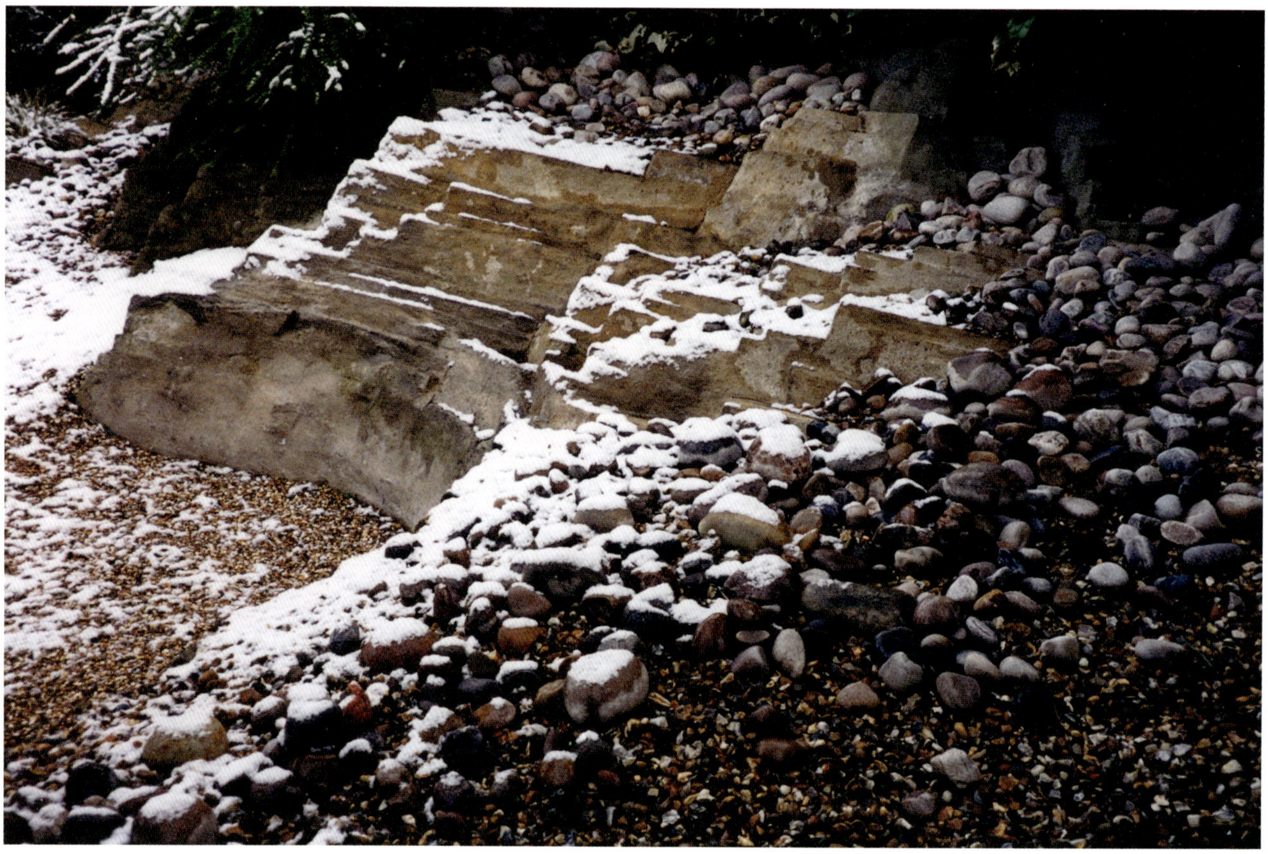

Right-hand side looking towards the end of the garden

7

The garden leads back into the studio which occupies the whole basement from the front to the back of the house, a dividing wall between two rooms having been knocked down in 1974. Now there are picture racks on the walls, two easels, a Bewick and Wilson printing press from Stockton on Tees – and an exercise bike. Sometimes if Frankland has a deadline for an exhibition he will stay here through the early hours of the night. The radio, particularly Radio 4, is his companion: its familiar sound fills the studio space and in engaging conscious thought perhaps more easily enables intuition to add significant colour, shape and form to the intellectual framework of an idea.

Frankland is first and foremost an intellectual artist, there is a concept or scheme behind every picture. After working for such a long time in the creation of relief structures and modular compositions with optical illusions, his work began to change. In 1976 he ceased doing reliefs and returned solely to painting. Eventually the wholly abstract, brilliantly coloured, lattice-work prints and paintings like *Shimmer* and *Regular Return* began to open up until by the end of the 1980s concrete images started to appear within them. In truth the purely abstract had become too limiting for him and realistic elements began to seem more gratifying and appropriate in the development of his ideas.

The acquisition of the press in September 1986 marked a return to printmaking and led to the development of new semi-abstract linocuts which could scarcely have been more different. They were much less detached, less interested in the cool principle of design and more dynamic than before. Although full of semi-realistic elements, as pictures they are quintessentially modernist; indeed lacking a correct vanishing point and a single point of reference they could almost be called Cubist. Again and again Frankland talks about the importance of structure. You might put different clothes on a clothes-horse but the structure remains the same. And he likes the answer given by Braque who would introduce a random object or shape into a still life for no apparent reason. 'Why put that shape there?' he was asked. 'The composition requires it,' he replied.

Once a picture is started and he begins to see the work in part there will evolve some random clue which will help determine how to continue – a process of clarity coming out of mystery in itself. A collage of, for example, photographs of paving stones, mirrors and abstract

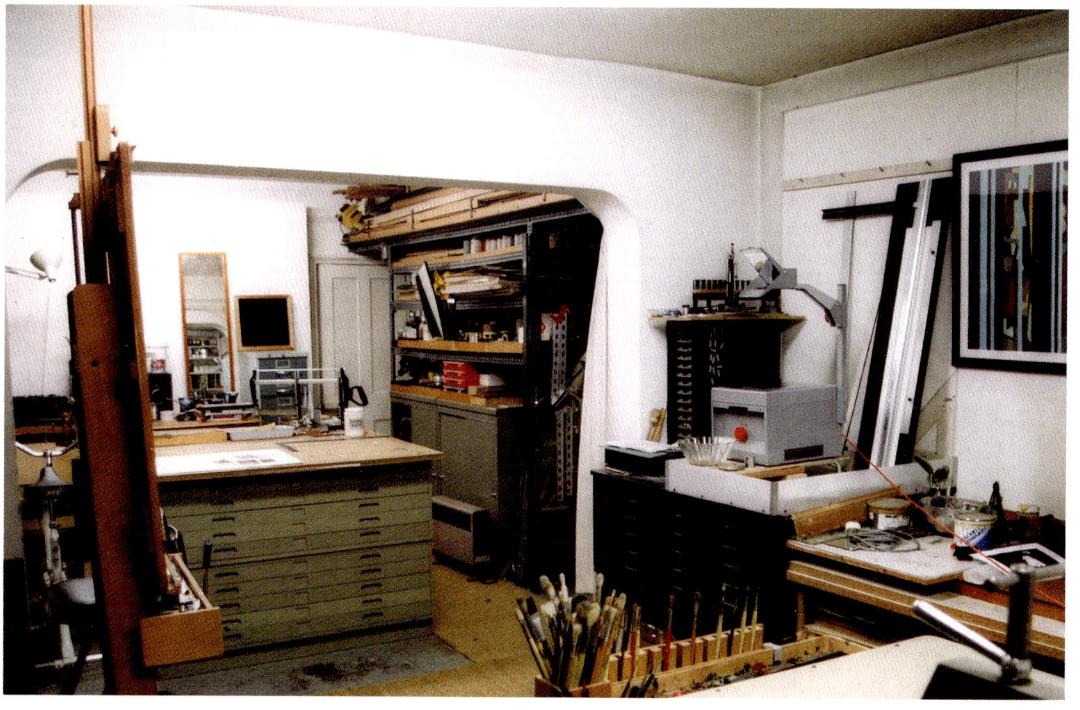

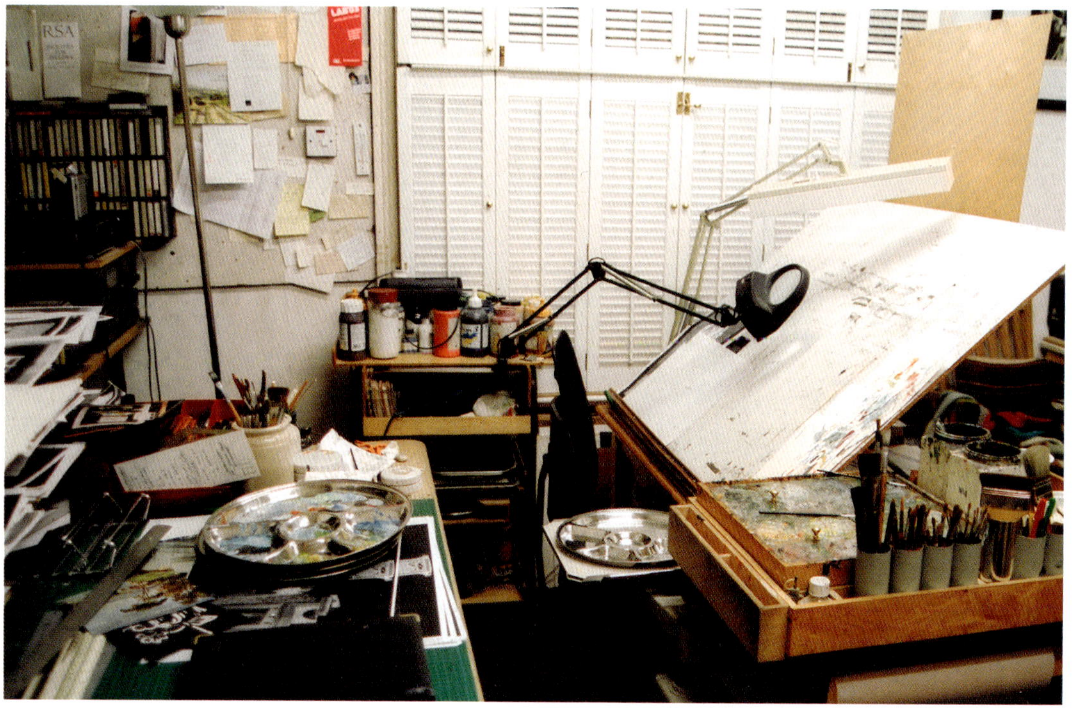

Lower studio layout

Upper studio layout

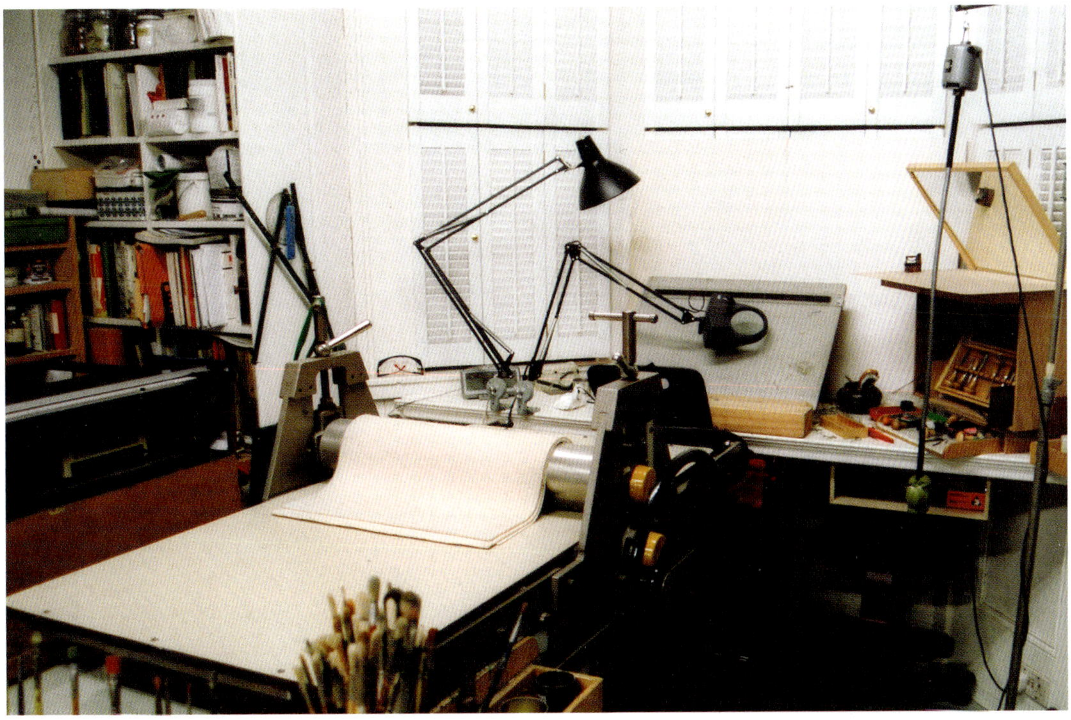

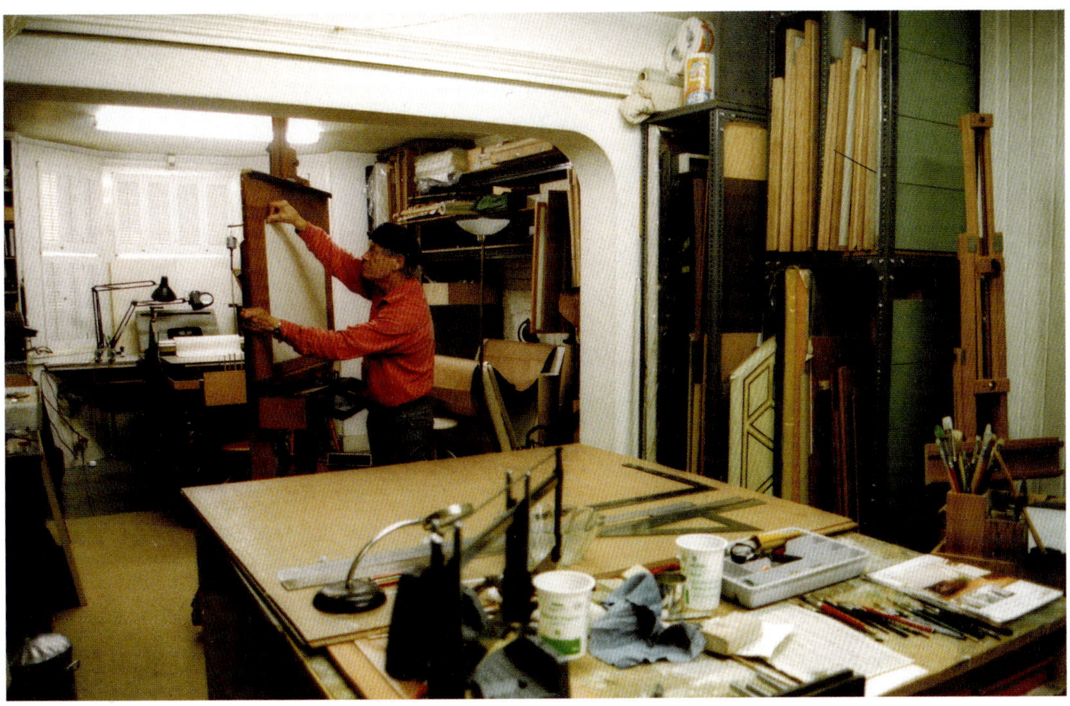

Lower studio layout

Lower studio layout

shapes added for purposes of composition will begin to evoke meaning. A firm believer in the delicacy of good draughtsmanship, he will work on a linocut with dental tools (which are employed by many printmakers) until a fine image has been achieved. He uses a special printing technique which requires heavy paper to keep the blacks intense.

A watercolour is first sketched in conté crayon which is then stippled and glazed with another colour so that the texture comes through and the images appear to float on top of a base. Although there may have been ten ideas going on at once before the intention becomes lucid in his own mind the final picture will have taken only two or three days of intensive painting.

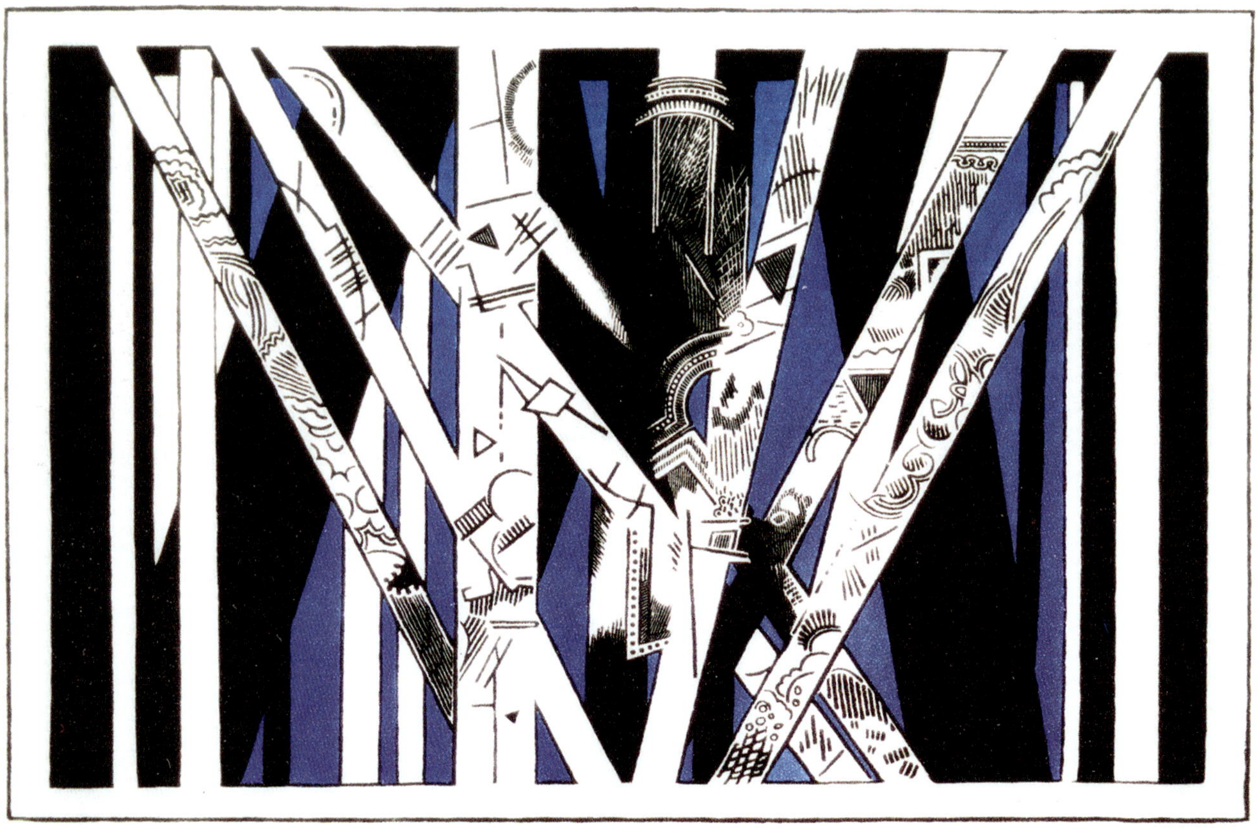

Although the interplay of perspectives between the representational and flat patterns has become his distinctive style, he uses perspective to disturb and enchant rather than to gratify. Nowhere is secure, nowhere is measurable. Frankland's imagery is mostly traditional and

Temple
700 x 460 mm, coloured linocut
Diploma print given on election to the Royal Society of Painter-Printmakers
(Ashmolean Museum)

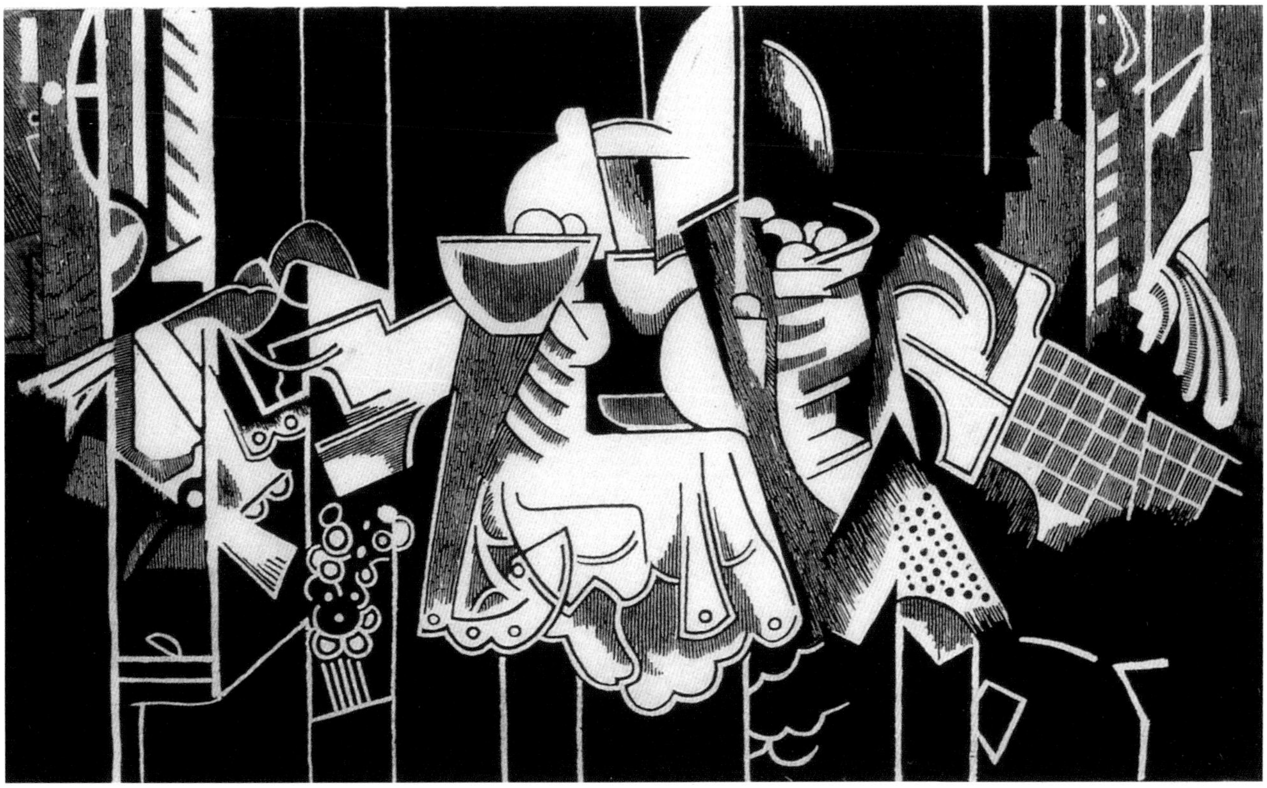

Interior No 1
750 x 460 mm, linocut

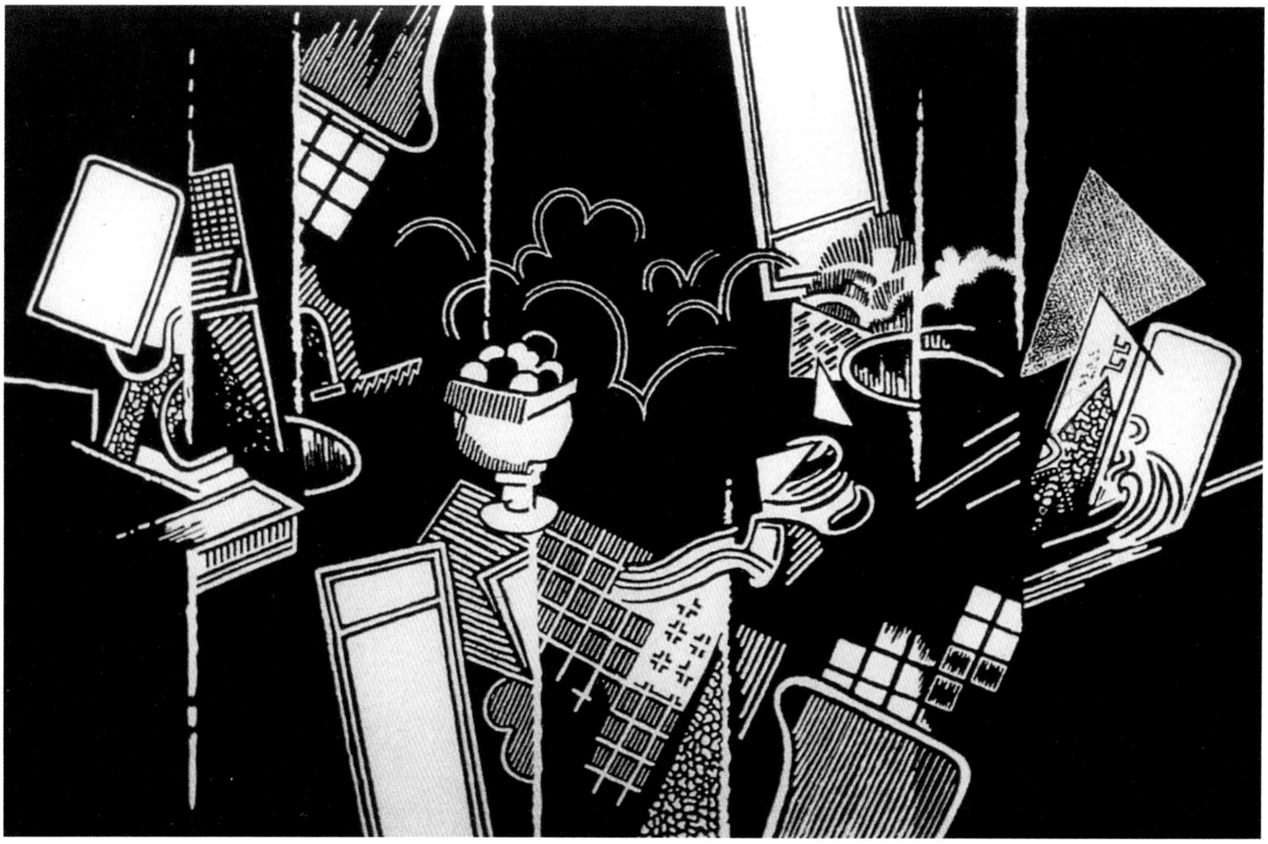

Summer Evening Reflection
615 x 410 mm, linocut

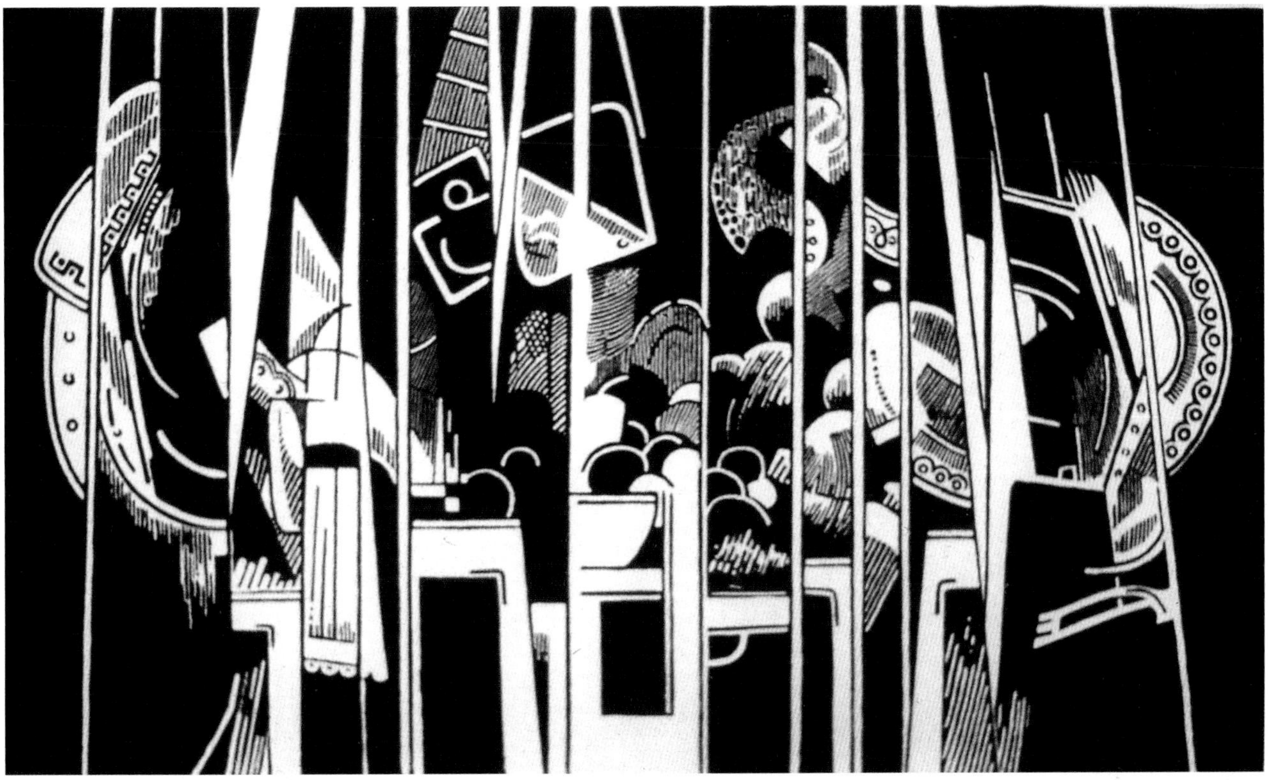

Still life with Brass Plate
710 x 430 mm, linocut

the individual items which recur in the foreground of his pictures make for the most part a quite tidy and homely still life. These, he calls 'domestic landscapes'. An inventory of objects would include cushions, garden furniture and plants, carpets, mirrors, a chess board, Chinese vases, Sigmund Freud's couch (appropriately for an artist so interested in the potency of symbols), a mosaic from Carthage, shutters, and Venetian blinds. Sometimes these are echoes of old material from his own pictures or from painters in history such as Claude but together the assembled objects seem to represent a private mythology which is retold again and again. Frankland comments only that the choice of these archetypal images creates a mood and the spectator can read or create whatever story he wants from a composition. Save for the odd statue or figurine there are no people, however. They are not needed, he says forcefully.

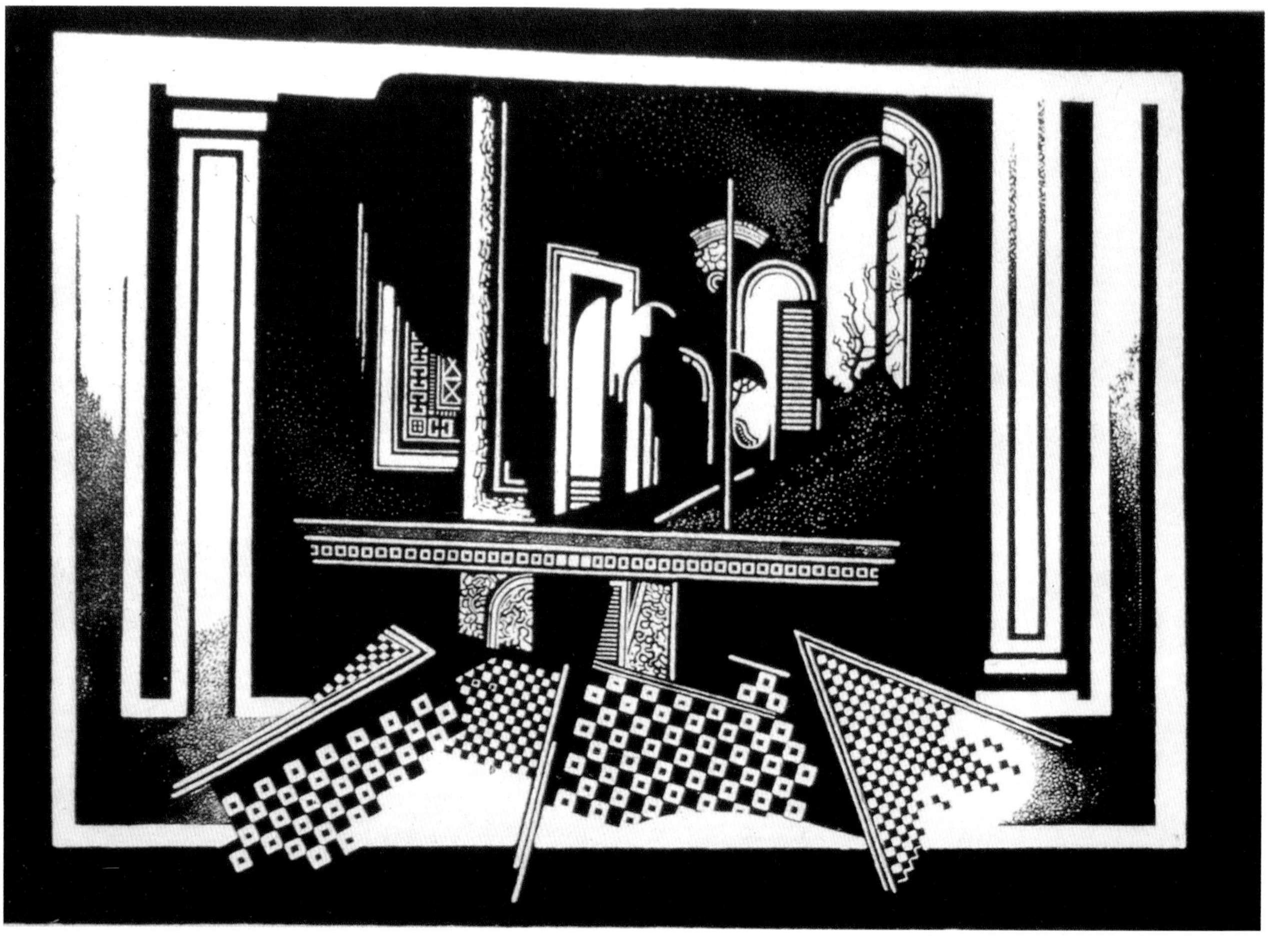

Recollections of a Great House no 3
750 x 550 mm, linocut

Between foreground and background there lies an unbridgeable no man's land. What exists here may belong to the completely abstract world of physics: the surface of things deprived of real content. In the tradition of Renaissance paintings these two-dimensional landscapes are glimpsed through archways and windows. Sometimes they just seem to be his back garden but the cities and towers are inspired by his own travels – whether to Esfahan, Palmyra or Milan – and then re-imagined and rebuilt on paper. Perhaps too these distant buildings contain their own entrances and exits: openings onto infinity. Background and foreground are held together in space by a single colour which creates a dramatic change in tone; most often it is that most fascinating and utterly suggestible of all colours – black, for blackness represents the precipitous mystery of the void.

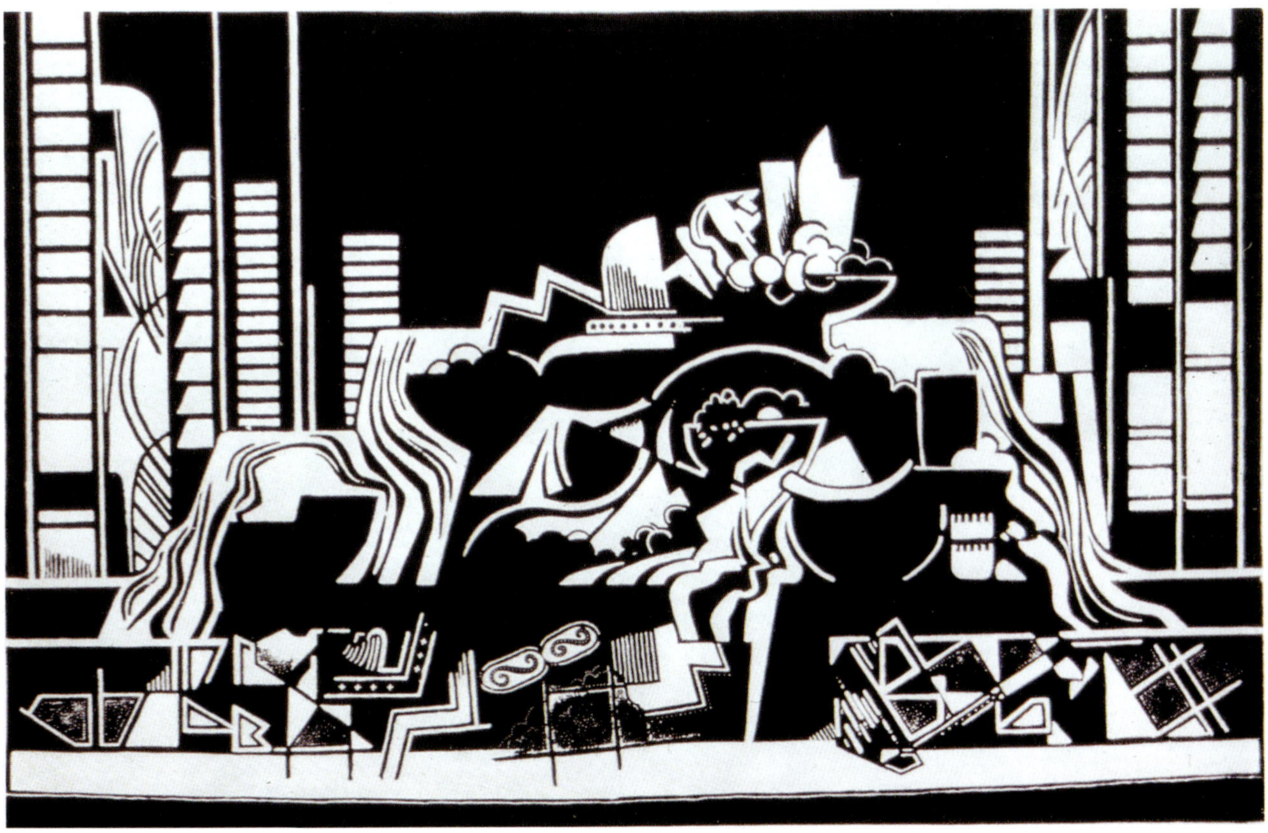

New York Interior
700 x 450 mm, linocut

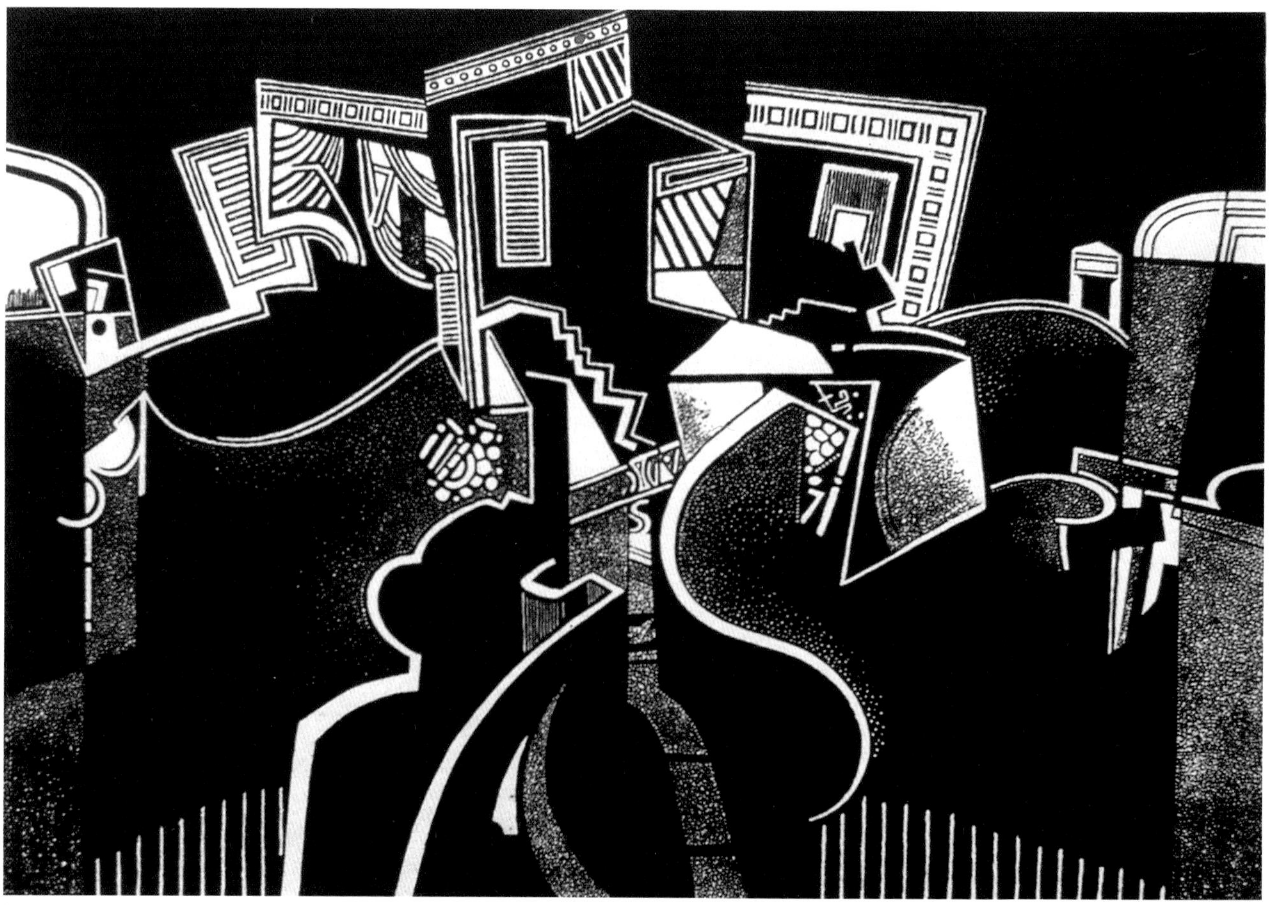

The House at L'Estaque
610 x 430 mm, linocut

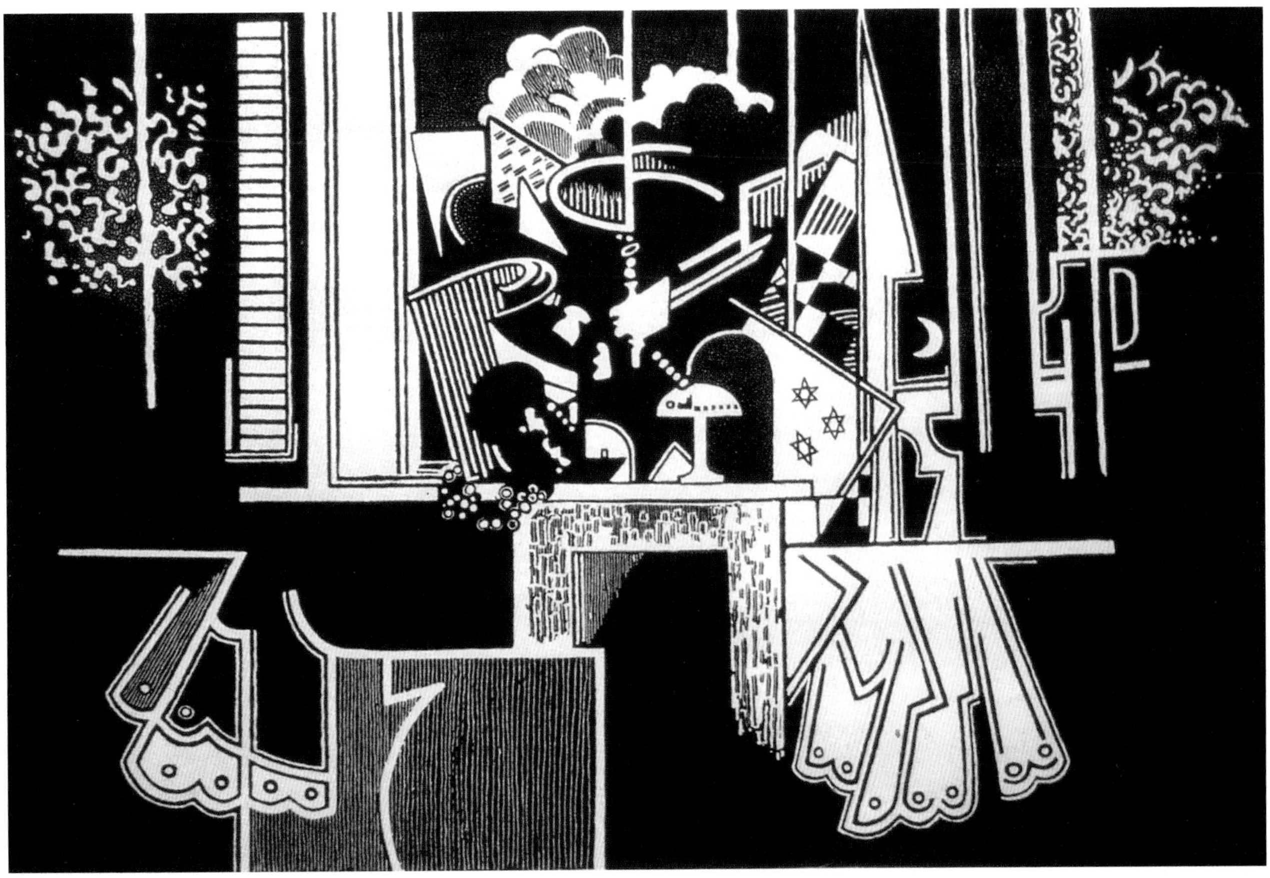

Interior View
595 x 405 mm, linocut

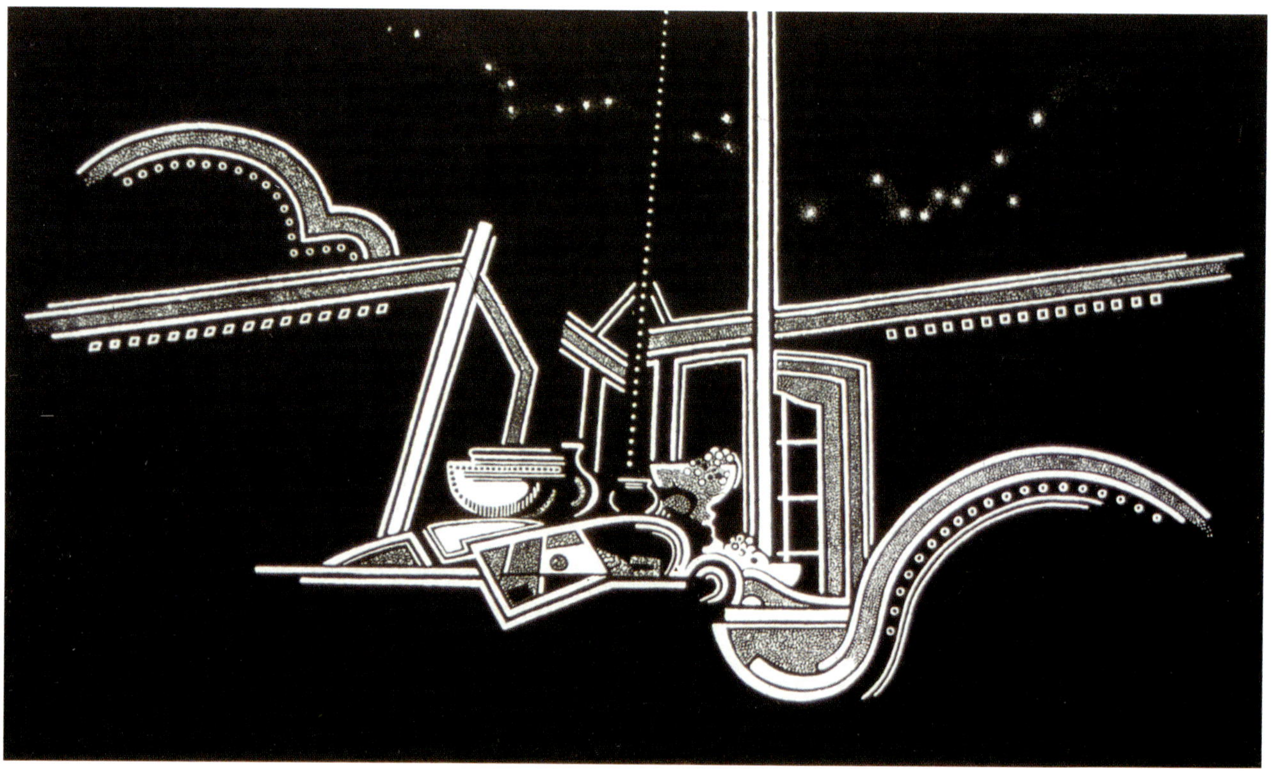

Solaris
750 x 450 mm, linocut

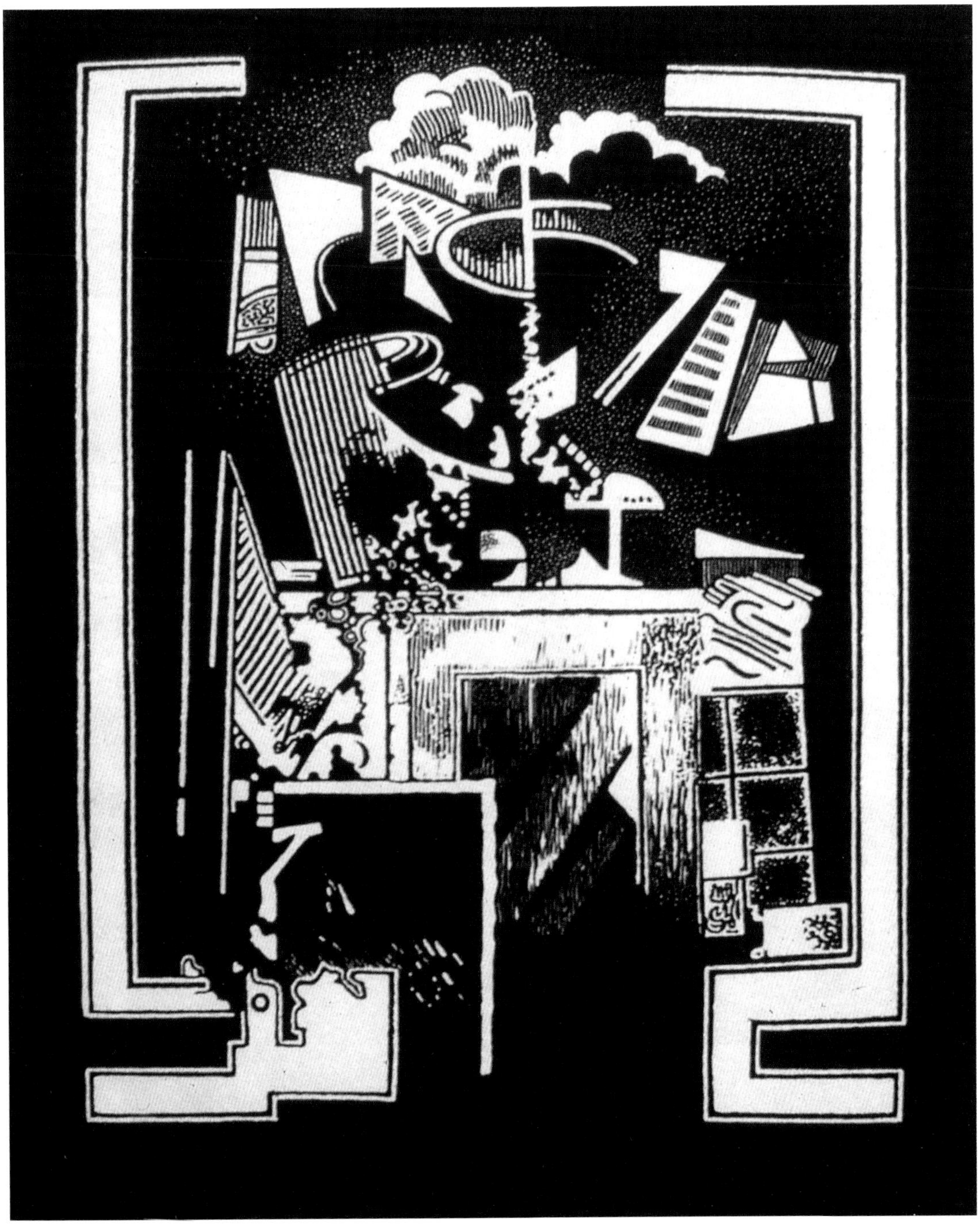

Summer Evening no 2
360 x 455 mm, linocut

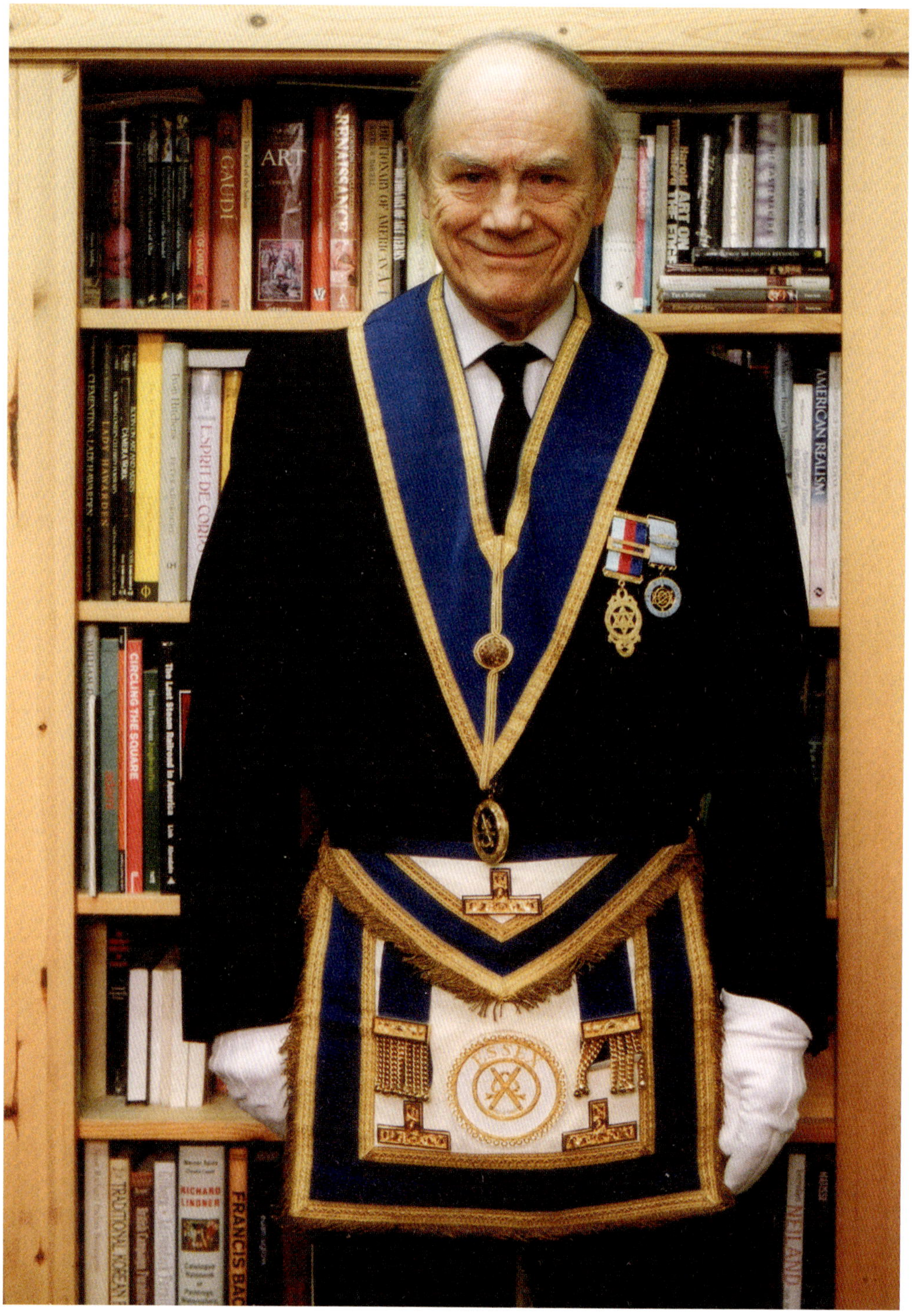

Wearing Masonic Regalia
Past Provincial Assistant Grand Director of Ceremonies for the Province of Essex, and Past Provincial Grand Sojourner for the Province of Surrey.

8

In February 1987, following the suggestion of a colleague of Dorothy's, Frankland was initiated into freemasonry at the Philbrick Lodge no. 2255 (the lodge is named after its founder, a nineteenth-century judge). Once introduced to the idea, it was perhaps inevitable that freemasonry should have fascinated him. Its origins in mystery (the secrets of a Master Mason), its patterns and ceremonies, rituals and fellowship, all this is grist to his own imagination and muse. There is also the appeal of the theatrical whereby the initiate is led through symbols and passwords from darkness into the triumph of light over shadow.

Two years later in 1989 to mark the centenary of his lodge Frankland presented a painting to the library and museum of the United Grand Lodge of England. The picture, *Ashlar*, had previously been exhibited at the Shipley Art Gallery in Gateshead. It is a composition based on a grid of equilateral triangles which symbolise the sacred word. At its centre is the perfect ashlar (a hewn building stone), which has a dual nature being both positive and negative. As the image is ever changing it points out the paradoxical nature of time, space and existence and although changing it remains constant and changeless. Its colours are yellow-gold, symbolising the sun and constancy; black which denotes silence and secrecy, and white representing purity, truth, innocence and hope. Its essence however represents the Grand Geometrician of the Universe, the Masonic name for God.

Freemasonry also offers an opportunity for socialising. He always takes pleasure in the idiosyncrasies of his fellow man. The household of the Academician Carel Weight, a near neighbour, which consisted of Weight, his wife, and Janey, who lived perpetually in her night attire and shared her room with an enormous birdcage, is a constant source of anecdote.

Part-time teaching did not guarantee continuous employment – teachers were only employed from one term to the next – until the lecturers' union (NATFHE) succeeded in persuading employers to give all long-term part-time lecturers fractional full-time contracts. At the beginning of the 1980s Frankland was finally appointed an Associate Senior Lecturer at what is now Middlesex University at 0.6 full-time for three days a week. He retired in 1996.

In the late 1980s and early 1990s Frankland began to take an interest in the exhibiting societies and started to show work with a number of them. As well as offering an outlet for sales the societies enable him to find out what other artists are doing, for companionship, and – since he is interested in their politics – for influencing their direction. And so in 1992 he was elected an Associate of the Royal Society of Painter-Printmakers (he had been exhibiting with them since the 1980s), and a Fellow the following year. He also served as its Honorary Treasurer from 1993 to 2003.

Subsequently in 1995 he became a member of the Royal Society of British Artists, and has been a Director, Trustee and Secretary of RBA Ltd since 2000. (Dorothy is now also a member of the RBA.) The following year he was elected to the London Group and served as Honorary Treasurer between 1997 and 2005. He is also a member of the Art Workers Guild and of the Small Paintings Group. He was made an Honorary Member of the Royal Institute of Painters in Water-Colour in 2003 and between 1993 and 2006 served on the Board of Directors of Bankside Gallery Ltd.

The Society to which he has been most dedicated however has been the Royal Watercolour Society of which he was elected an Associate in 1997 and, which is exceptional, a full Member in the following year. (It would be normal to have to wait for a longer 'probationary' period.) In 1997 he was elected the Society's first ever Honorary Curator. He found that no diplomas – a member's document of entitlement on election which is signed by the Queen – had been issued for over a decade. Furthermore many members had never deposited a 'Diploma picture' to the Society's collection as is their duty following RWS rules. The die for the official seal was lost and more than half the artists had not signed the roll of membership. Record keeping within the Society has now been considerably improved and diplomas are regularly presented.

In 2003 a member of Council suggested to him that he might like to stand as President. He was not the obvious choice since he had never served as Vice-President, the normal route. Trevor agreed, as long as Dorothy was happy for him to do so – which she was. There were three candidates and, following the usual procedures, he was duly elected for the Society's bicentennial. His first task, together with Anita Klein the President of the Royal Society of Painter-Printmakers and Angela Bliss the Deputy Director of the Gallery, was to assist in modernising the Gallery. Both Societies had, for many years, wanted to get rid of its red walls and paint them white but the projected cost presented by the then Director was far too high. It was not until the new Deputy Director was appointed that an acceptable estimate

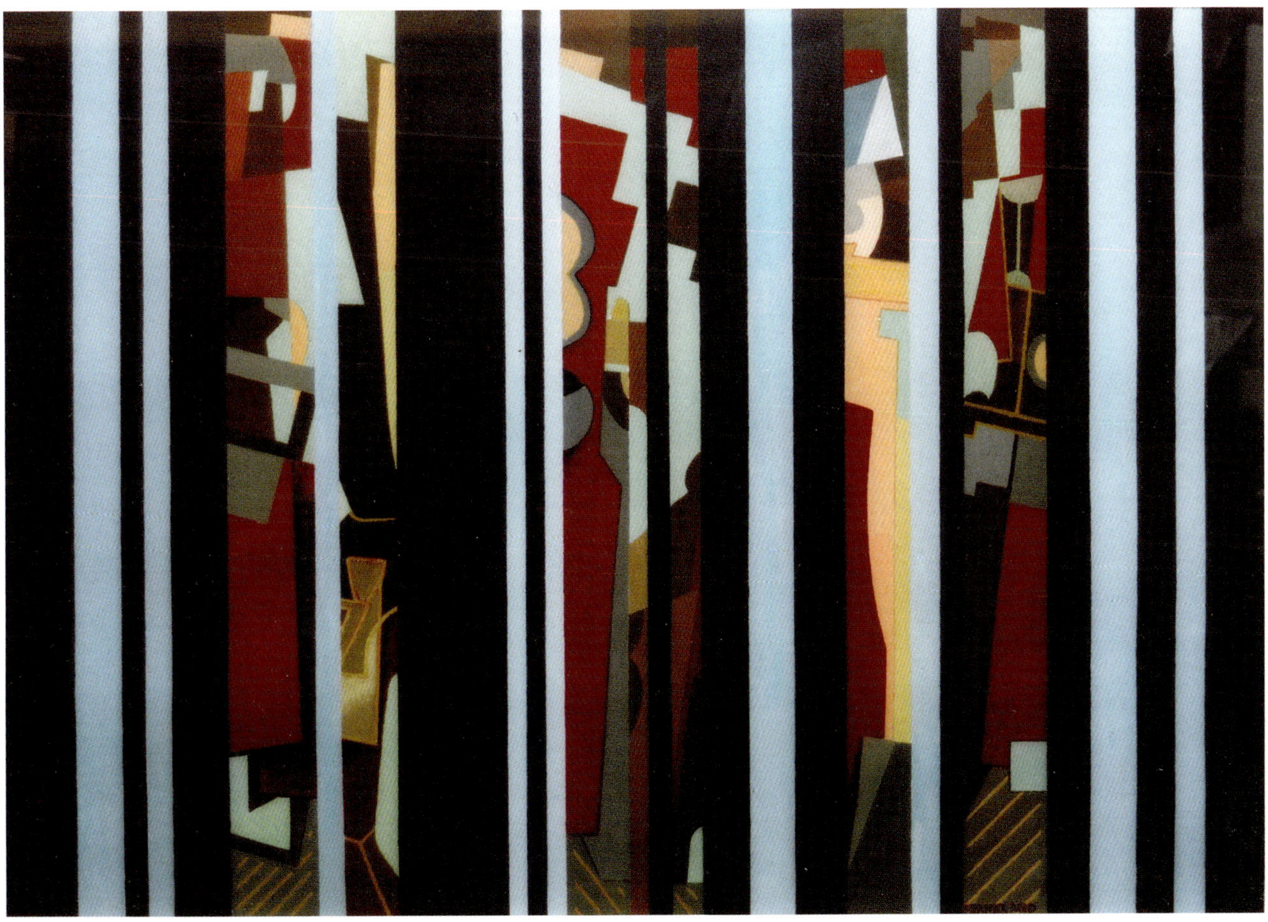

Villa Carillo
880 x 640 mm, acrylic

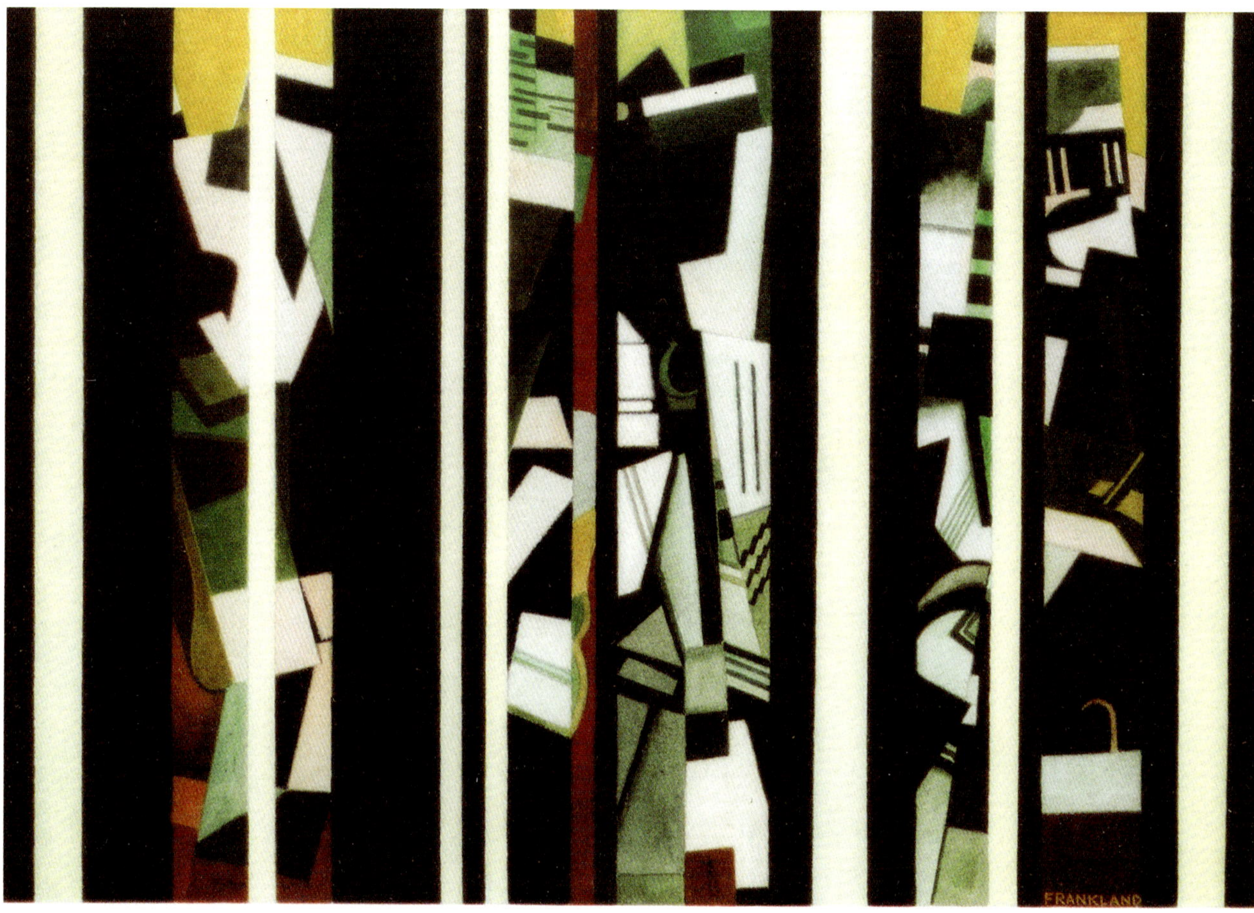

Spanish Village
540 x 380 mm, watercolour and acrylic

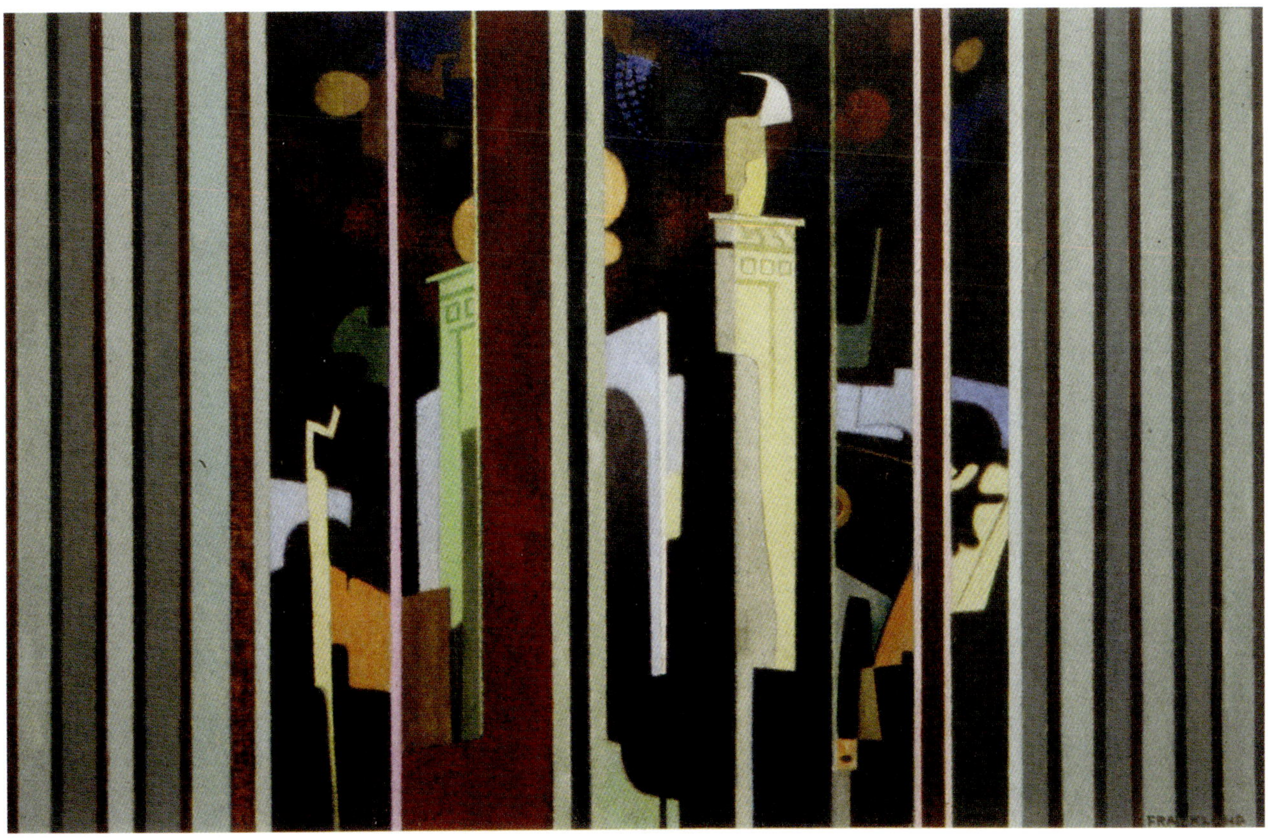

Studio Interior
610 x 400 mm, acrylic and watercolour

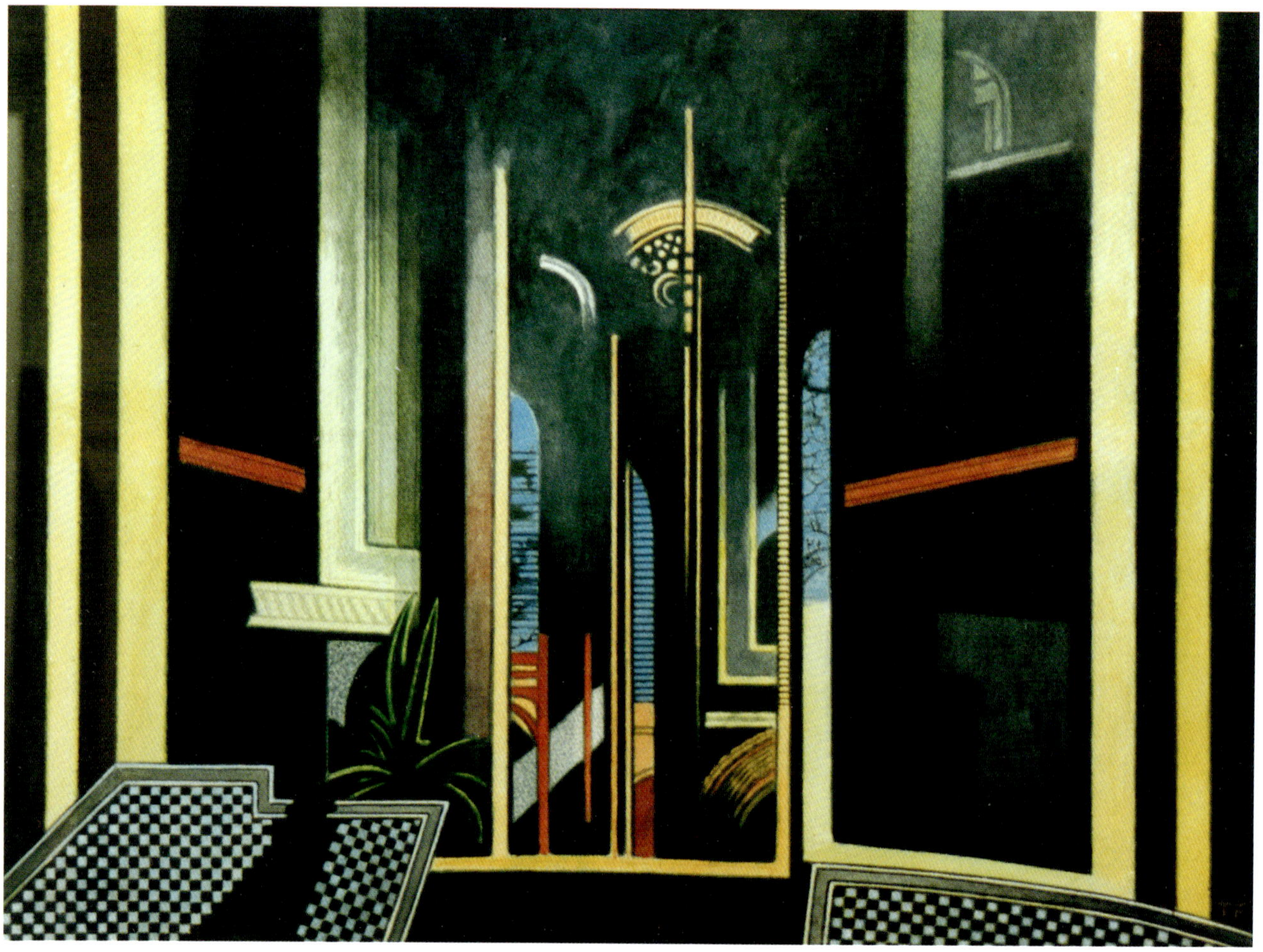

Moroccan Interior
550 x 430 mm, watercolour and acrylic

was obtained and the two Presidents agreed that the cost to both Societies was now sustainable. The year 2004 marked the bicentennial of the founding of the RWS in 1804 which was celebrated by exhibitions at Bankside, the Dulwich Picture Gallery and the Whitworth Art Gallery in Manchester. There were visits from both the Queen, the Society's Patron, and from the Prince of Wales, an Honorary Member. There was also a celebratory dinner in the House of Lords.

Despite this, Frankland's presidency was not an easy period. 2004 started with a large financial deficit and Frankland had to get the RWS to agree to support the Gallery in order to prevent its immediate closure. During the course of the year the fall in the value of the Society's investments and the slowdown in trading created increased financial problems; many members began to question the viability of keeping the Gallery. At the beginning of 2005 the situation was even more critical. Frankland sought the support of the Prince of Wales through his charitable trust. He was invited to Clarence House where the Society learnt that the Trust would give their professional advice. This encouragement eventually meant that the gradual slide which would have entailed the closure of the Gallery and sale of its lease was halted. He was enabled to steer the Society through a period of turmoil when many members, who feared that they might be liable for the Society's debts, saw the Gallery as the root cause of all their problems. However, because of the excellent management of Angela Parker, the new Director, by 2006 it was evident that the worst was over and confidence returned to the Gallery as the home of the Royal Watercolour Society.

After three years, the usual Presidential term in office, Frankland stood down as President of the Society but stayed on as Honorary Curator although he was no longer a member of Council. He had a particular interest in the role and in that capacity helped raise funds for the new research room for its archives – one of the most important collections of documents in British art – which was opened in March 2008. Despite this a few Society members questioned the necessity of its existence because of what they imagined was the expense involved. But it is a failing of artistic and professional societies that they should be inward-looking and often unaware as to how they might appear to the world outside. Over the weeks and eventually months I have spent in writing I was reminded of the reflecting mirrors which Frankland had installed in his house, and – for life imitates art – I have watched with a certain consternation certain members who echoed the words of the White Queen in *Alice Through the Looking-Glass*: 'Why, sometimes I've believed as many as six impossible things before breakfast.'

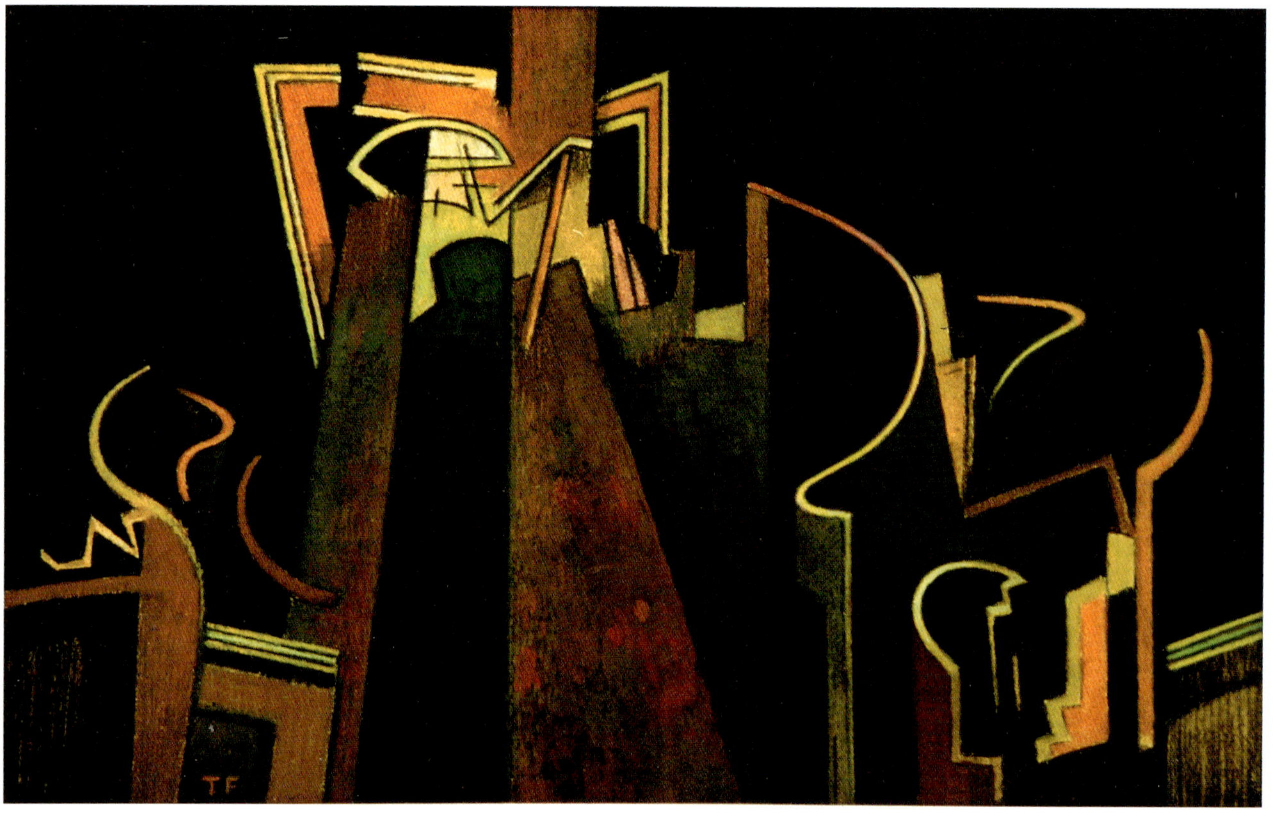

Cityscape no 1
410 x 260 mm, acrylic

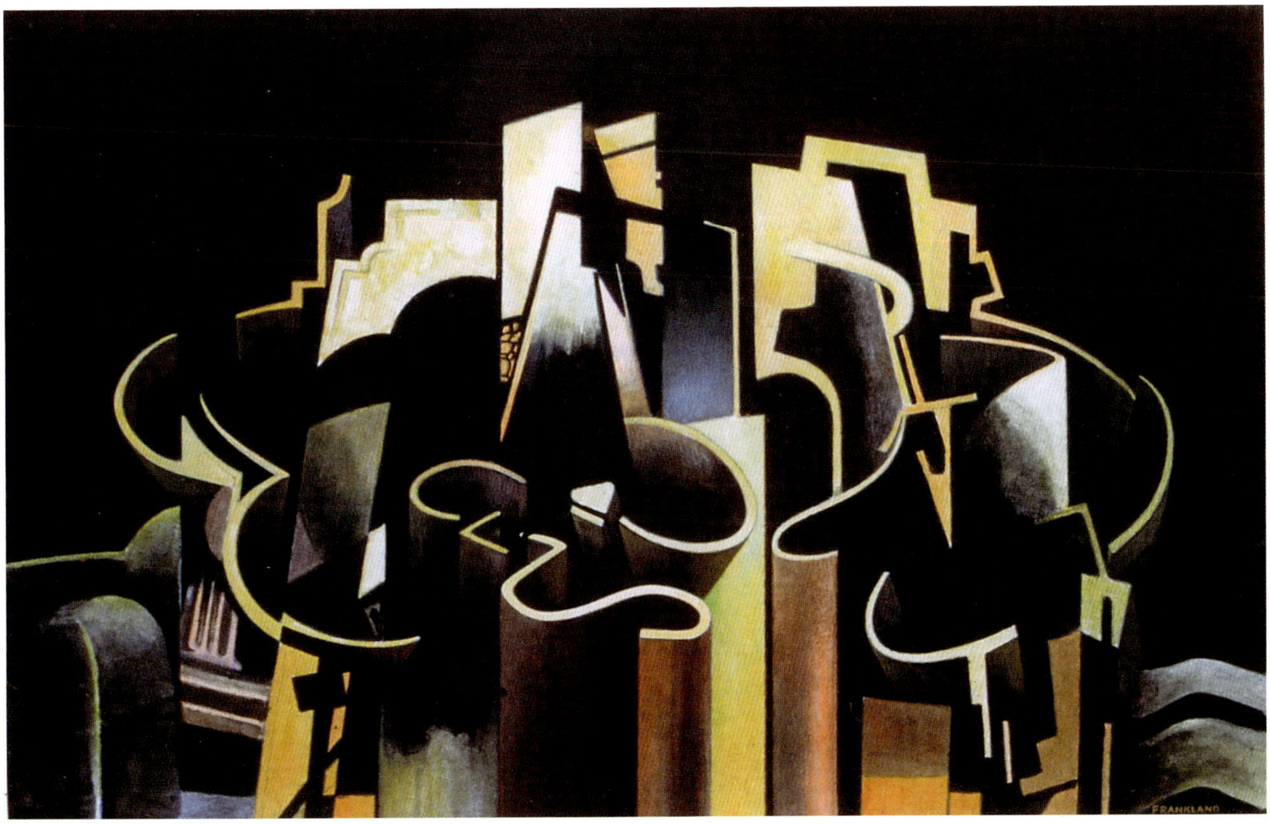

Neonlit Cityscape no 2
670 x 430 mm, acrylic and watercolour

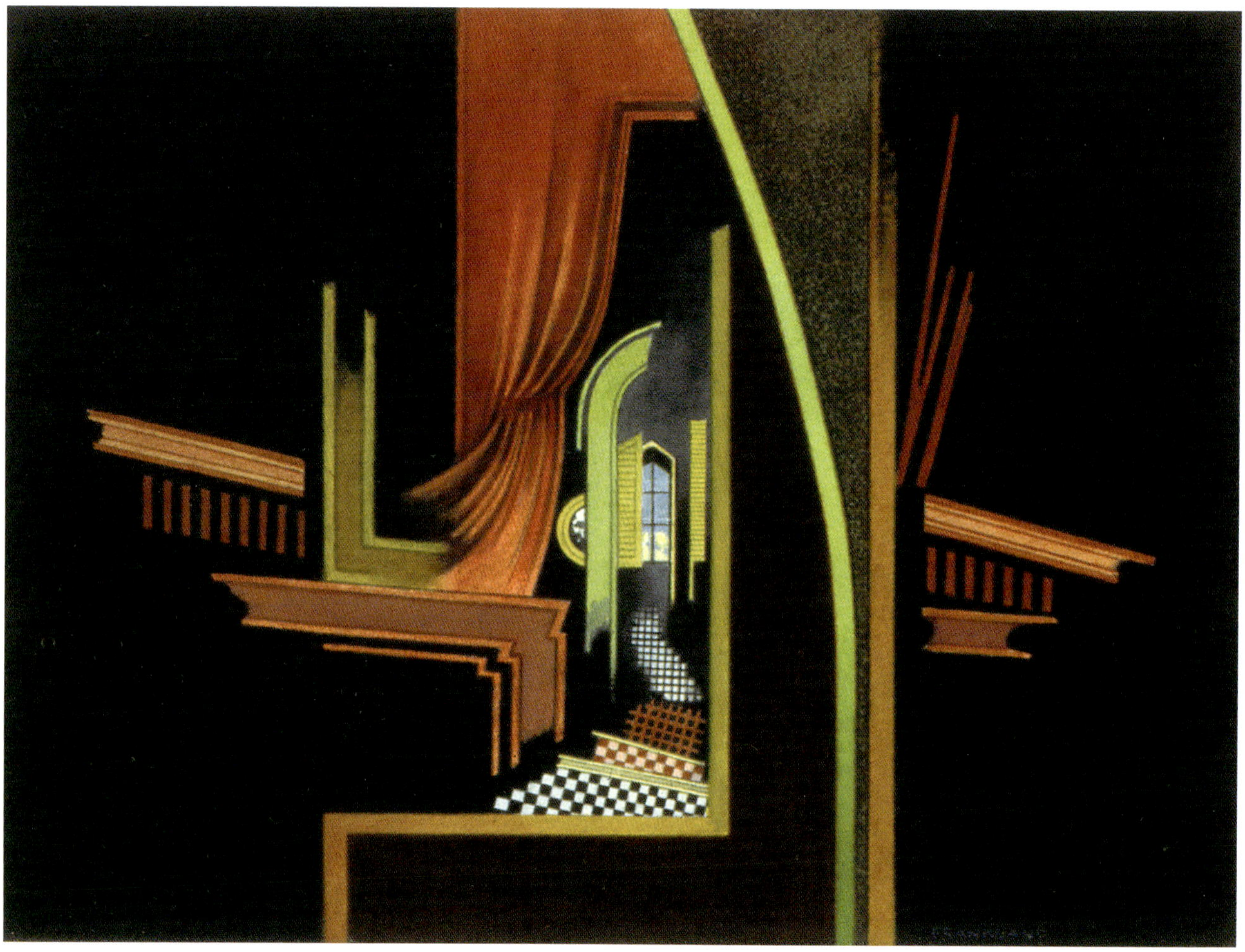

Homage to De Hooch no 3
670 x 500 mm, watercolour and acrylic

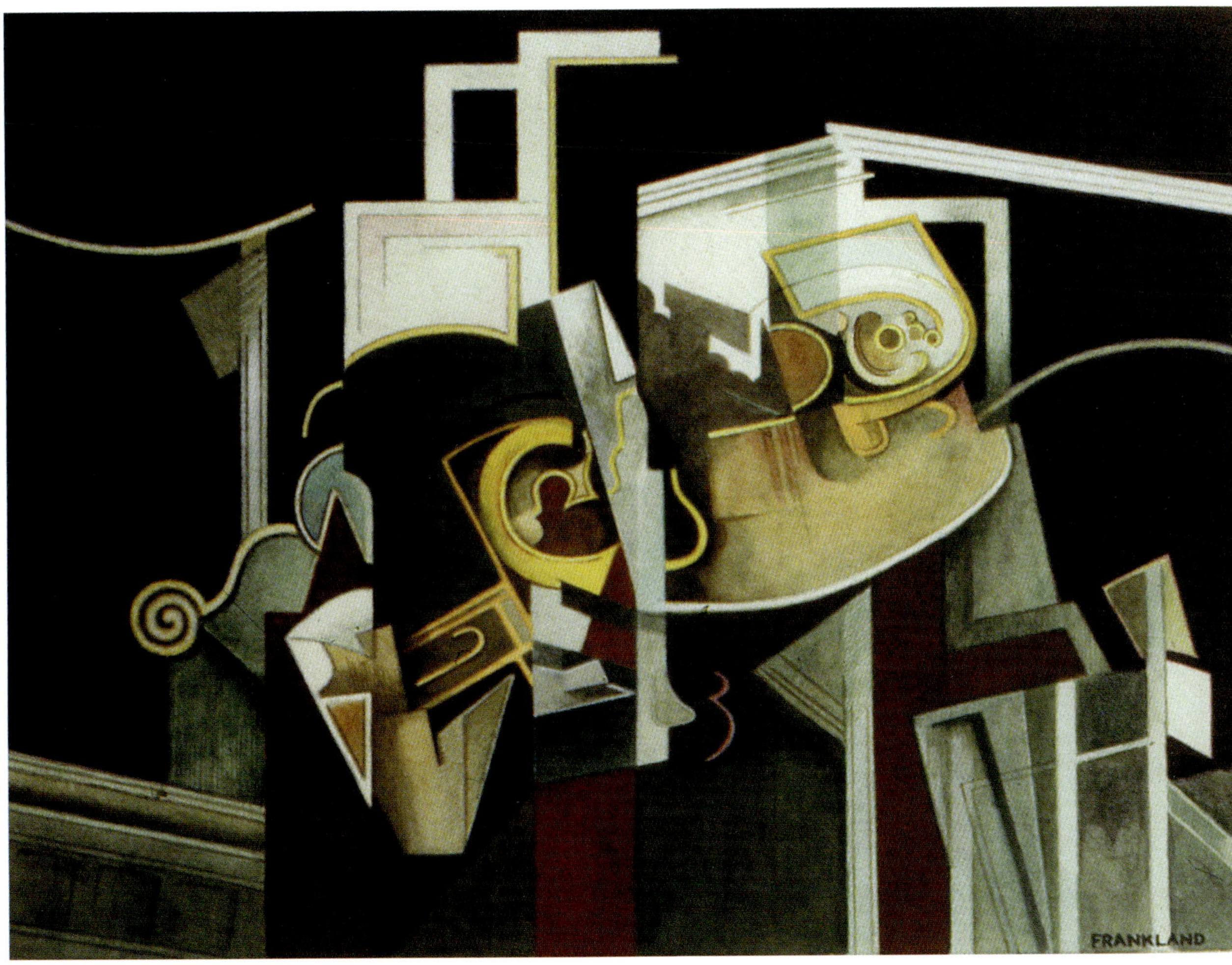

Metal Forms, Midnight
440 x 320 mm, watercolour and acrylic

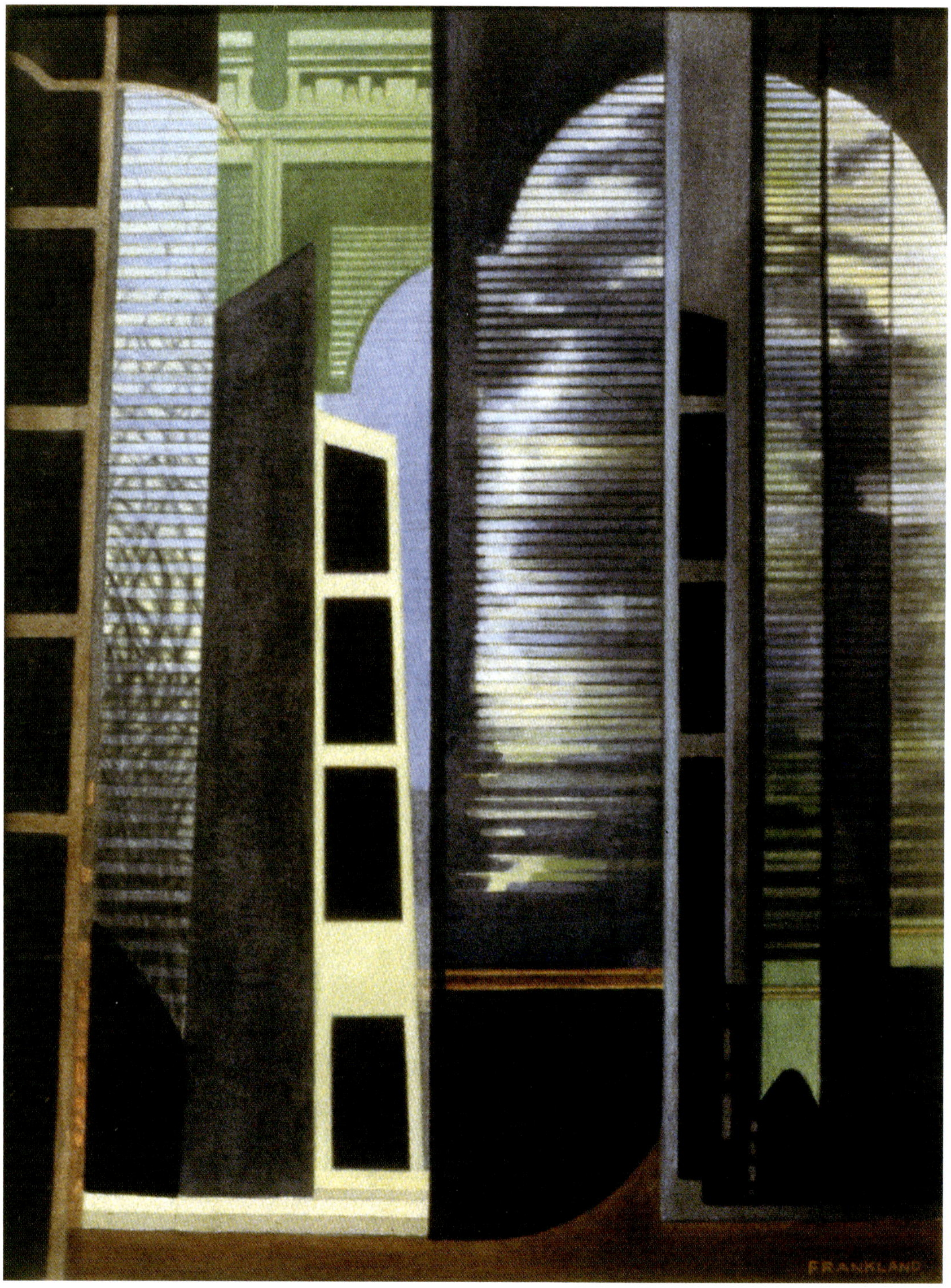

Villa D'Este no 2
310 x 400 mm, watercolour and acrylic
Royal Watercolour Society Diploma Picture

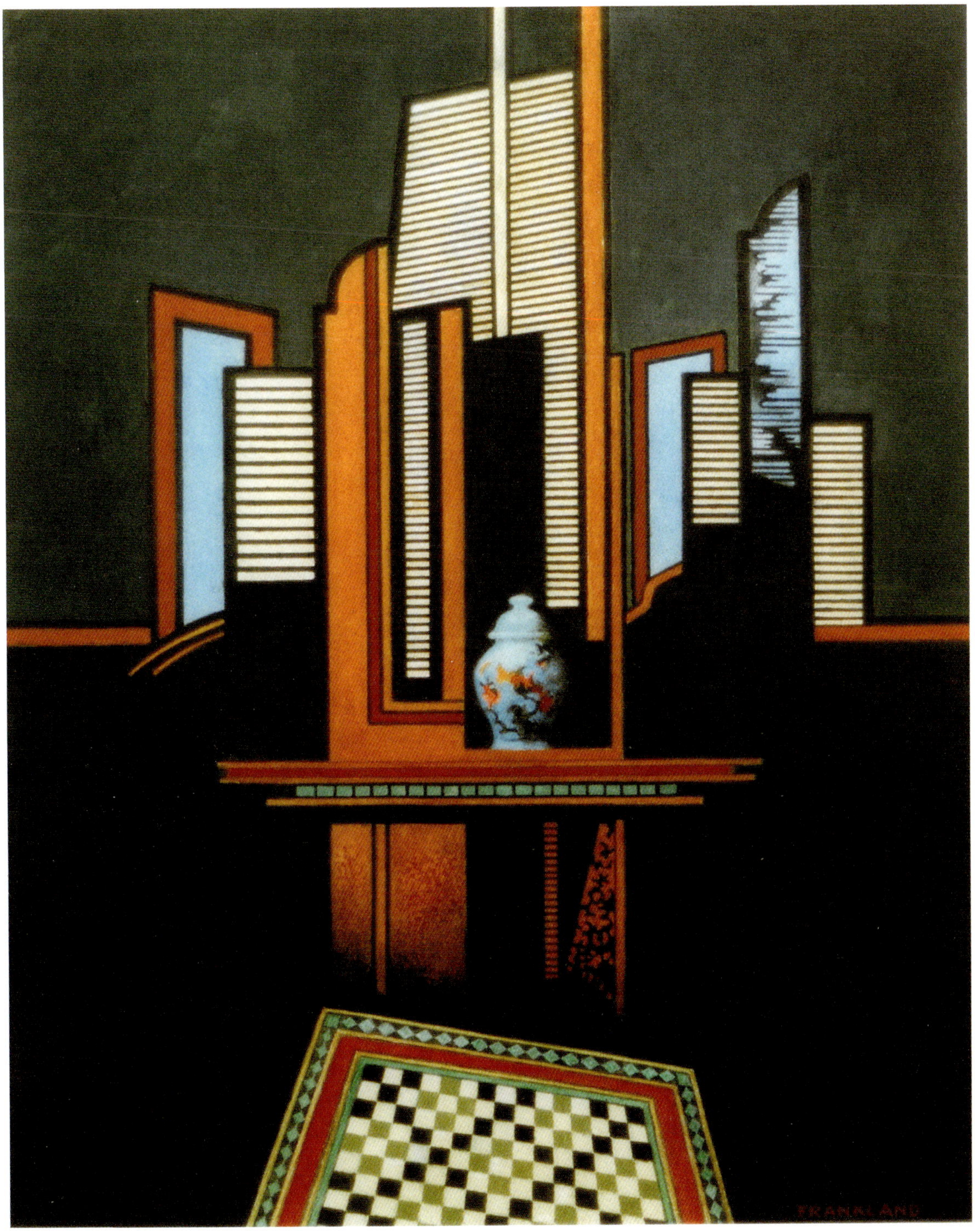

Oriental Pot
470 x 590 mm, acrylic and watercolour

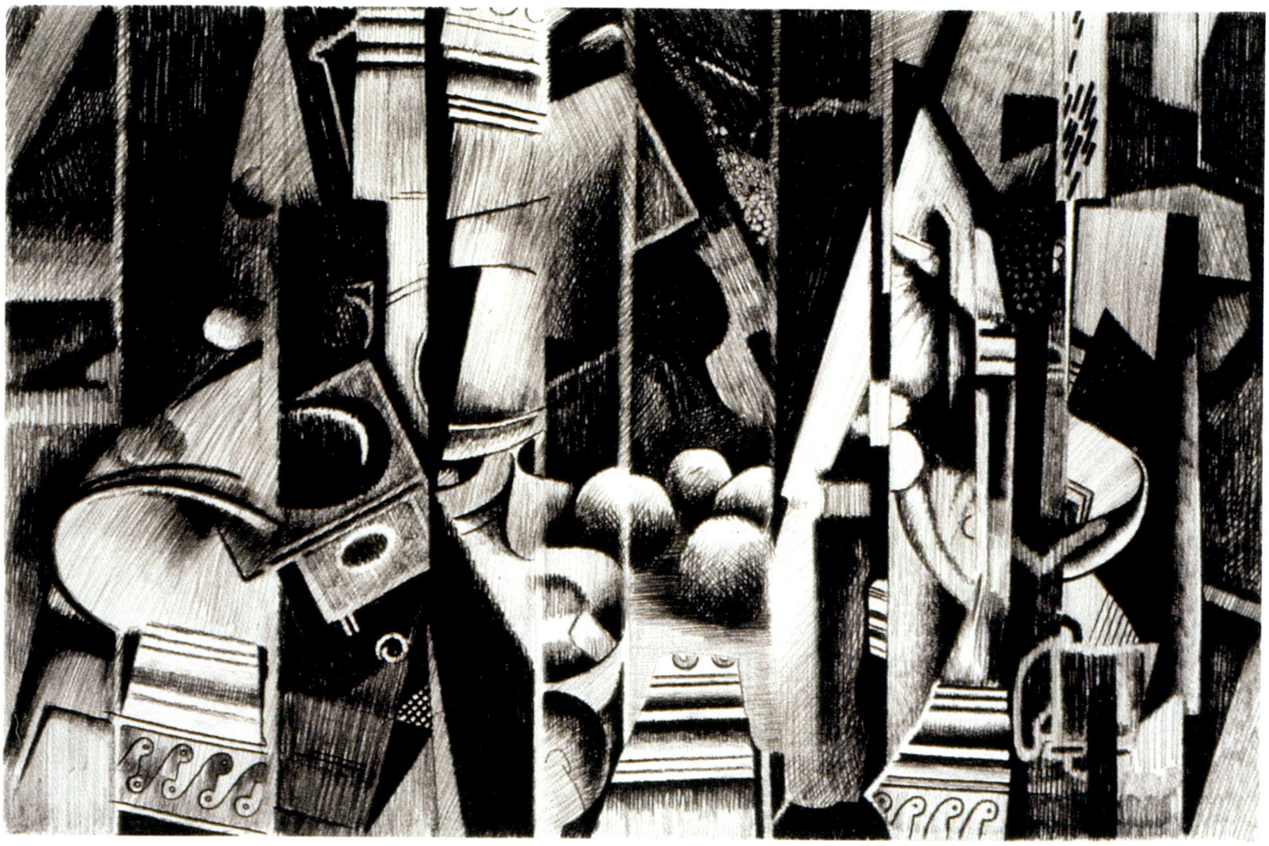

Still Life
980 x 660 mm, conté crayon

9

A staircase leads from the studio back up into the house. An Italian landscape by David Gluck hangs on the stairs. Gluck was a close friend who died in 2007 leaving a generous legacy from his estate to the Royal Watercolour Society. In the hall there are more pictures by friends and colleagues: Leslie Worth, Bert Irvin, Mark Vaux, Jules de Goede, Dave King, a signed print by Max Bill, as well as a nude by Eric Hebborn and a sketch of a barn Frankland made during a visit to Dedham Vale in Suffolk with Hebborn when they were still students. A Japanese quiver vase, which again comes from the Cliveden sale, stands on side table holding dried flowers.

Upstairs on the ground floor there is a second studio. For Trevor and Dorothy it began as their bedroom where, on their first morning, they awoke to the sun shining into the room and felt how after the confines of living in one room they had space at last. Now the room is occupied by the usual impedimenta of an artist – pots crammed with pencils, brushes and pens, rulers and set-squares, jars of paints and varnish, photographs and portfolios. On the walls hang a couple of Frankland's prints, a painting by Dorothy; beneath them are pinned notes and telephone numbers. A plan chest is filled with old prints and work in progress. (I asked Trevor what he does with pictures which fail; he replies that he cuts them up and re-uses them – virtually nothing is wasted.) This is essentially the room where pictures are planned, drafted, worked out. It is this process which he enjoys the most. He keeps here a small early-nineteenth-century percussion pistol given to him by Hebborn in exchange for a canvas, and on top of a filing cabinet in a corner of the room there stands a tall rectangular wooden box made by Frankland himself. The box contains a handful of the bamboo sticks which, following the directions of the *I Ching*, the Chinese book of divination, Frankland casts and interprets when he wishes to make a decision and no obvious solution is apparent. As with the optical illusion in his garden, he is content simply that it appears to work.

There are also more bookshelves. Frankland loves the theory behind the creation of a work, though believing in a Zen teaching which Wittgenstein stated as 'showing is more important than saying'. When I visit, a book on Nicolas Poussin lies behind us in the studio as we talk. Poussin is a great, perhaps Frankland's greatest, love in all art. The cool, near mathematical clarity of the artist, one of the founders of the ideal in landscape painting, serves to bring out the intense poetic

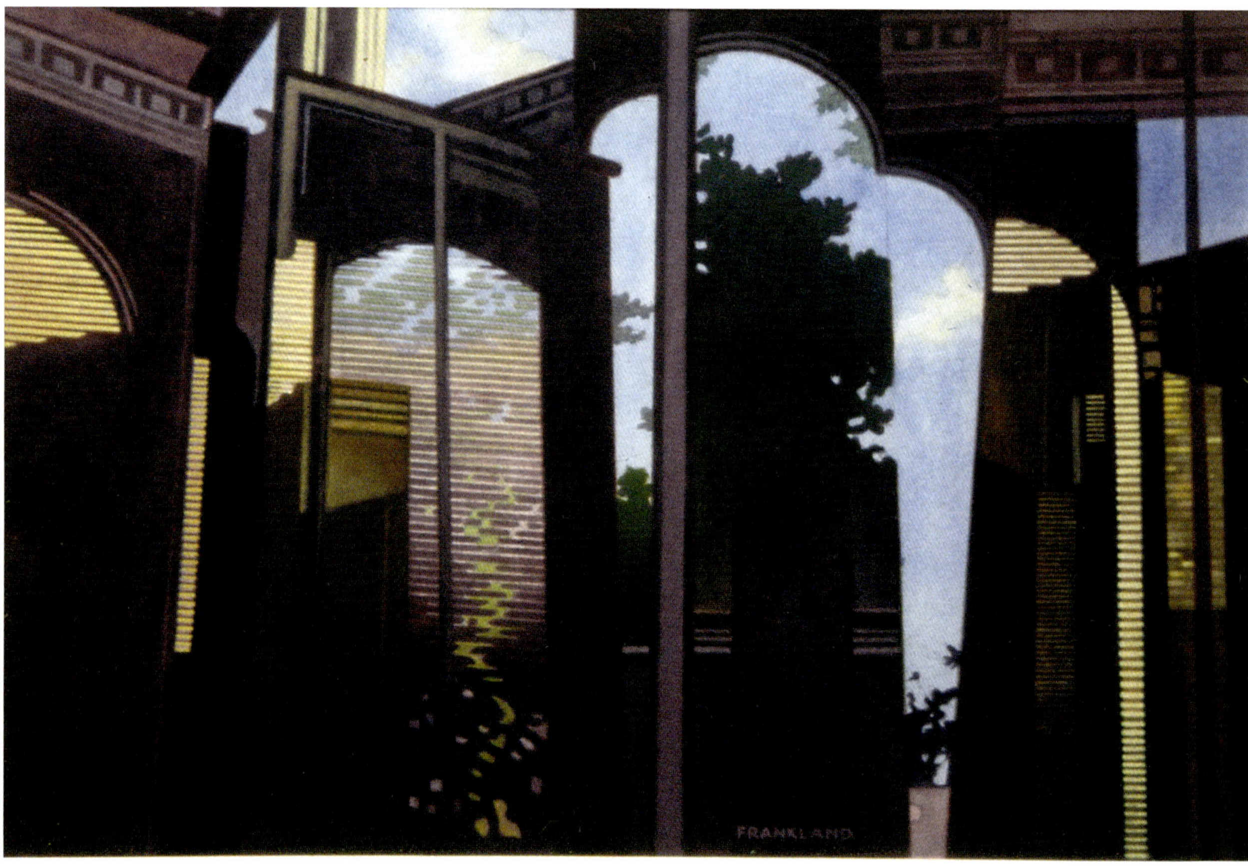

feeling of his paintings. It is the perfect balance. He also mentions Gustav Klimt, Giorgio de Chirico, Balthus and Frank Stella as important influences. Broadly speaking all these artists could be called classical rather than romantic. 'Whether we know it or not "we crave the expressive in art", Bernard Berenson wrote .... "there's more force in controlled passion than in exuberant passion. That's the idea I like. I like it slowly to creep out on you."'

This might serve as motto for Trevor Frankland's own work.

Villa D'Este no 3
720 x 480 mm, acrylic and watercolour

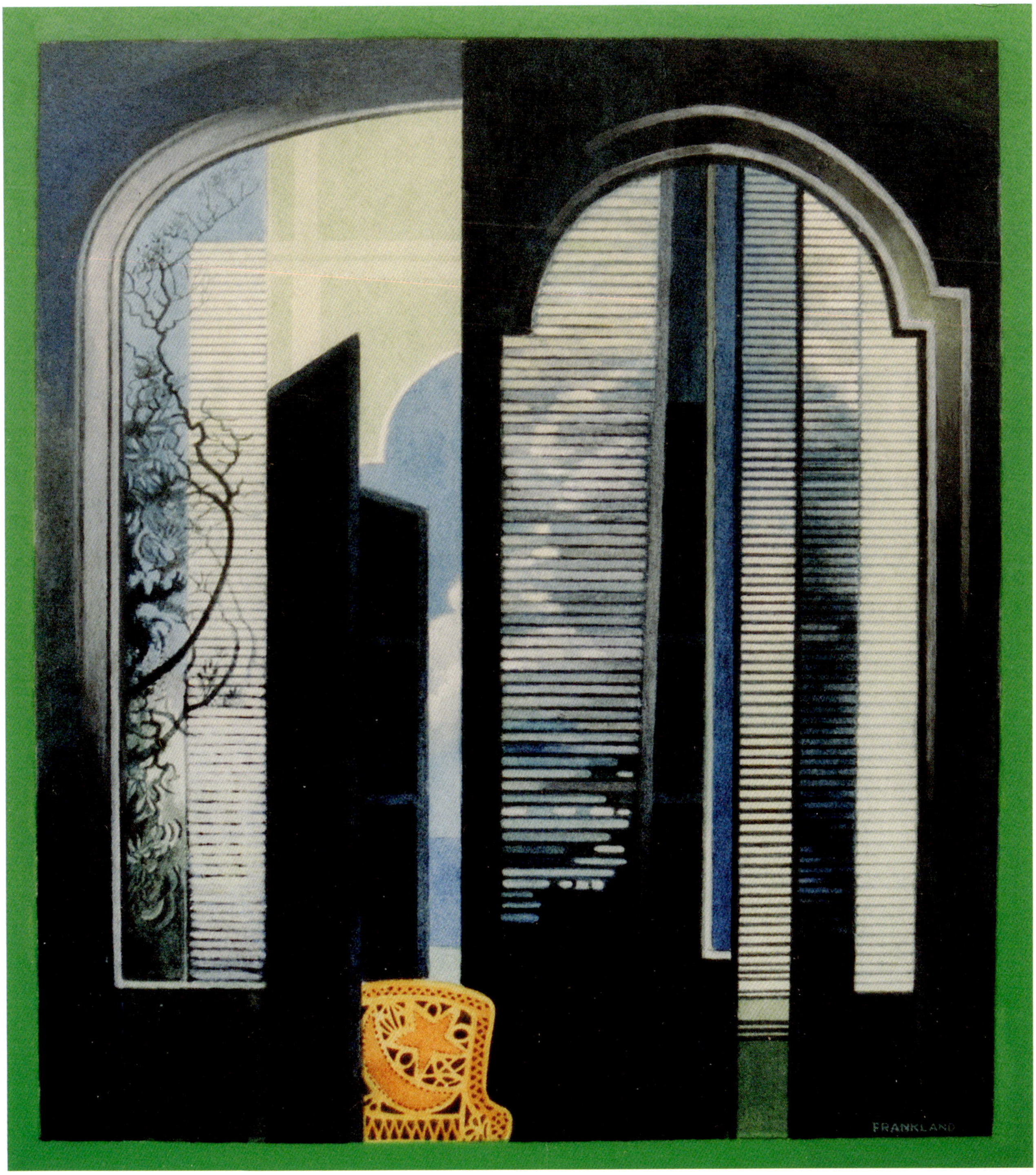

Chair with Moon and Star
445 x 510 mm, acrylic and watercolour

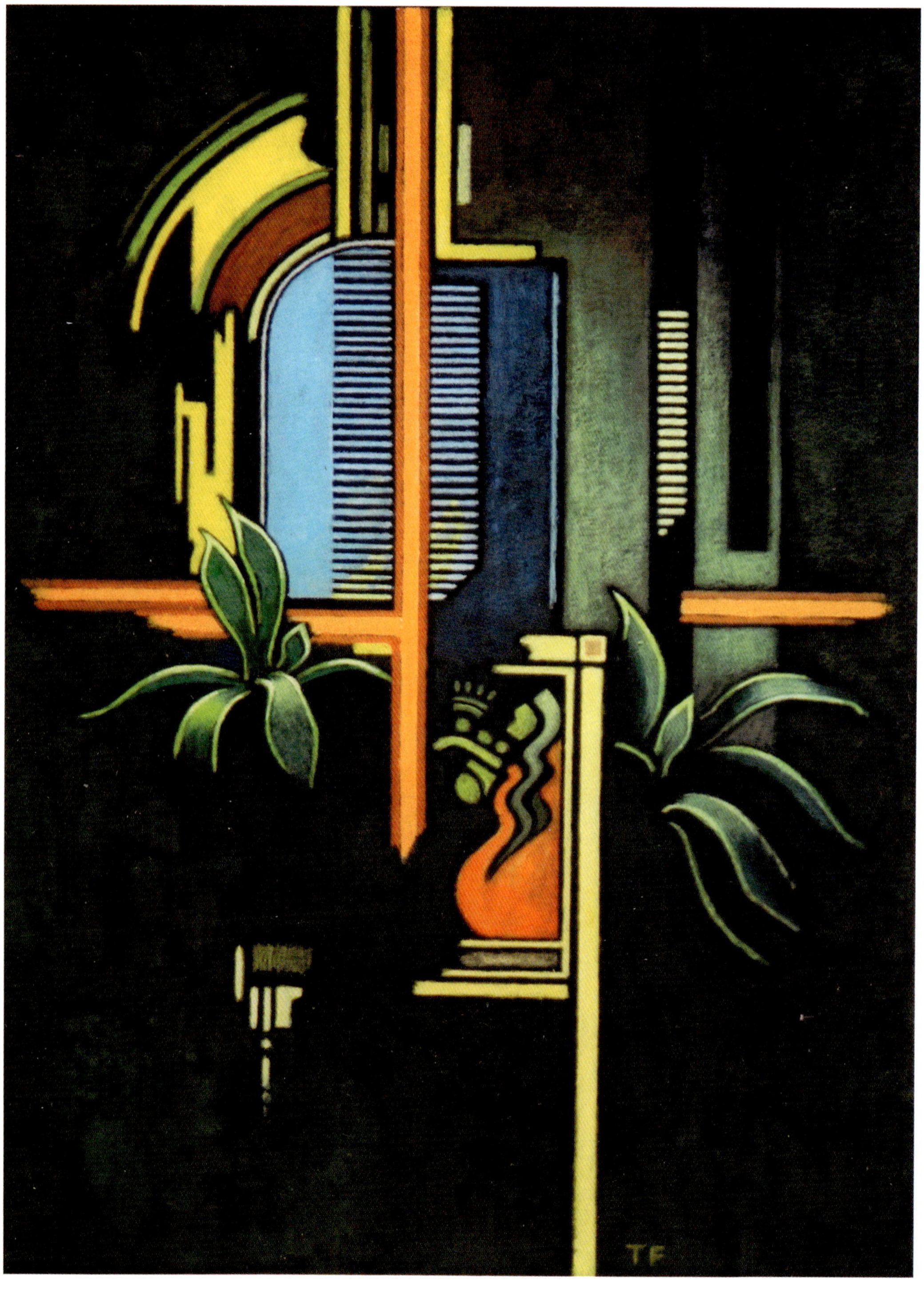

Study for Venetian Villa no 1
280 x 360 mm, watercolour and acrylic

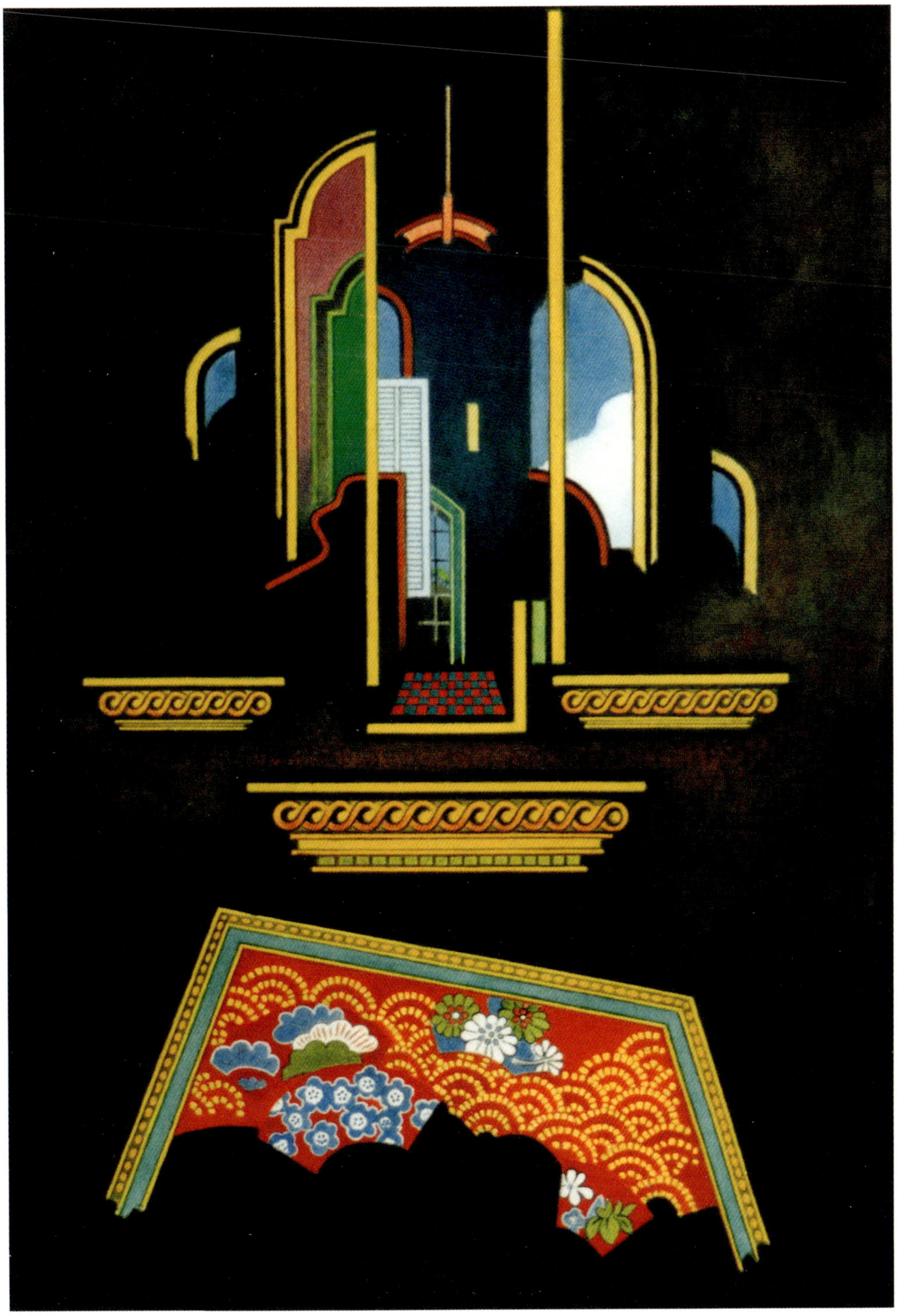

Magic Carpet
480 x 720 mm, acrylic

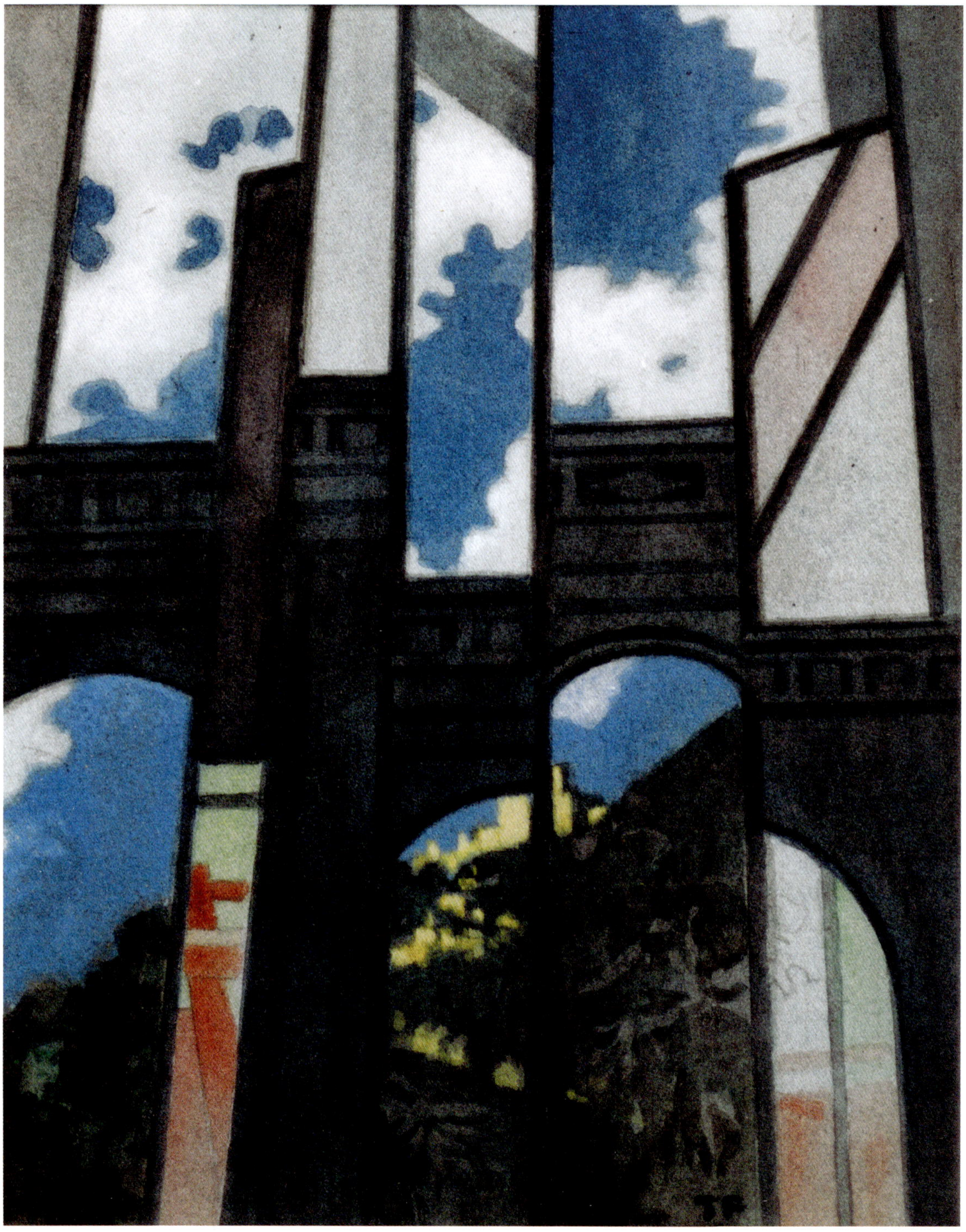

The Entrance
500 x 610 mm (frame size), watercolour and acrylic

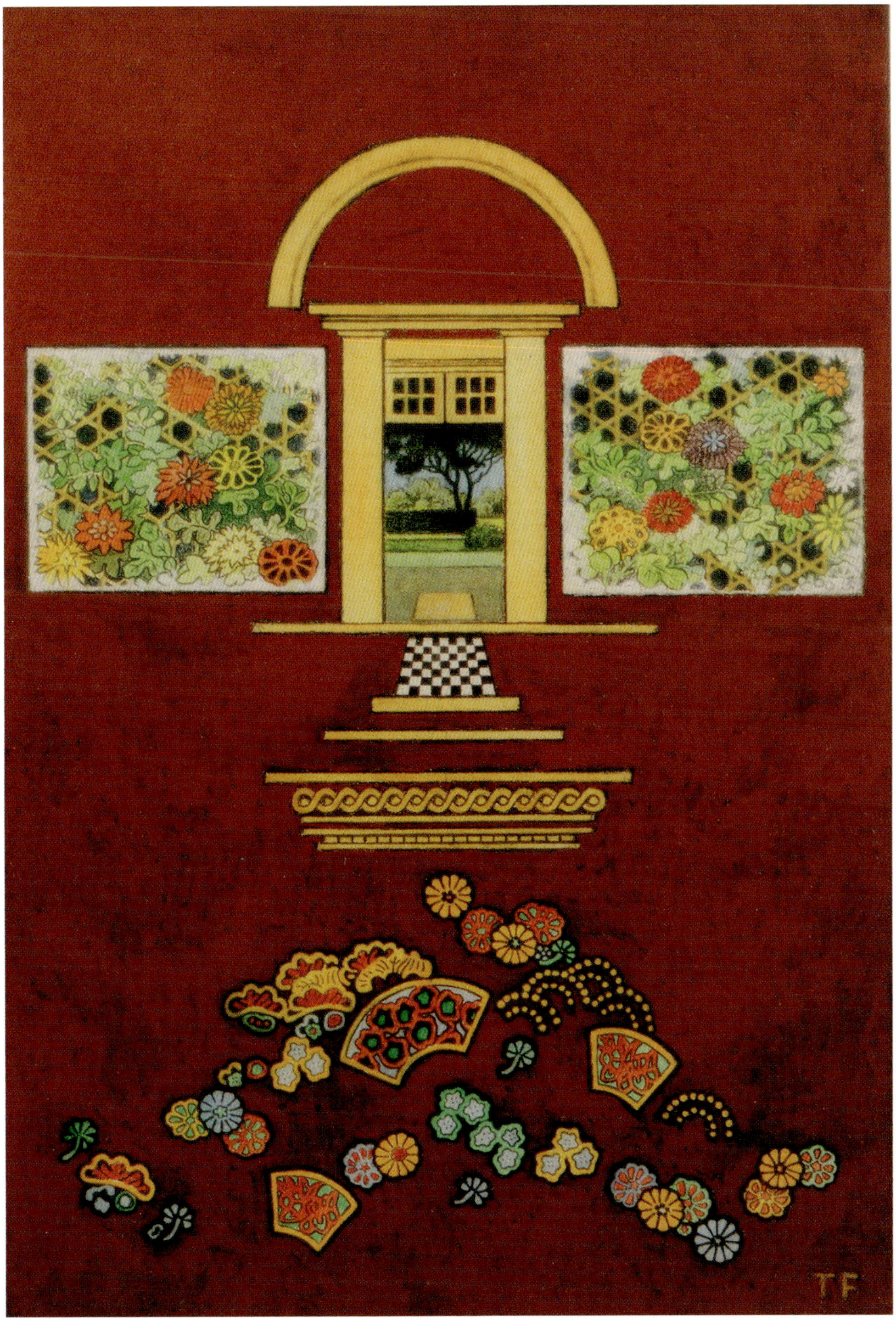

Garden of Delights no 2
390 x 550 mm, acrylic and watercolour

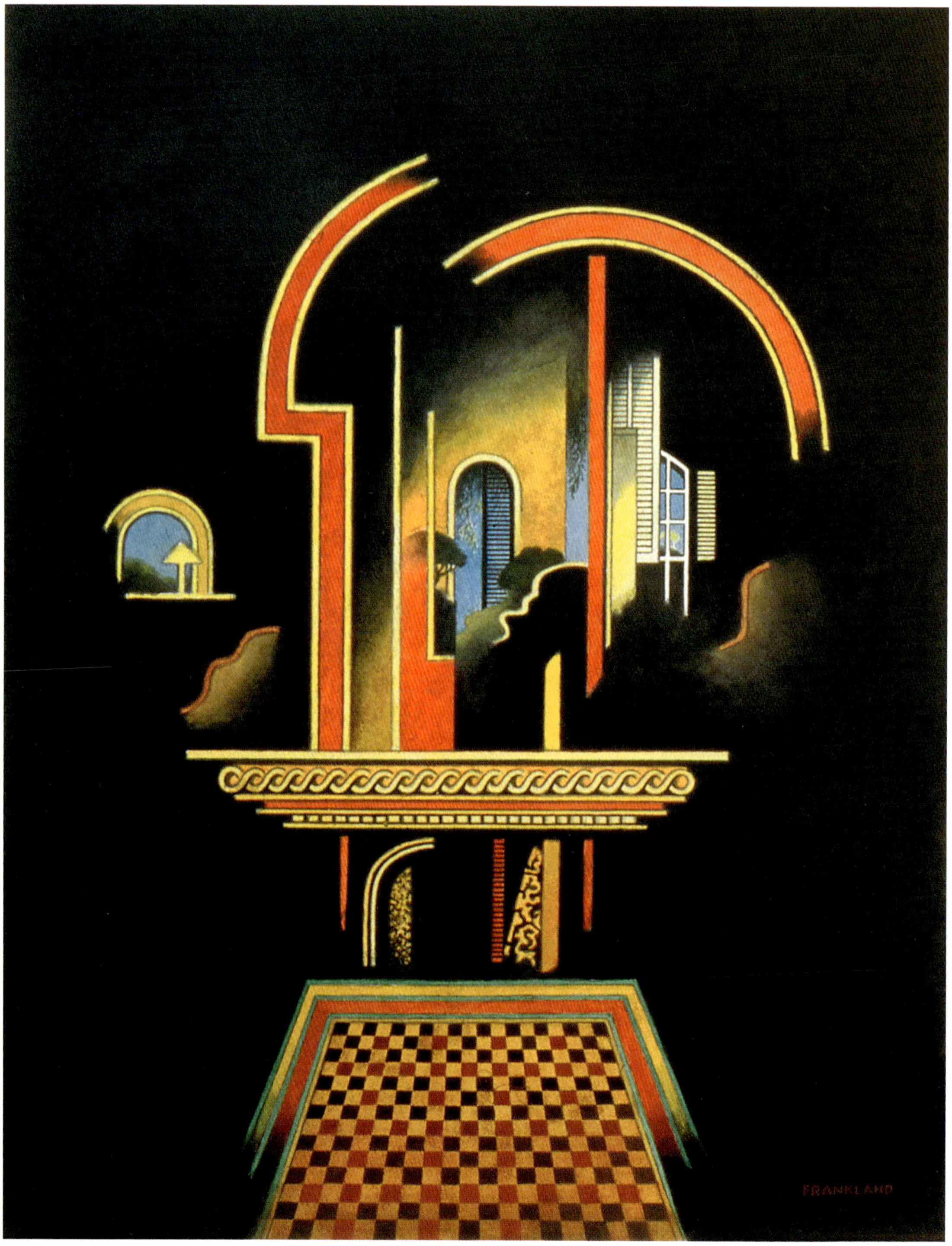

Villa Contarini no 2
500 x 640 mm, acrylic and watercolour

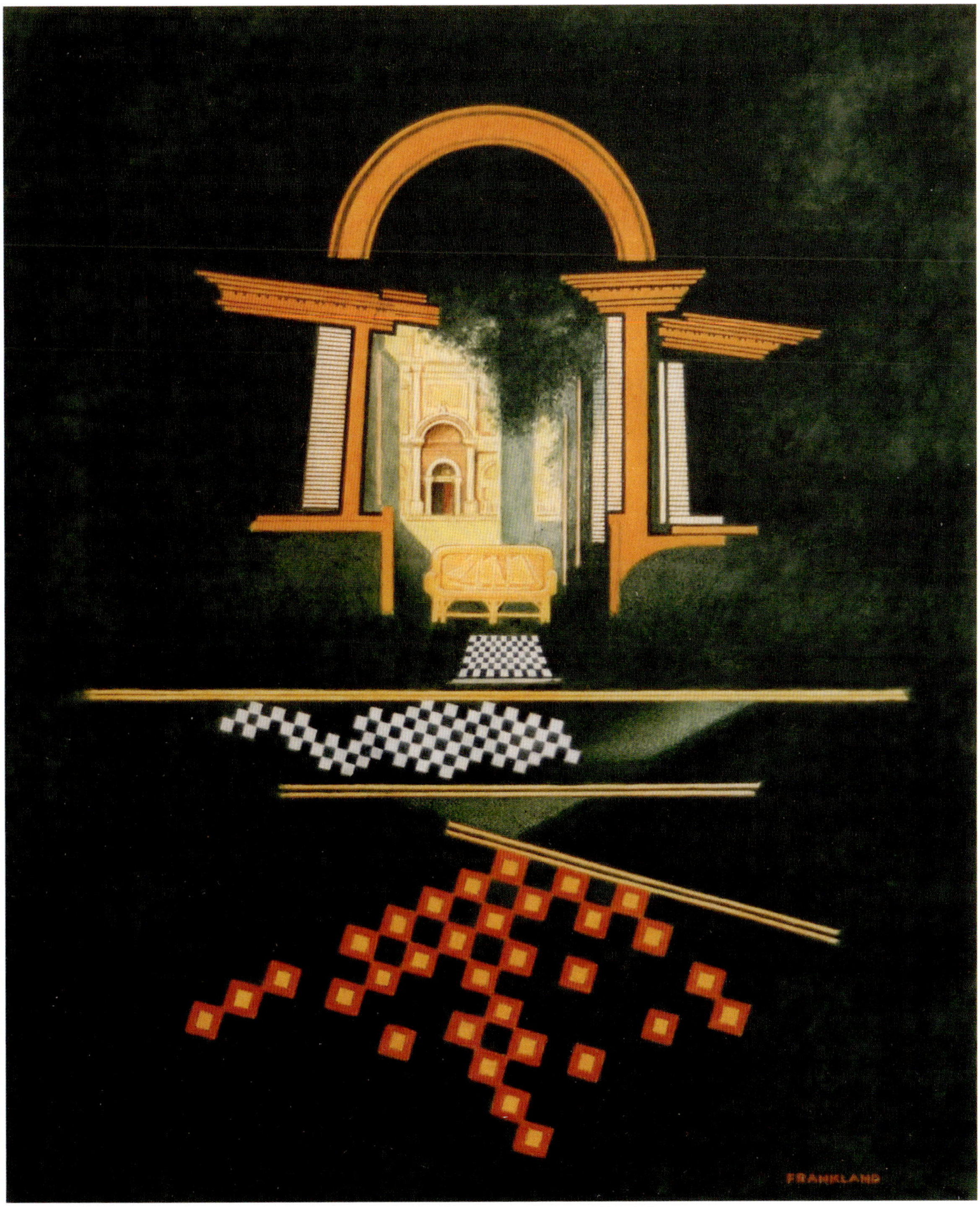

Grand Tour no 2
500 x 640 mm, acrylic and watercolour

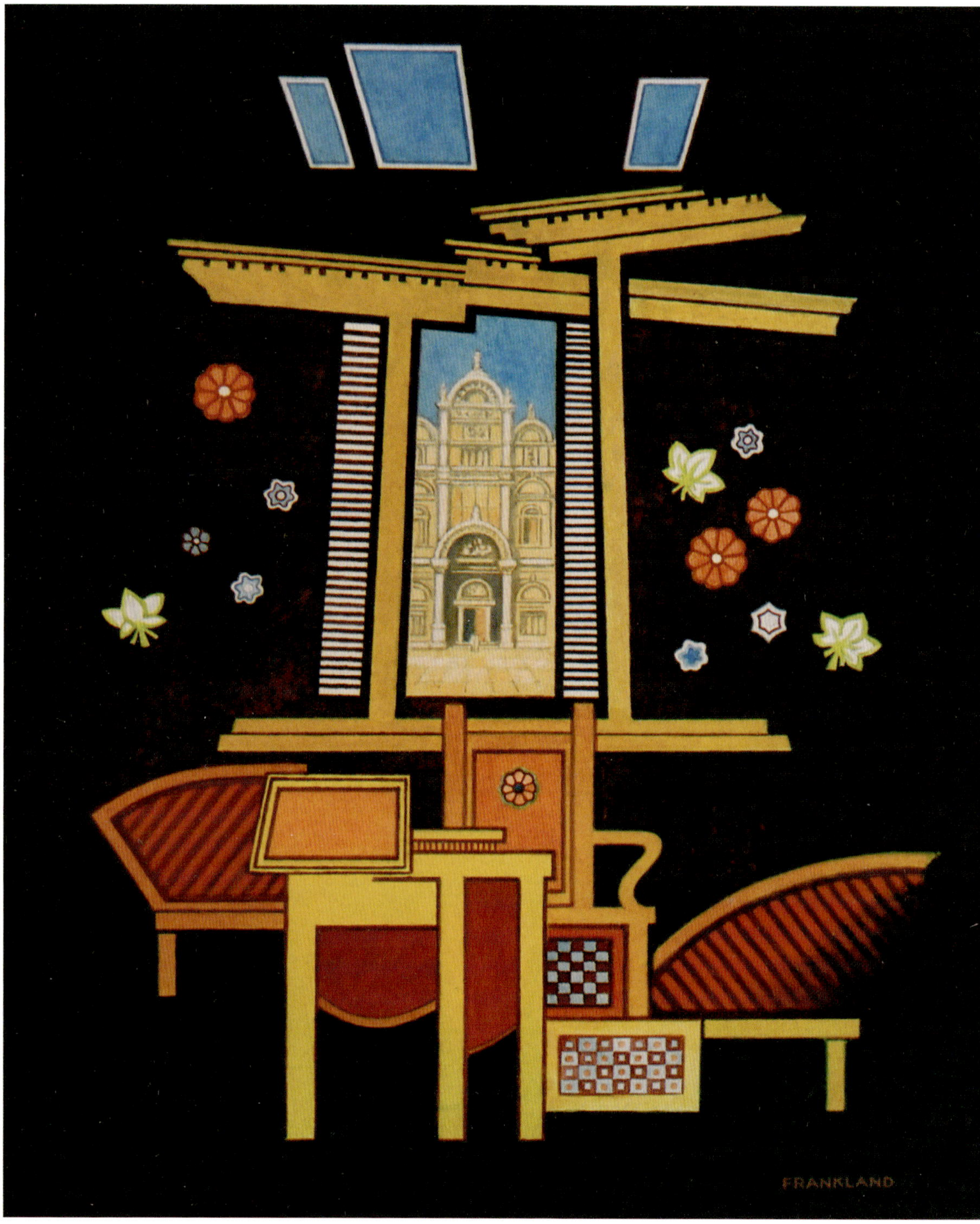

Venetian Apartment no 3 (study)
510 x 670 mm, watercolour and acrylic

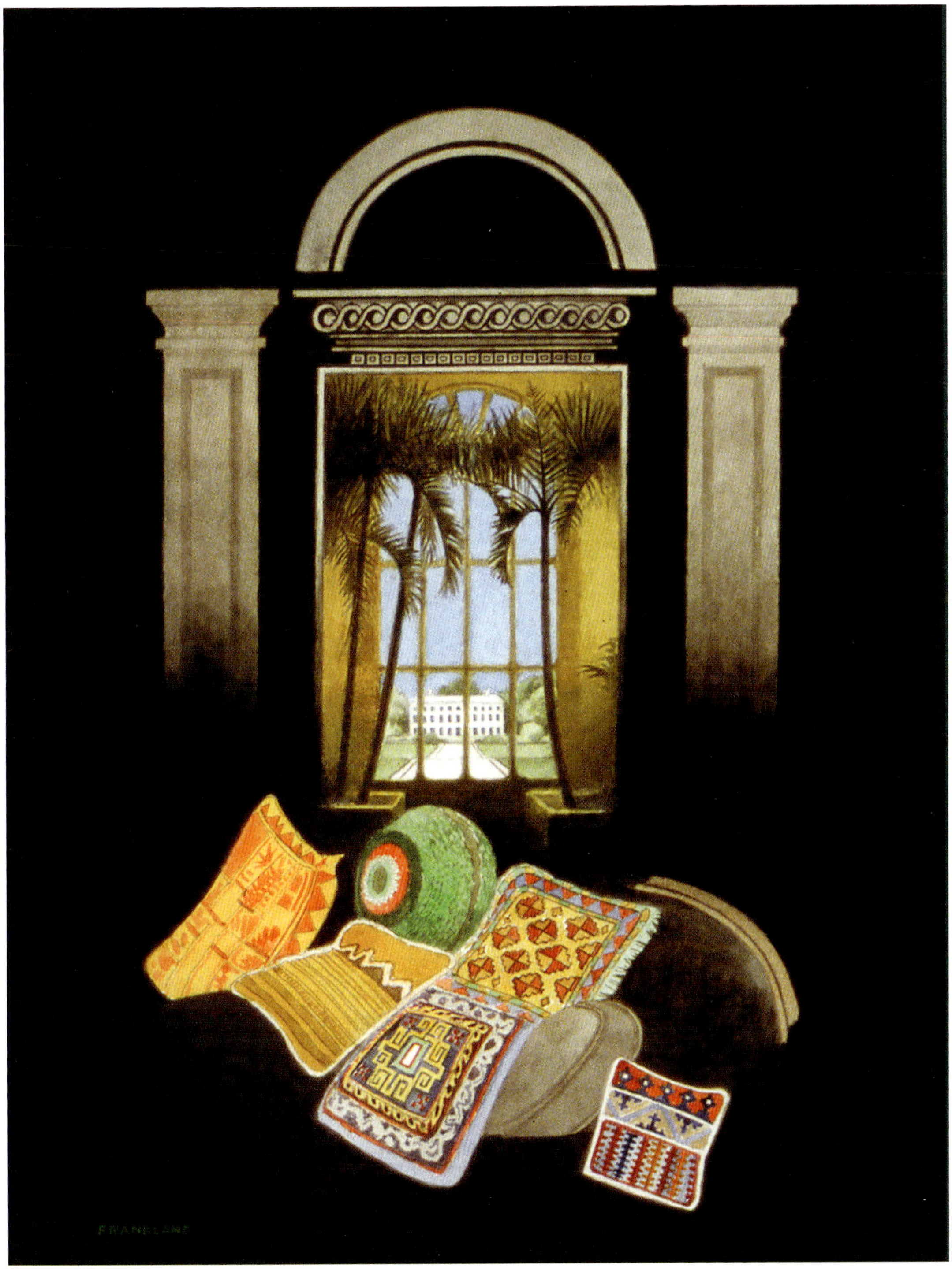

Cool Interior no 4
410 x 550 mm, watercolour and acrylic

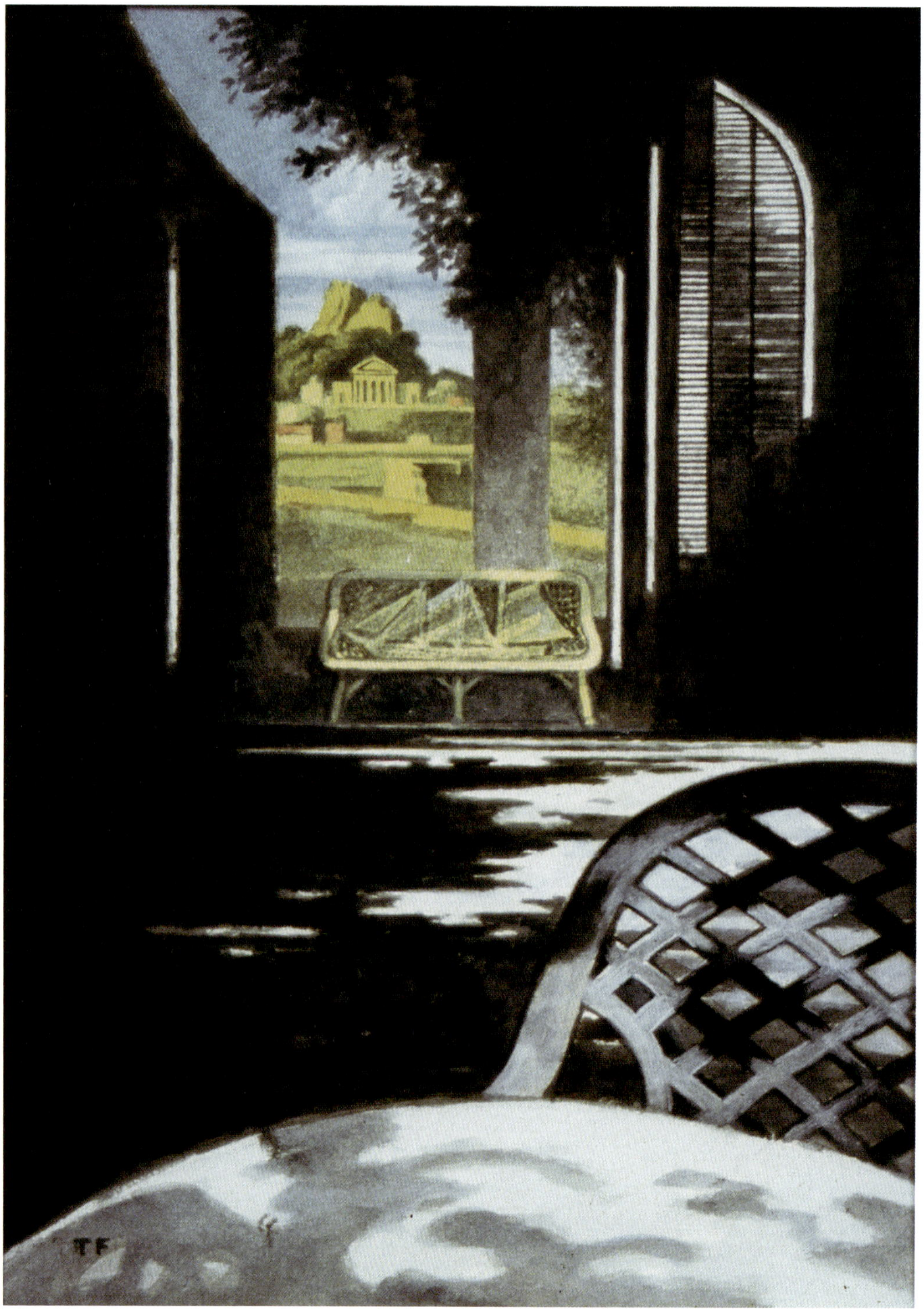

The Grand Tour Revisited
280 x 360 mm, watercolour and acrylic

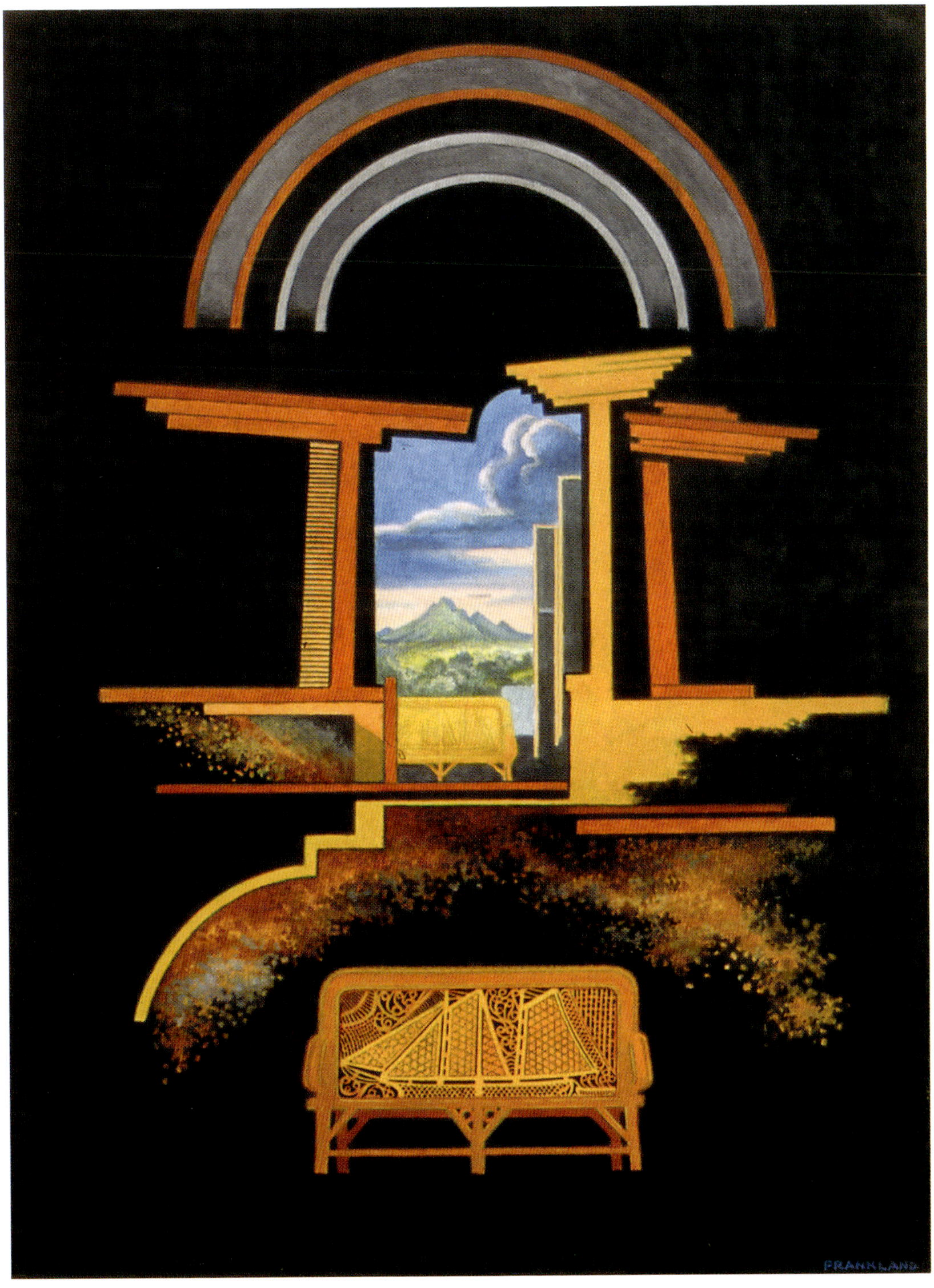

The Grand Tour no 4
720 x 940 mm, watercolour and acrylic

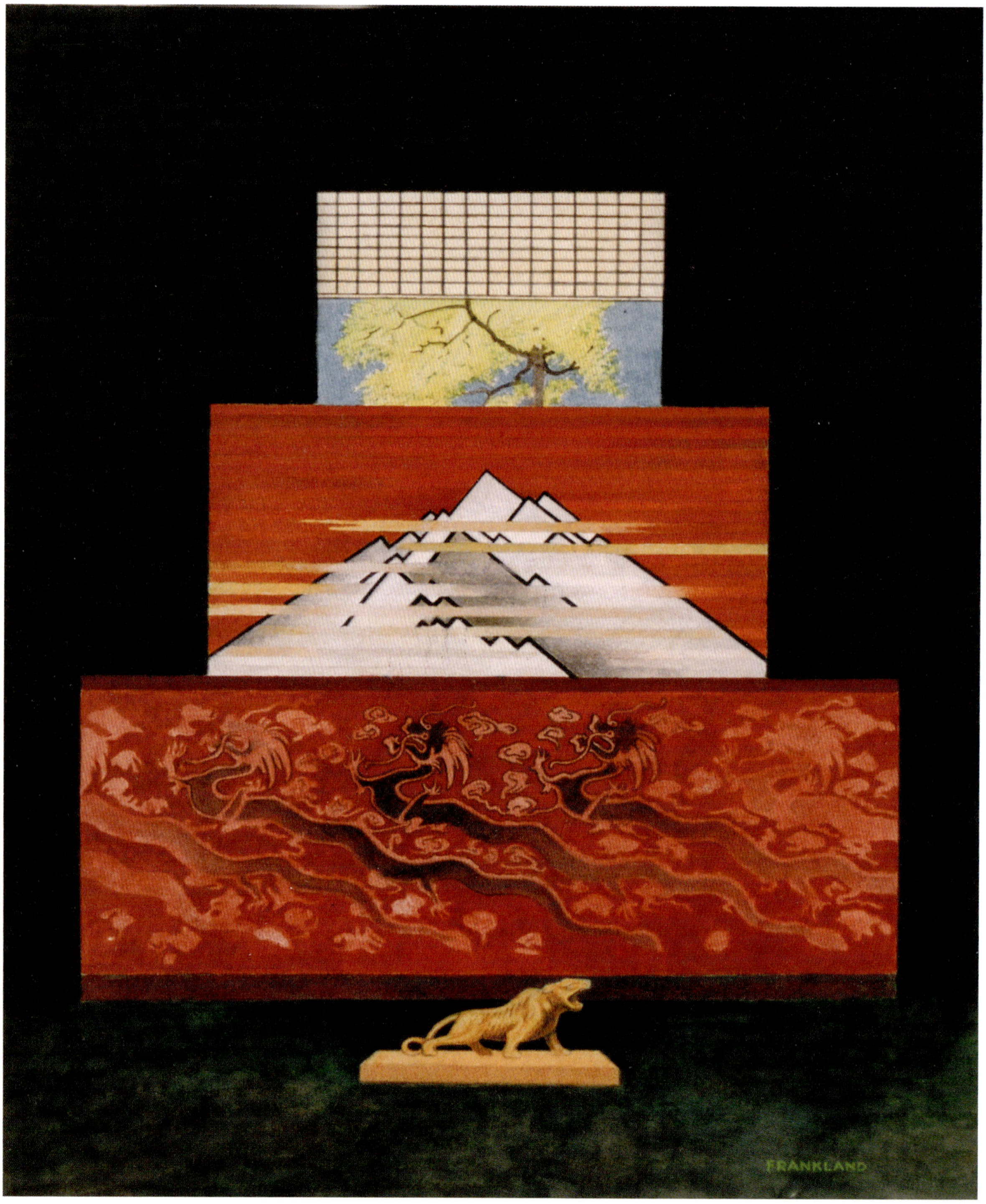

Dream Time
480 x 600 mm, watercolour and acrylic

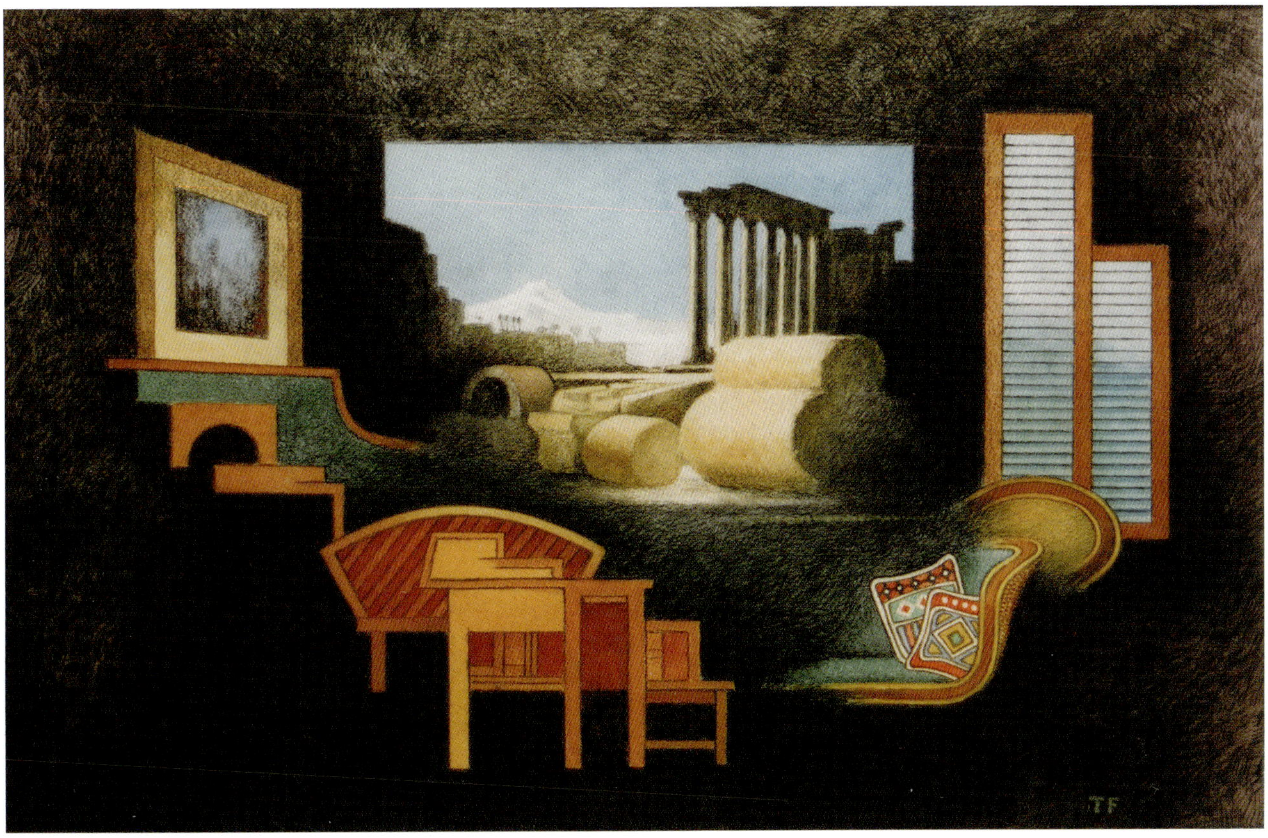

The Grand Tour Revisited no 5
680 x 460 mm, watercolour and acrylic

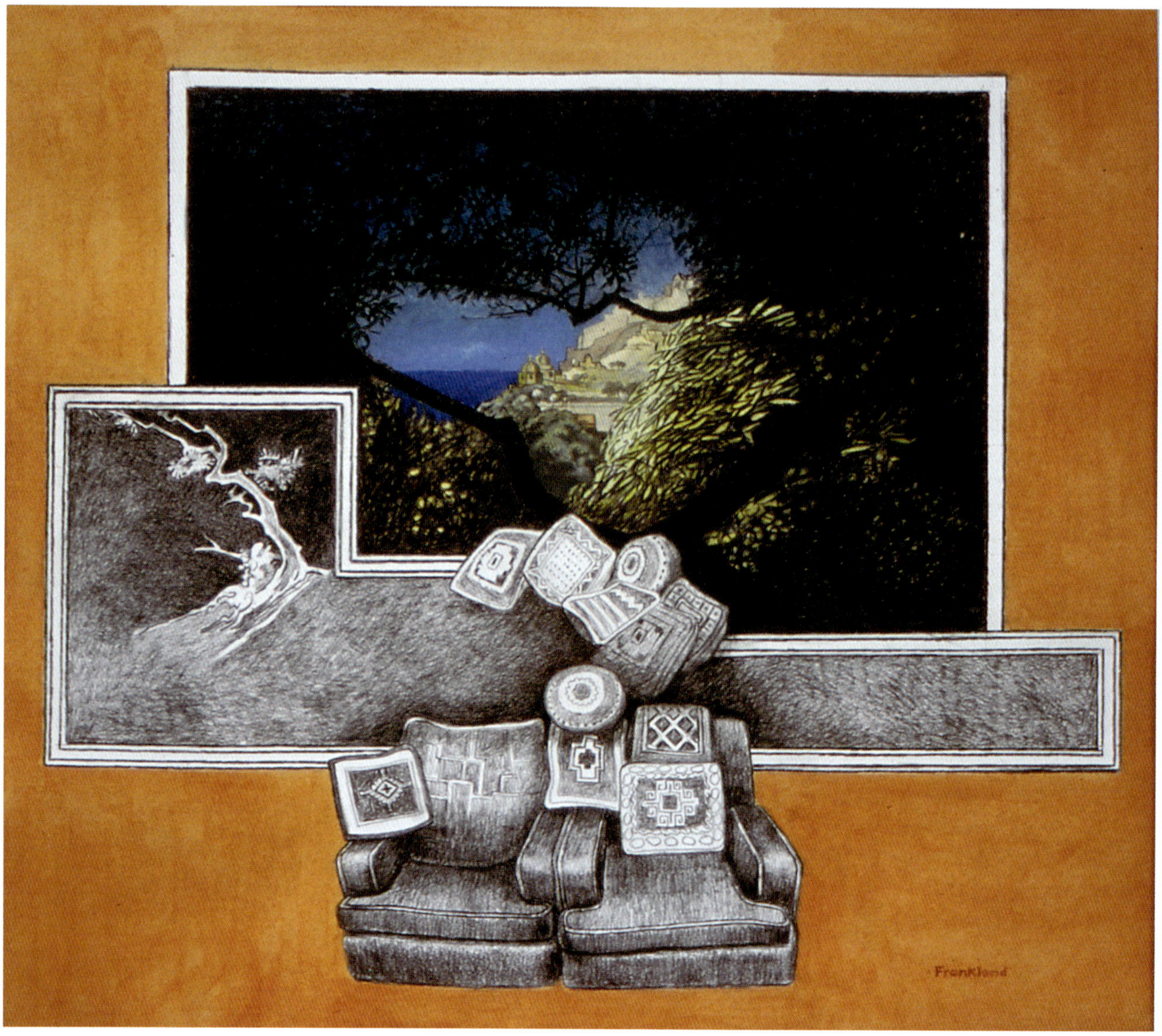

Recollections of a Distant View
670 x 510 mm, conté crayon and acrylic

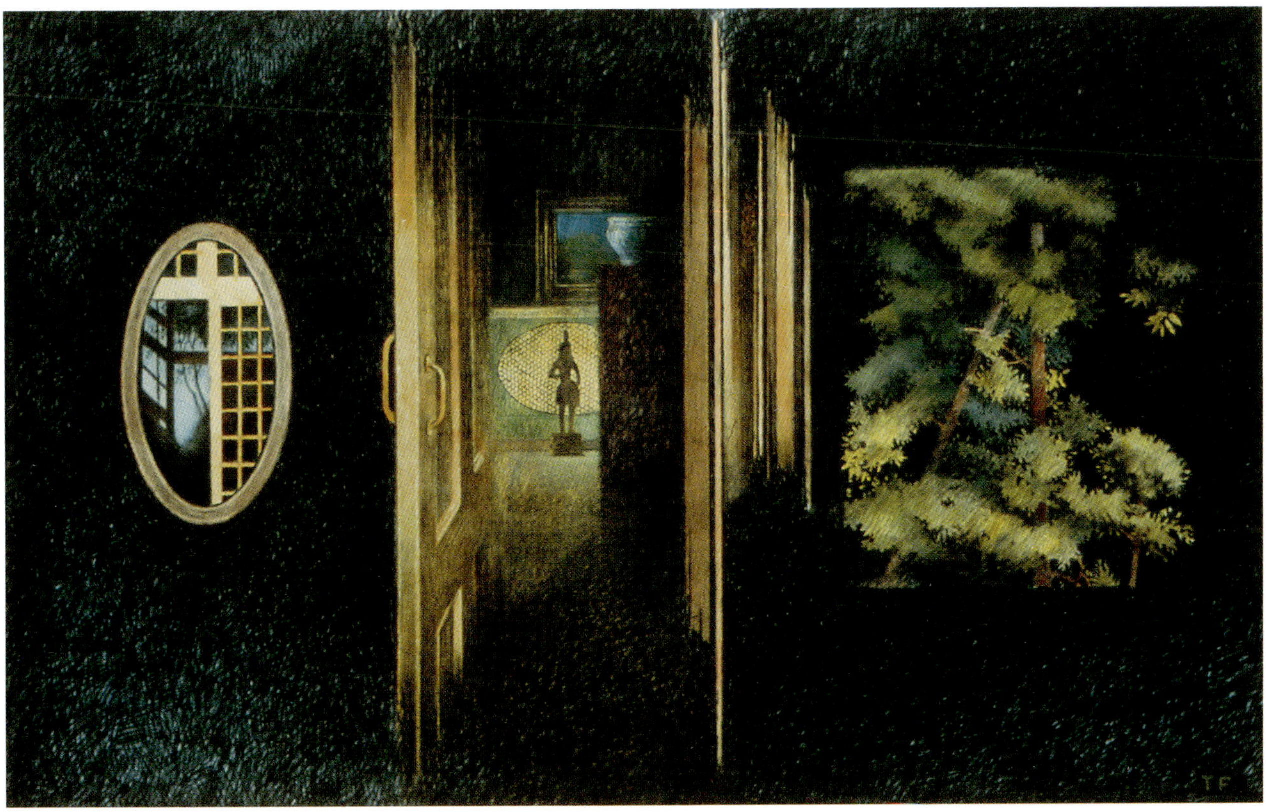

Outside Inside
910 x 580 mm, acrylic and conté crayon

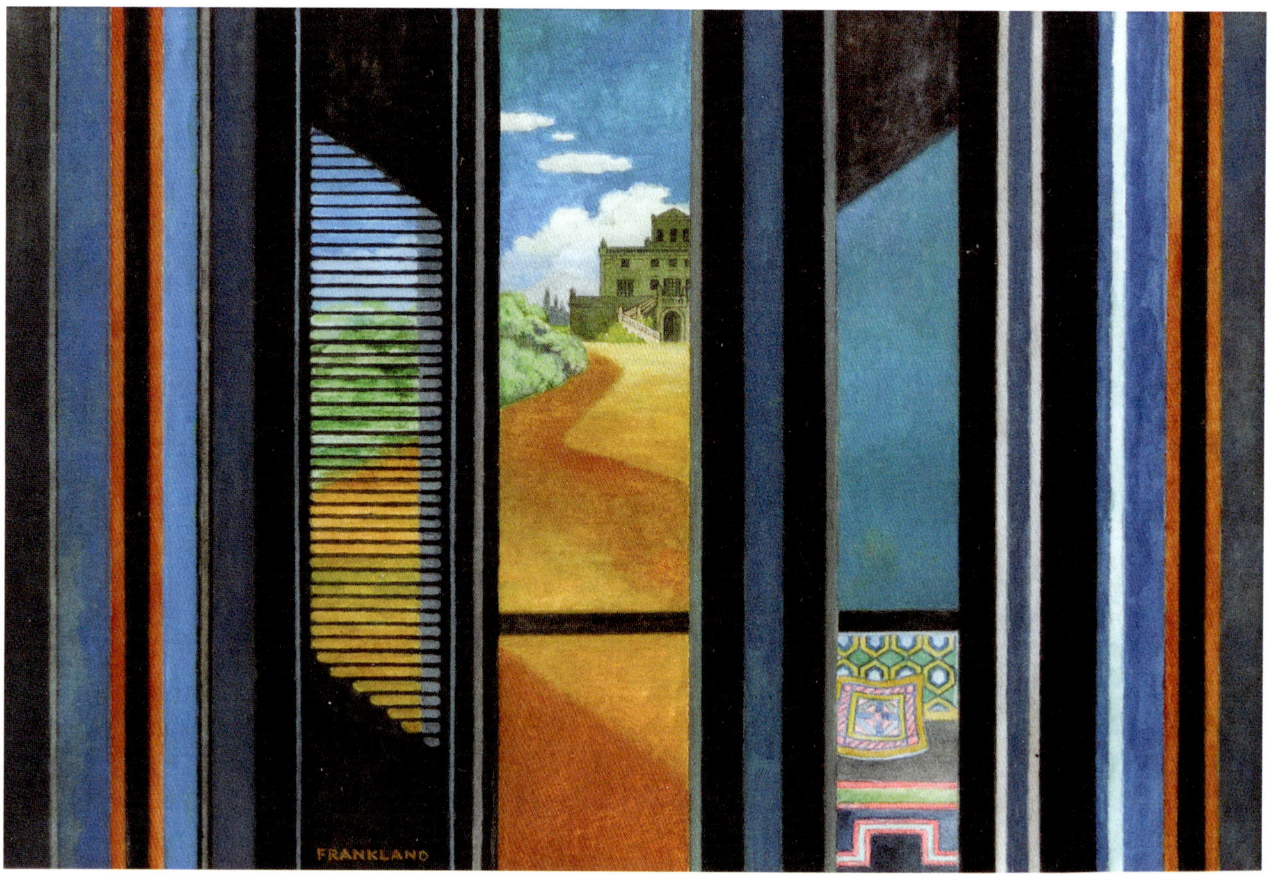

View of the Villa
520 x 450 mm, acrylic

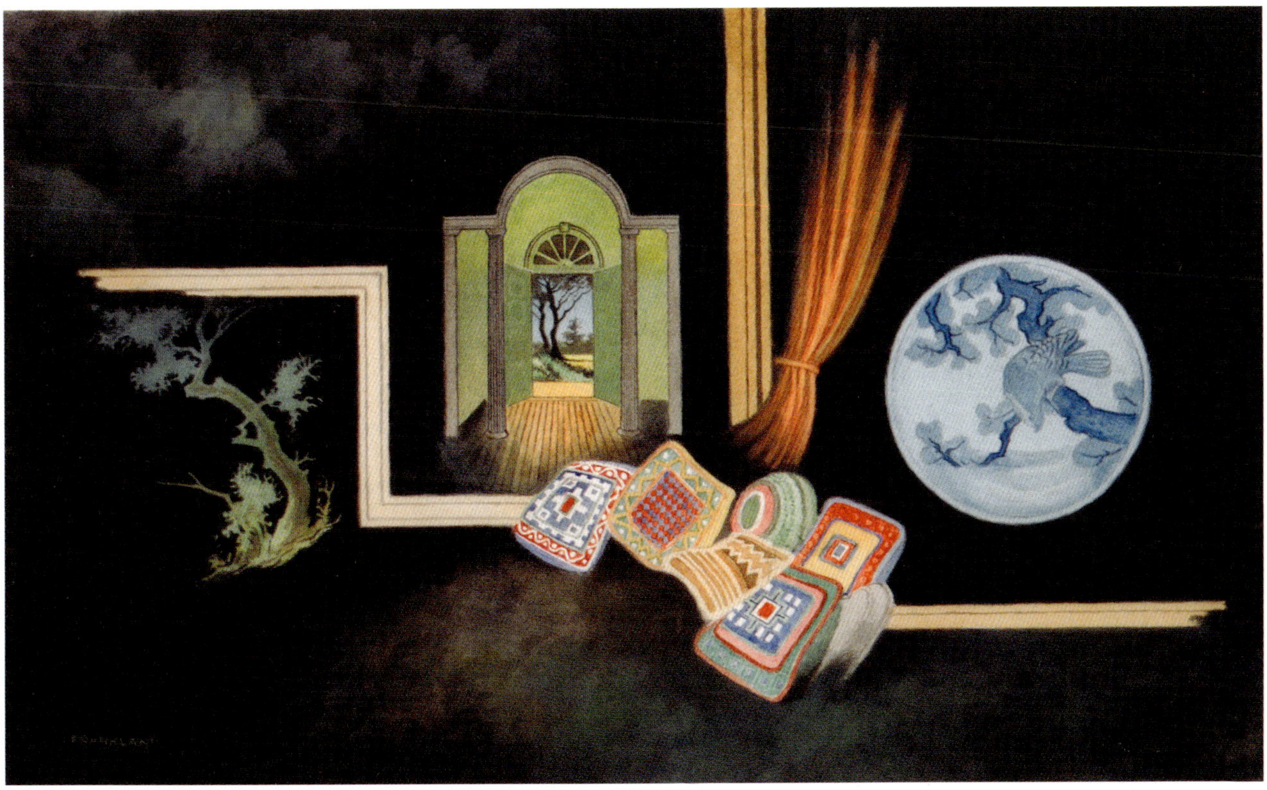

Time Suspended
680 x 420 mm, watercolour and acrylic

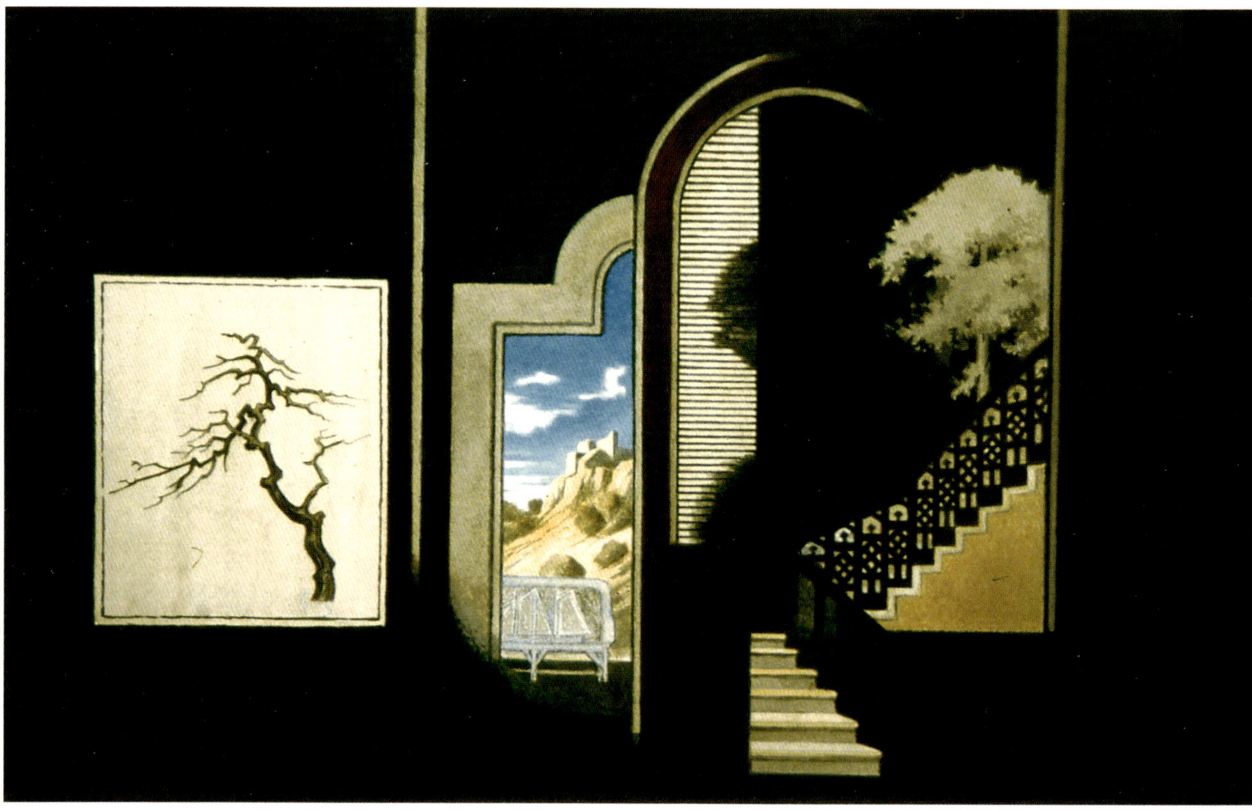

Castle on the Hill
620 x 390 mm, watercolour and acrylic

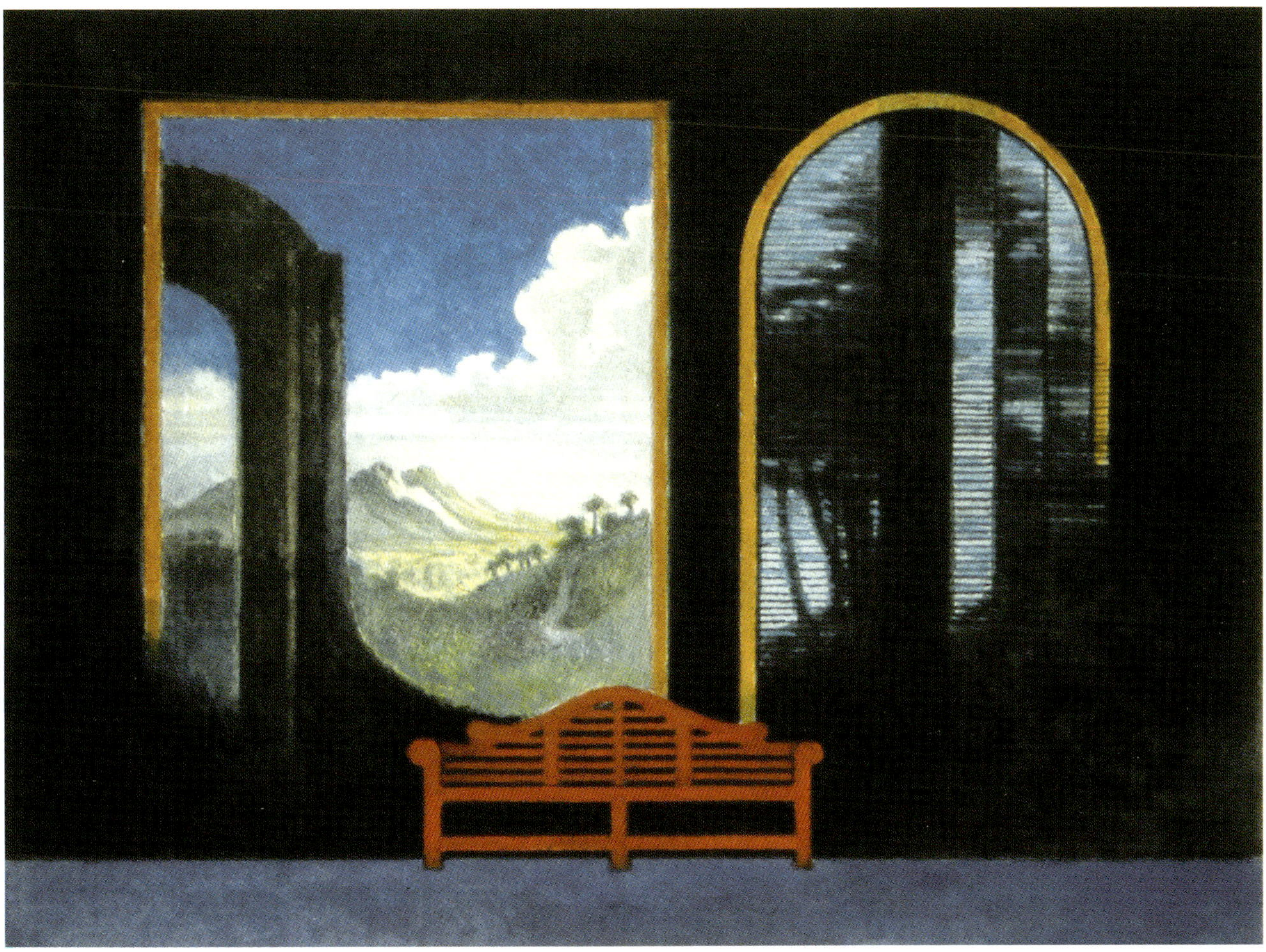

Return from the Grand Tour no 3
340 x 260 mm, watercolour and acrylic

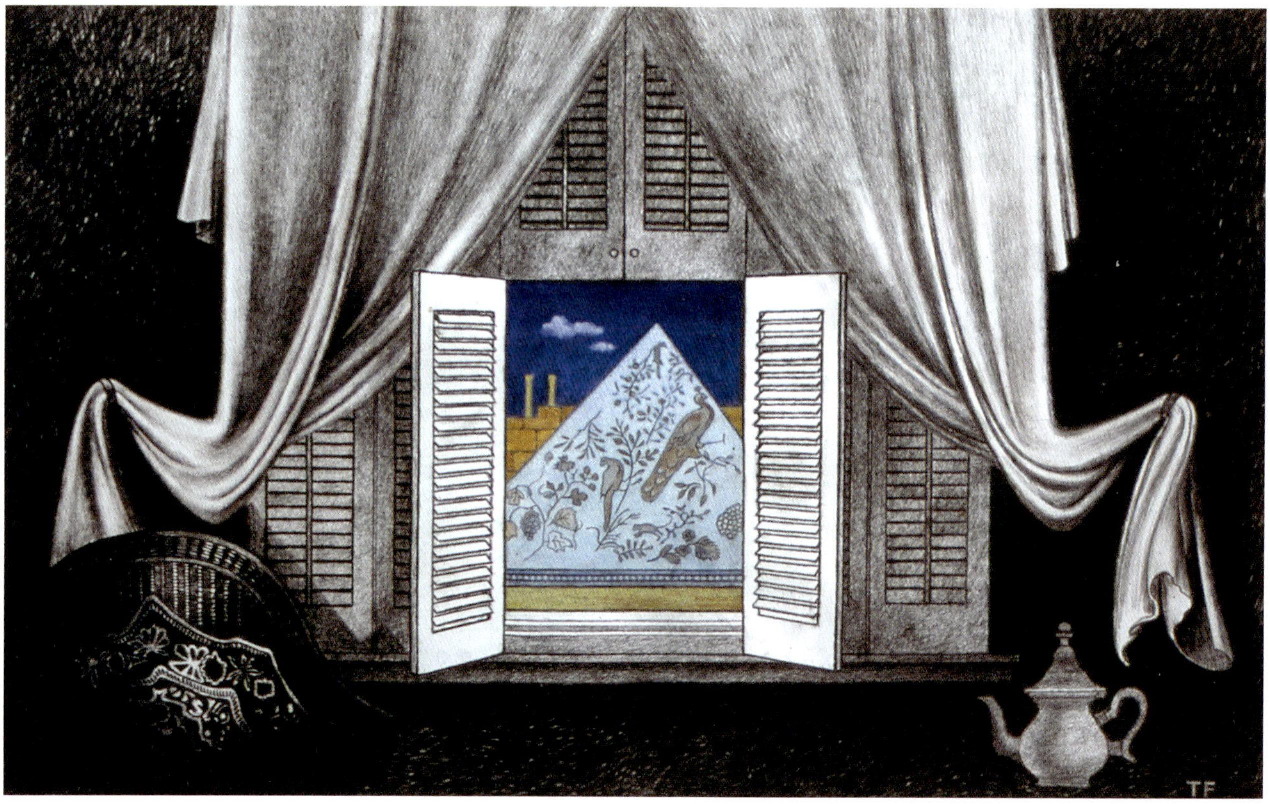

Discovery of Carthage
880 x 560 mm, watercolour and conté crayon

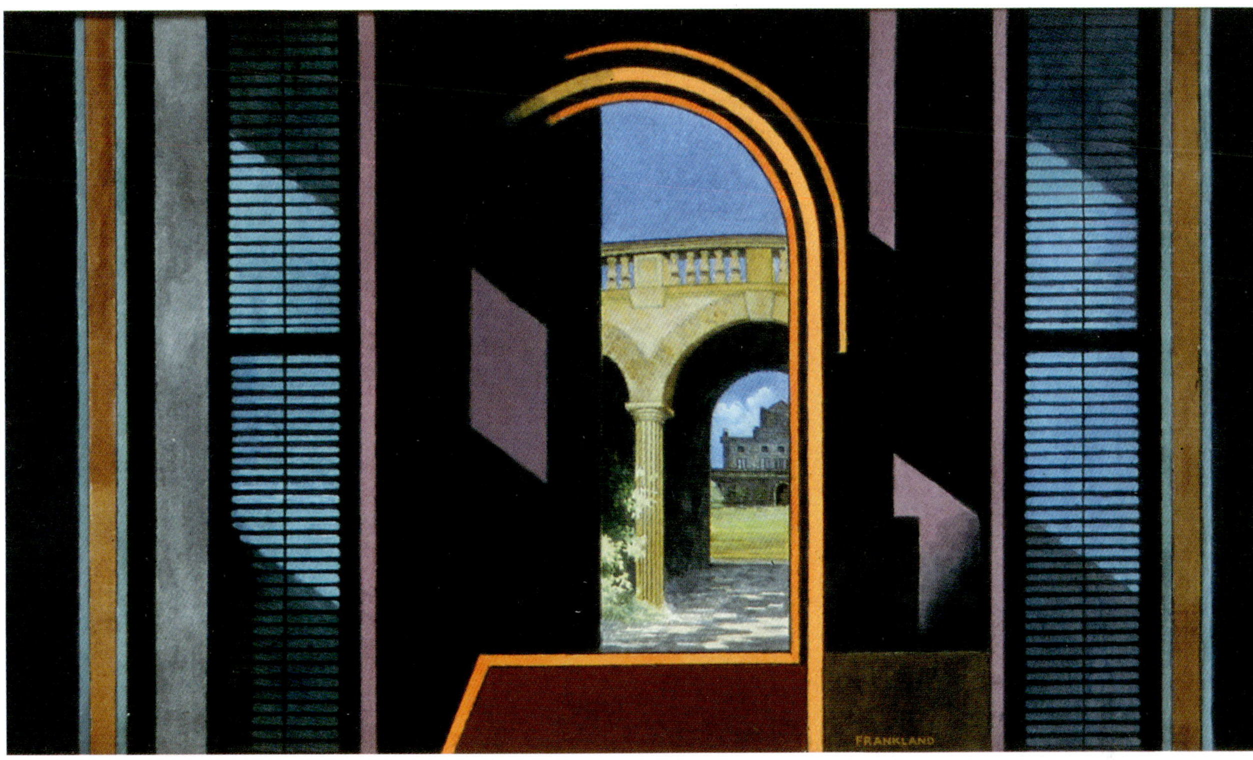

Sicily Revisited
710 x 420 mm, watercolour and acrylic

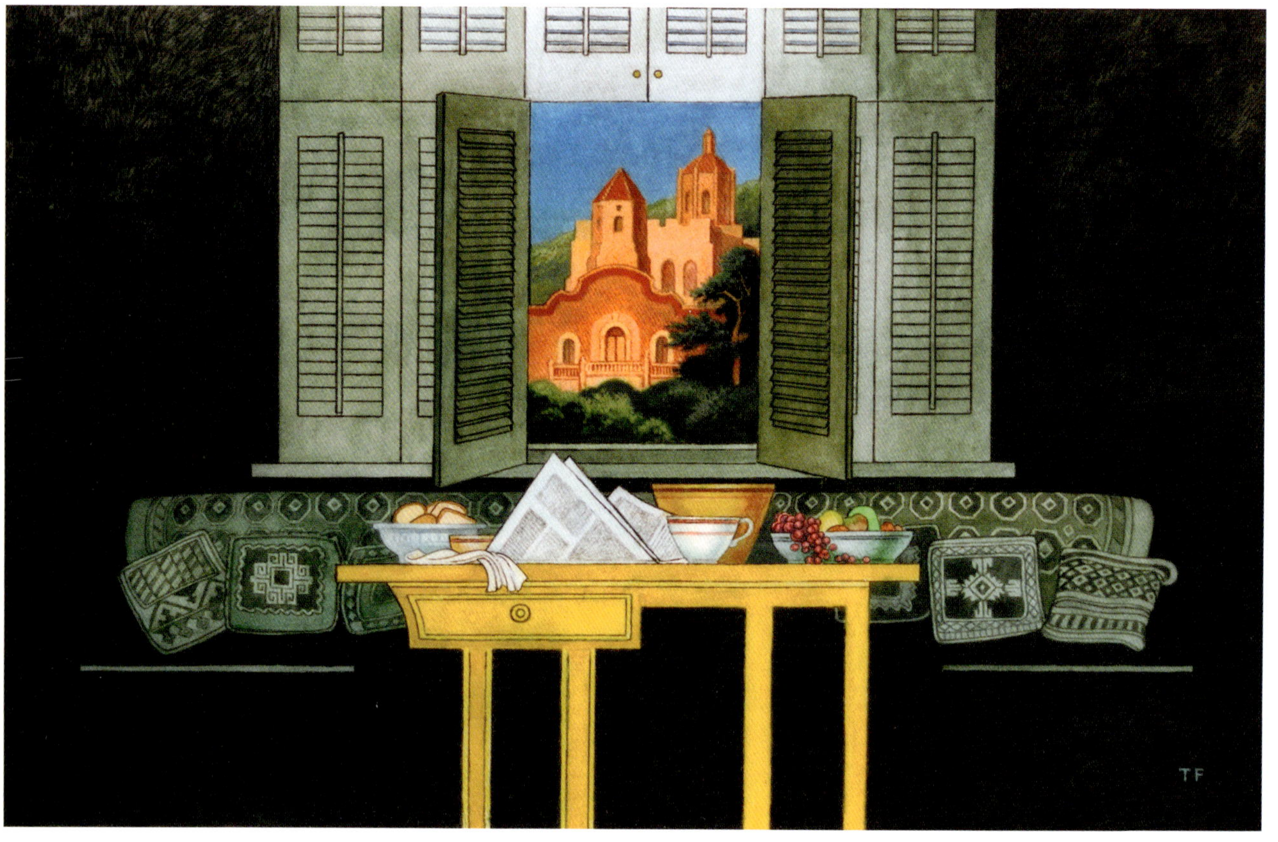

Continental Breakfast
850 x 550 mm, watercolour and acrylic

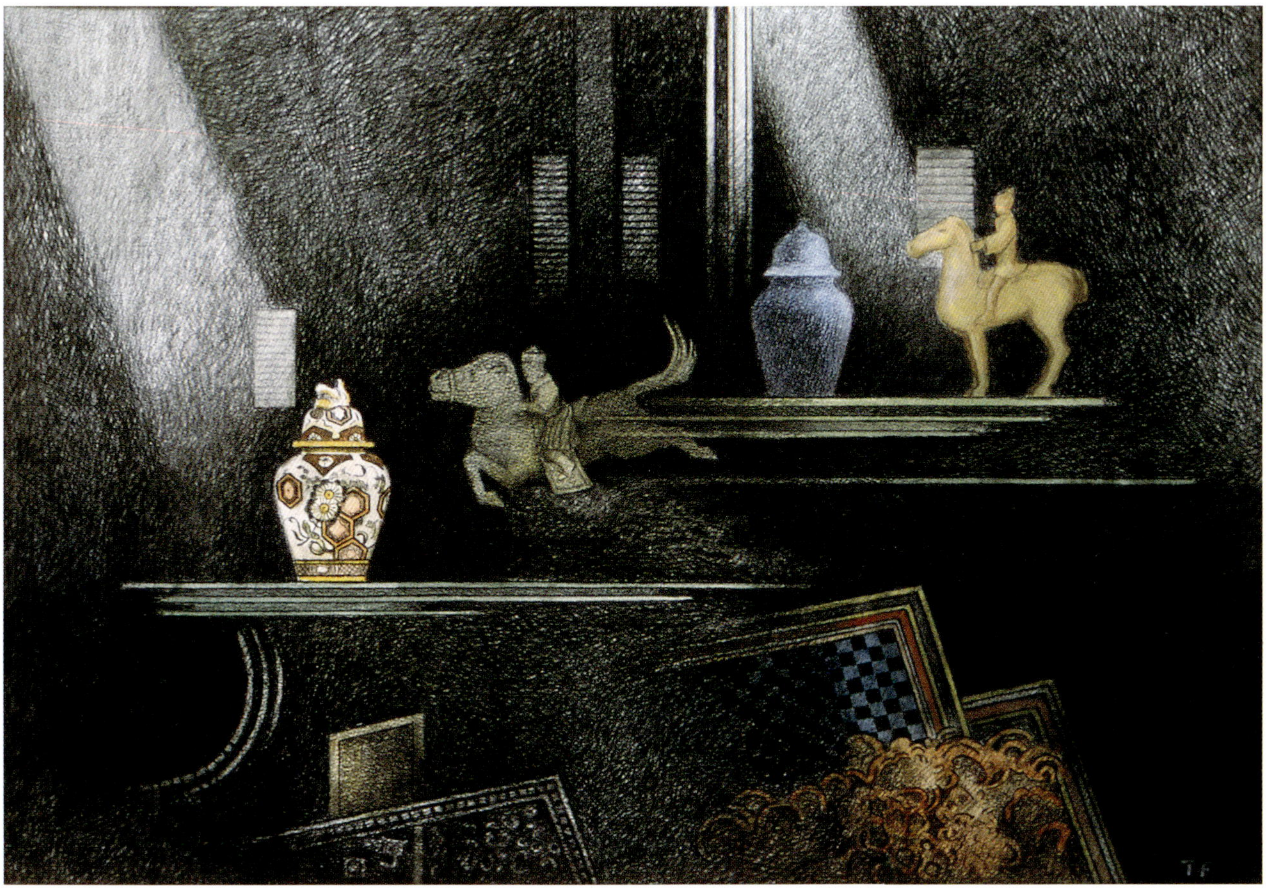

Museum Nightrider no 2
820 x 580 mm, watercolour and conté pencil

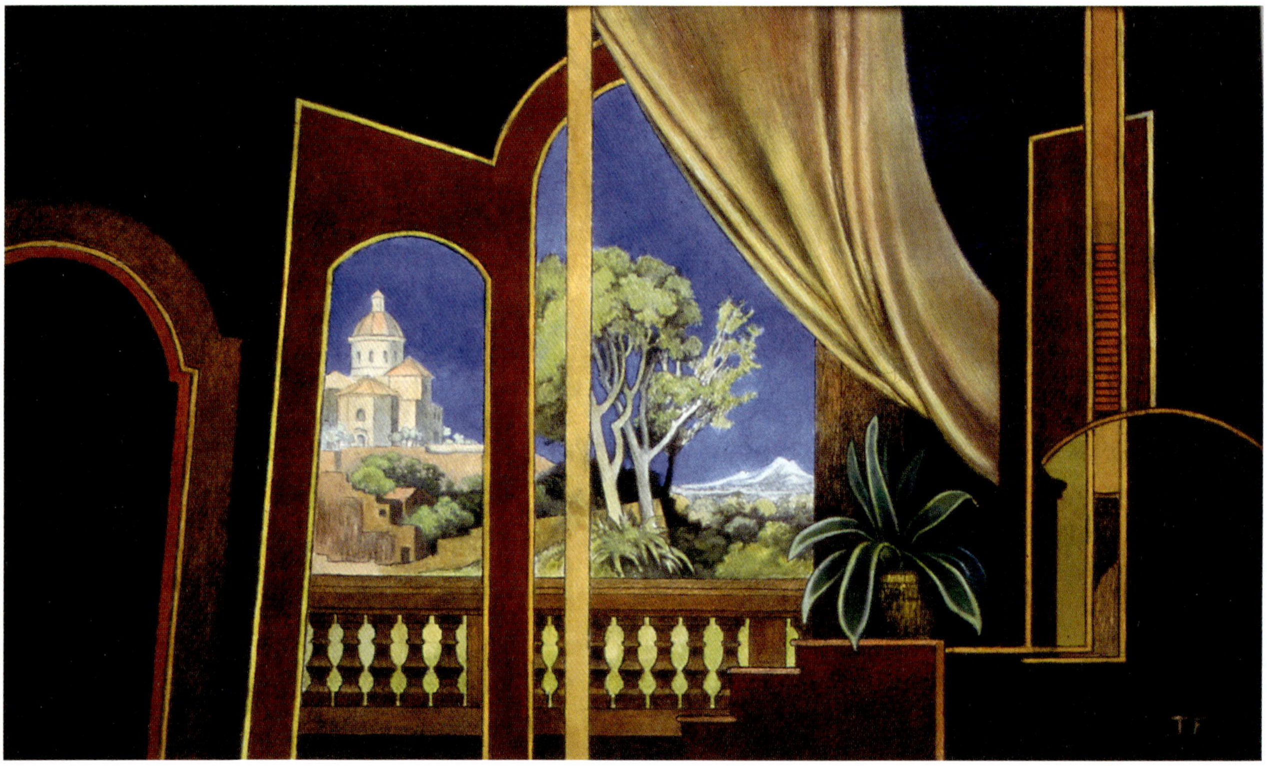

Screening the View
1000 x 740 mm, watercolour and acrylic

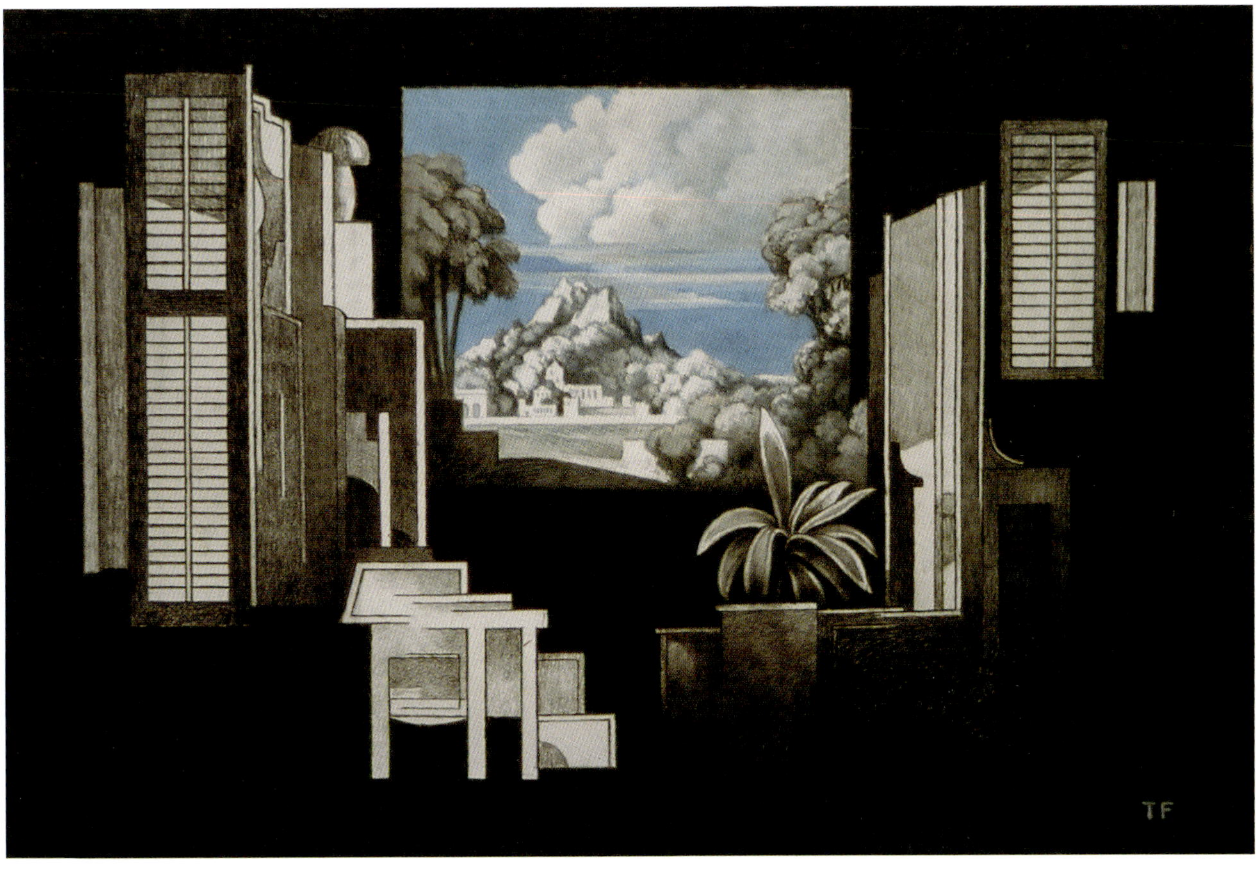

Italian Journey, The Grand Tour Revisited
1020 x 760 mm, watercolour and acrylic

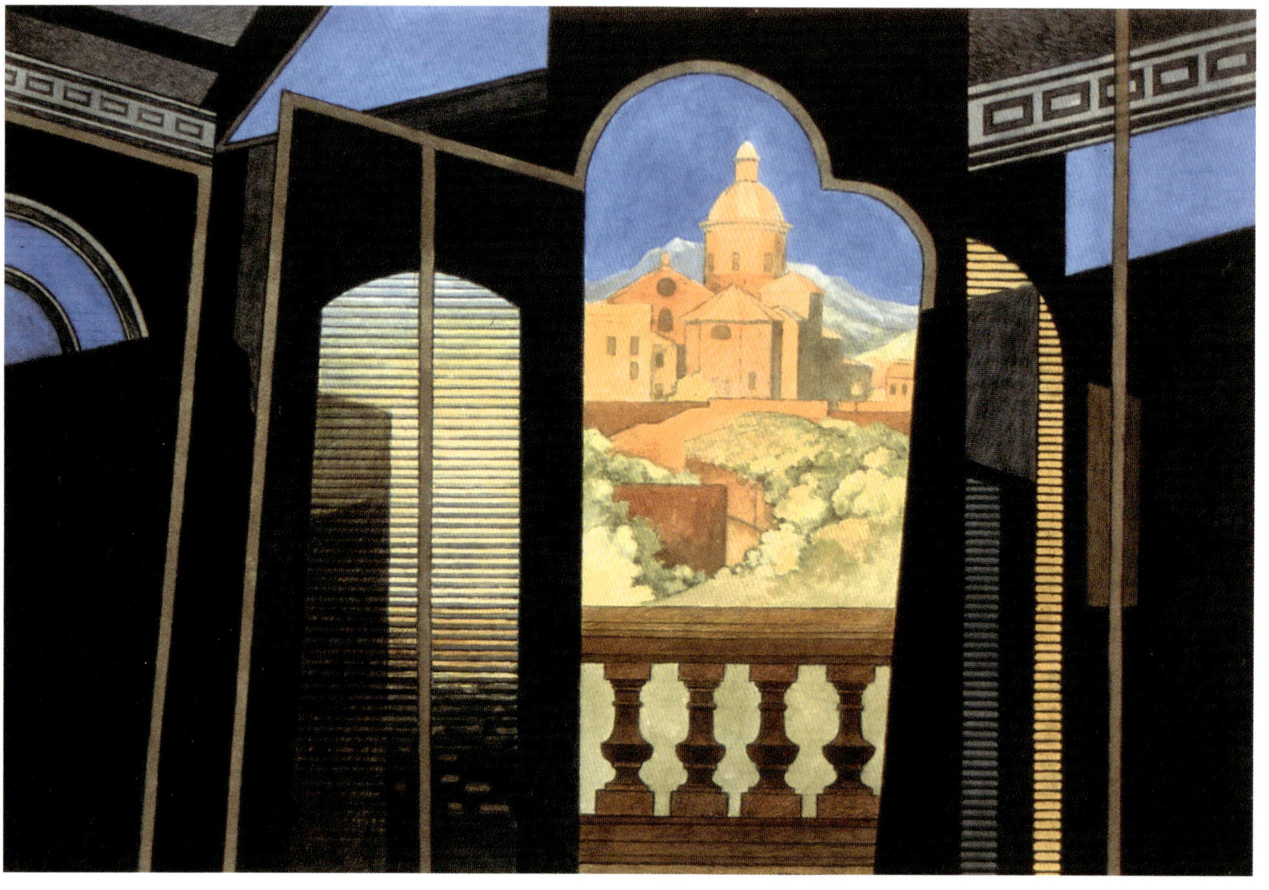

View from the Balcony
800 x 560 mm, acrylic and watercolour

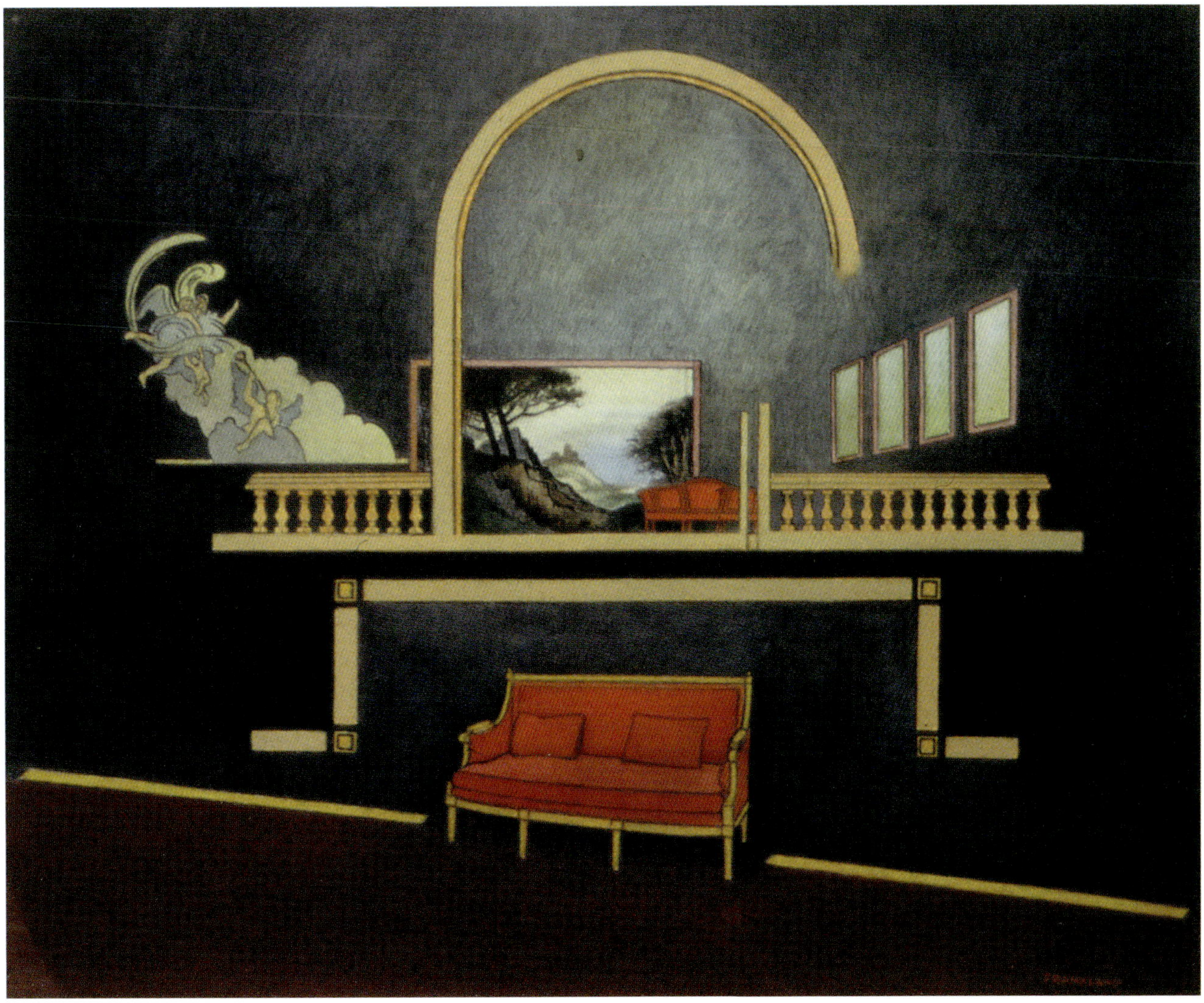

Recollections of a Great House no 4
800 x 610 mm, watercolour and acrylic

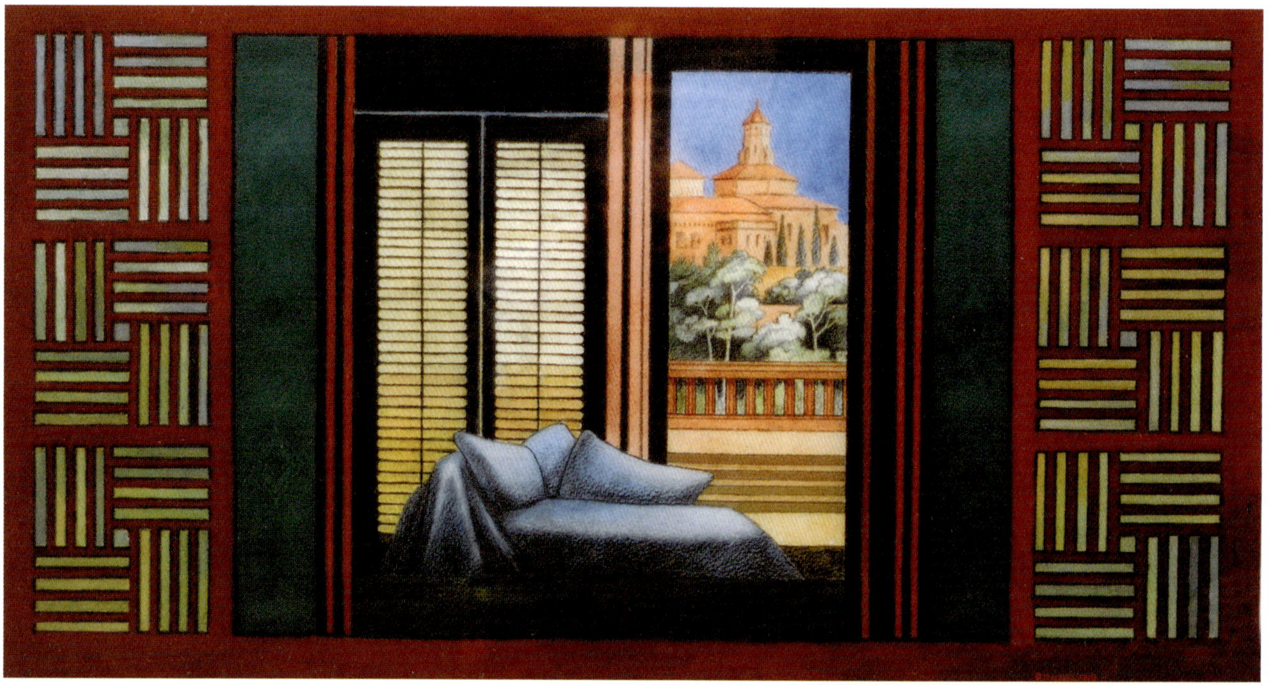

Summer Evening
1070 x 620 mm, watercolour and acrylic

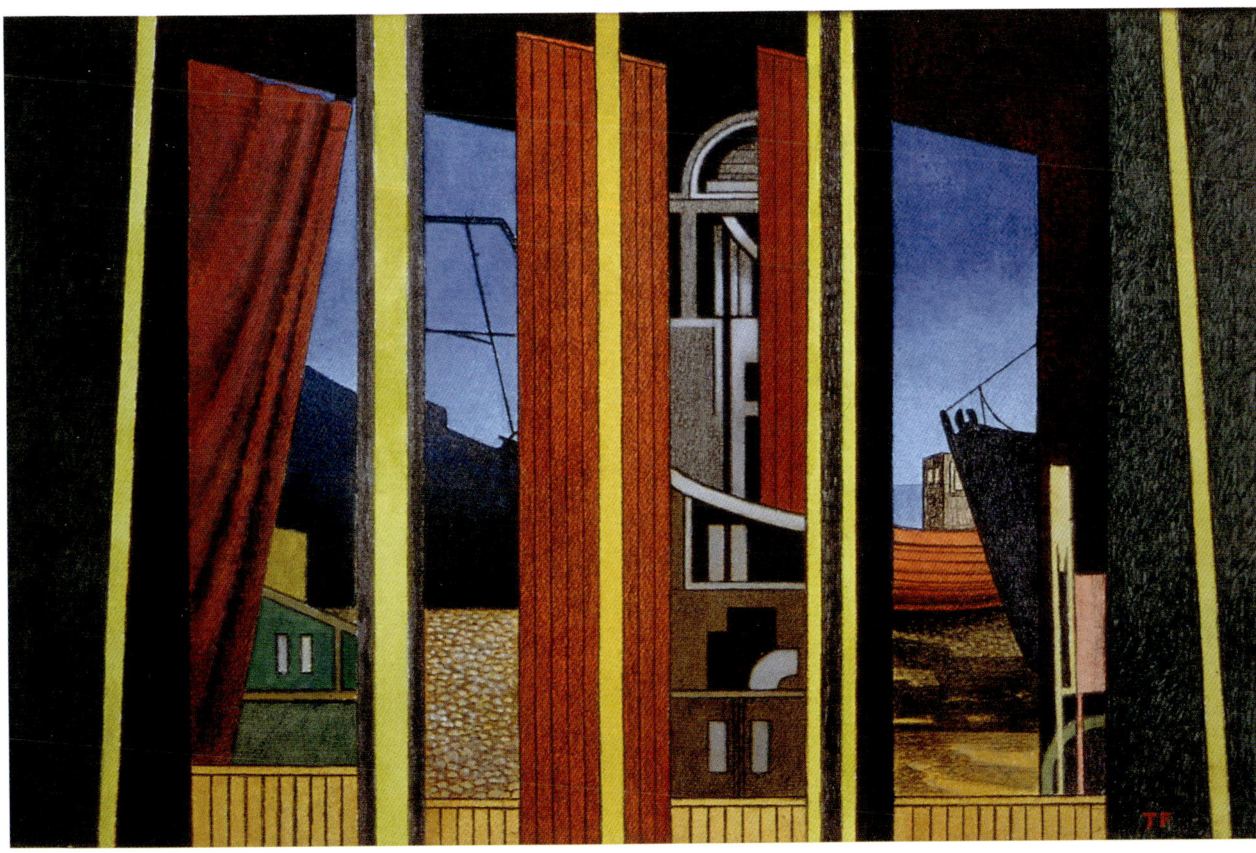

Boat Yard
600 x 390 mm, watercolour and acrylic

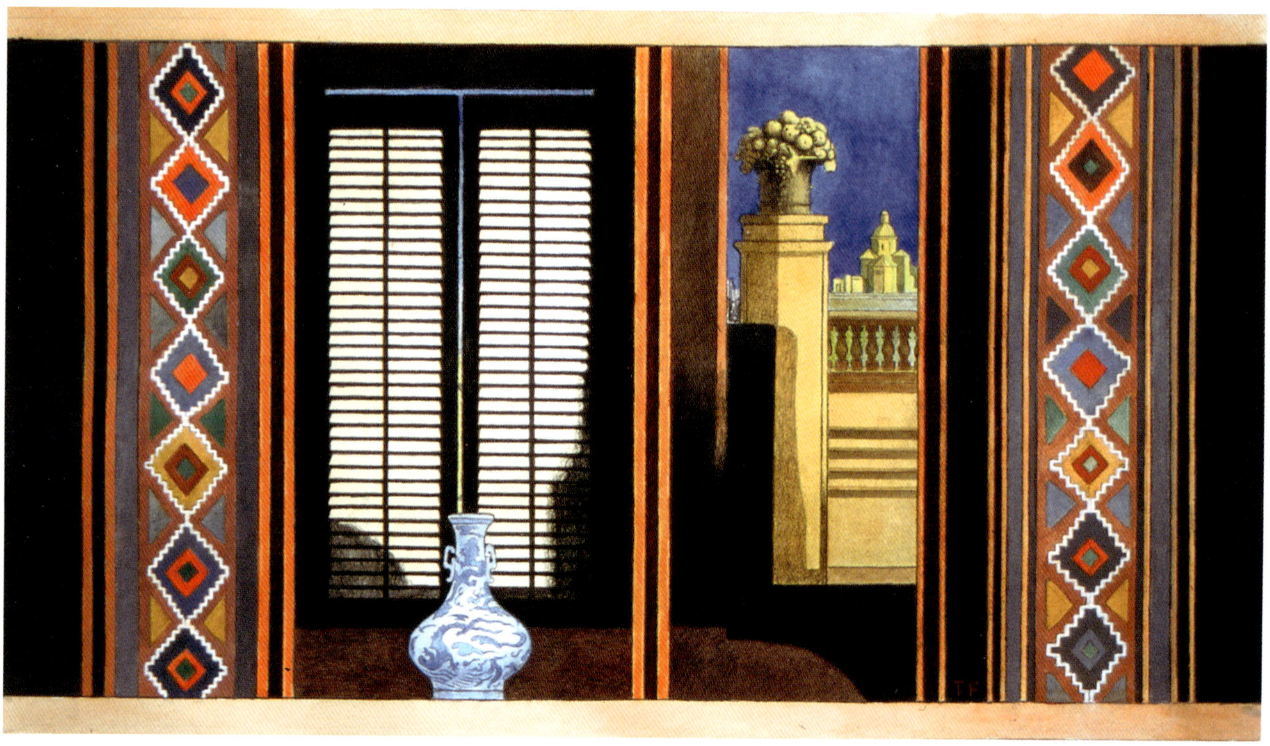

Sicilian Villa
1060 x 620 mm, watercolour and acrylic

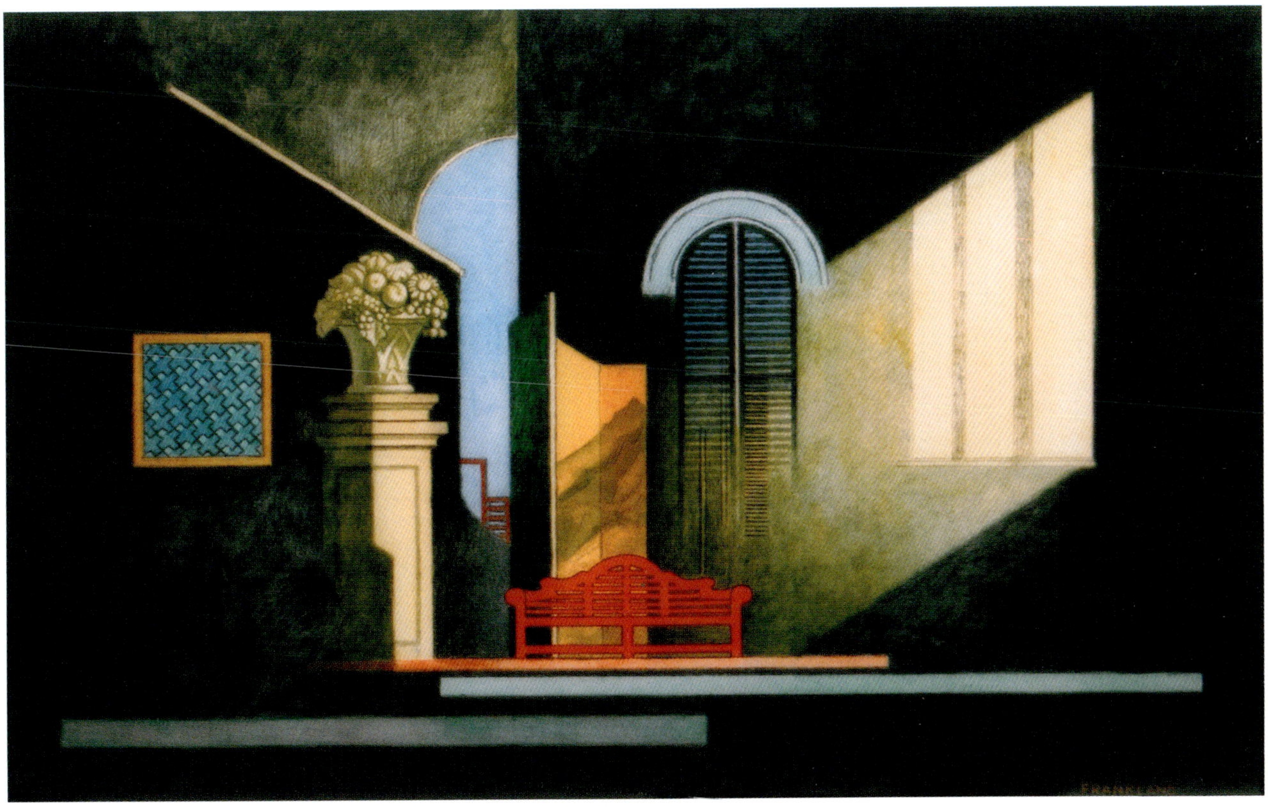

The Return Visit
700 x 430 mm, watercolour and conté crayon

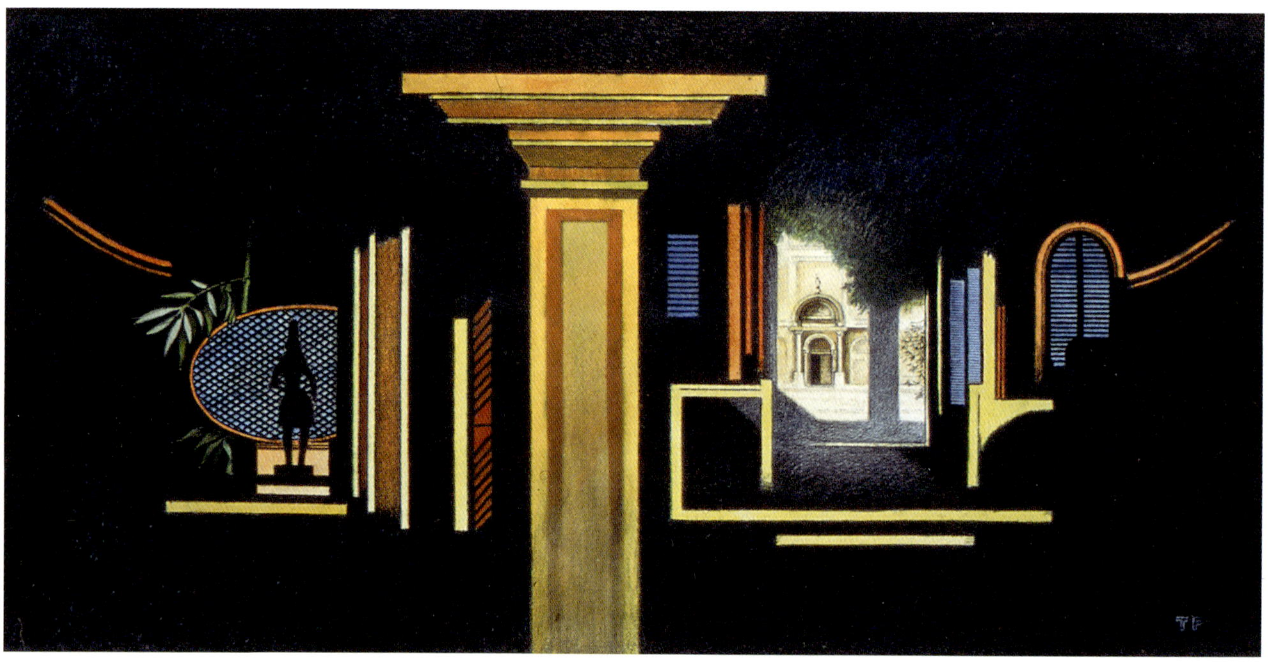

Fragments of Time no 2
690 x 370 mm, acrylic and conté crayon

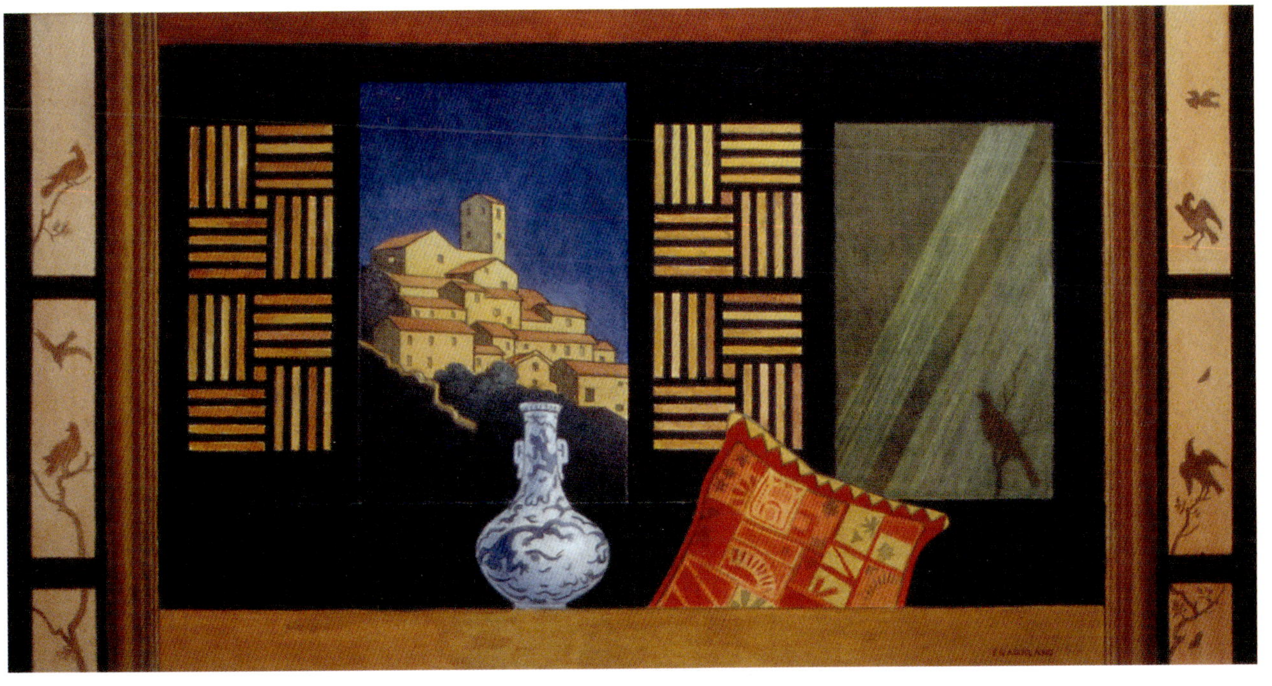

Mysterious Promise no 2
1070 x 620 mm, acrylic and conté crayon

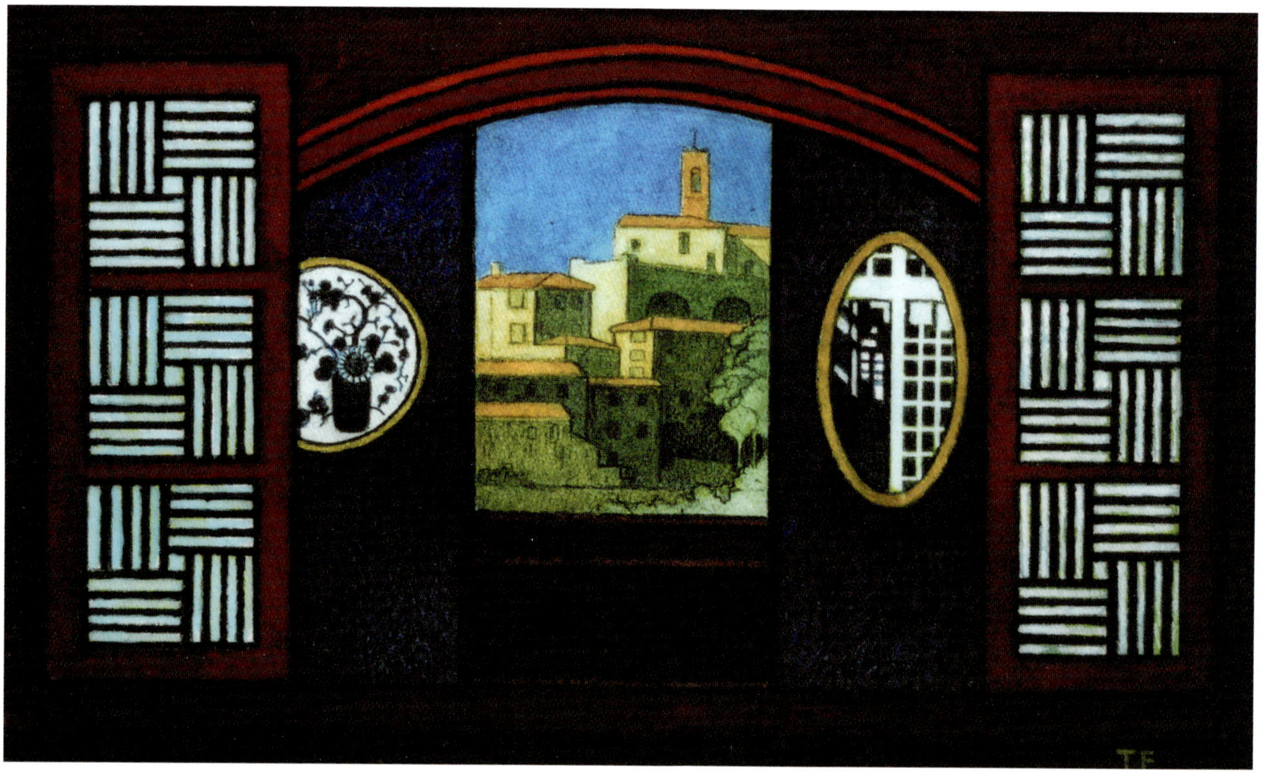

Study for Beyond the Screen
370 x 180 mm, acrylic and conté crayon

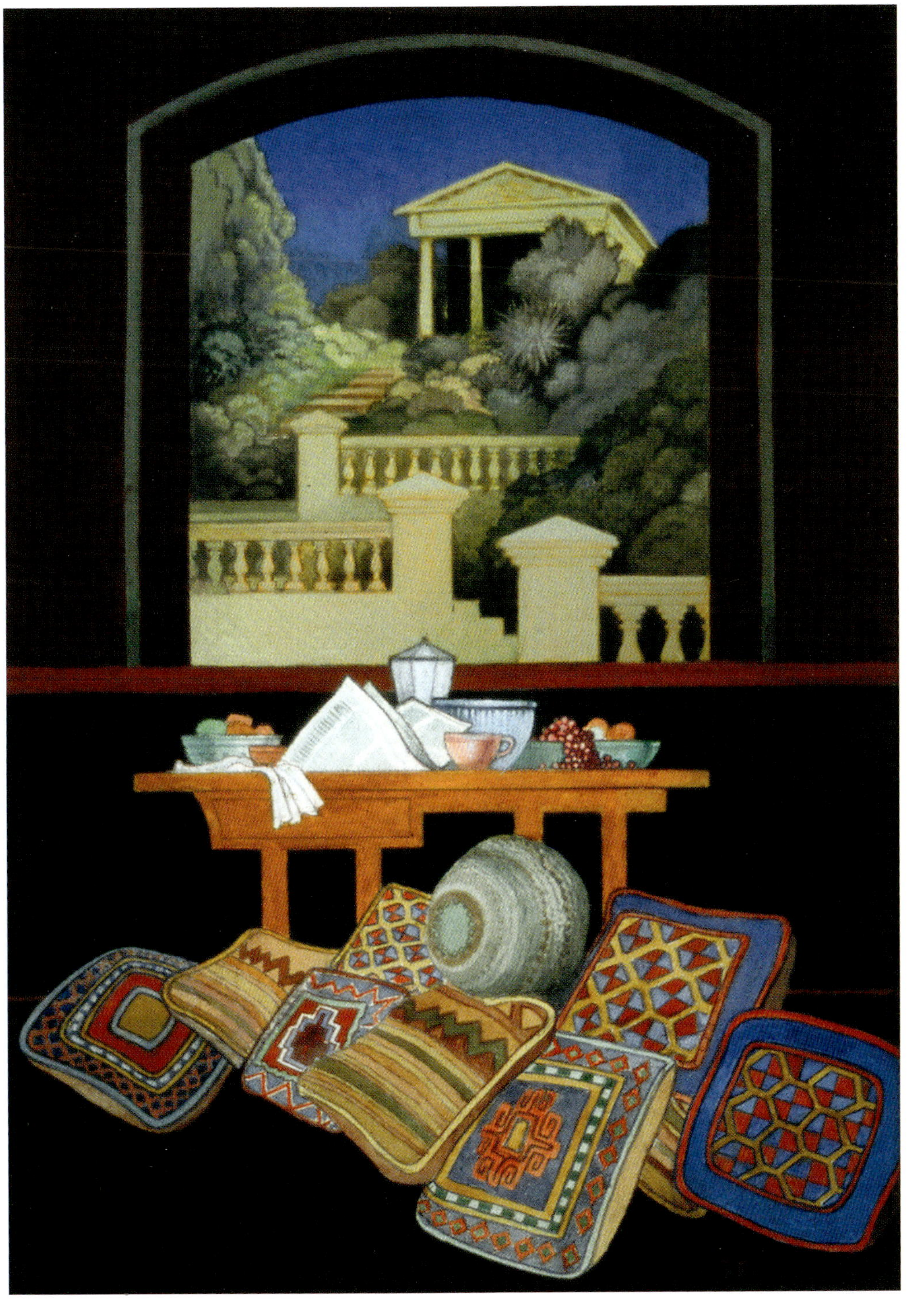

Continental Breakfast no 2
400 x 590 mm, acrylic, watercolour and conté crayon

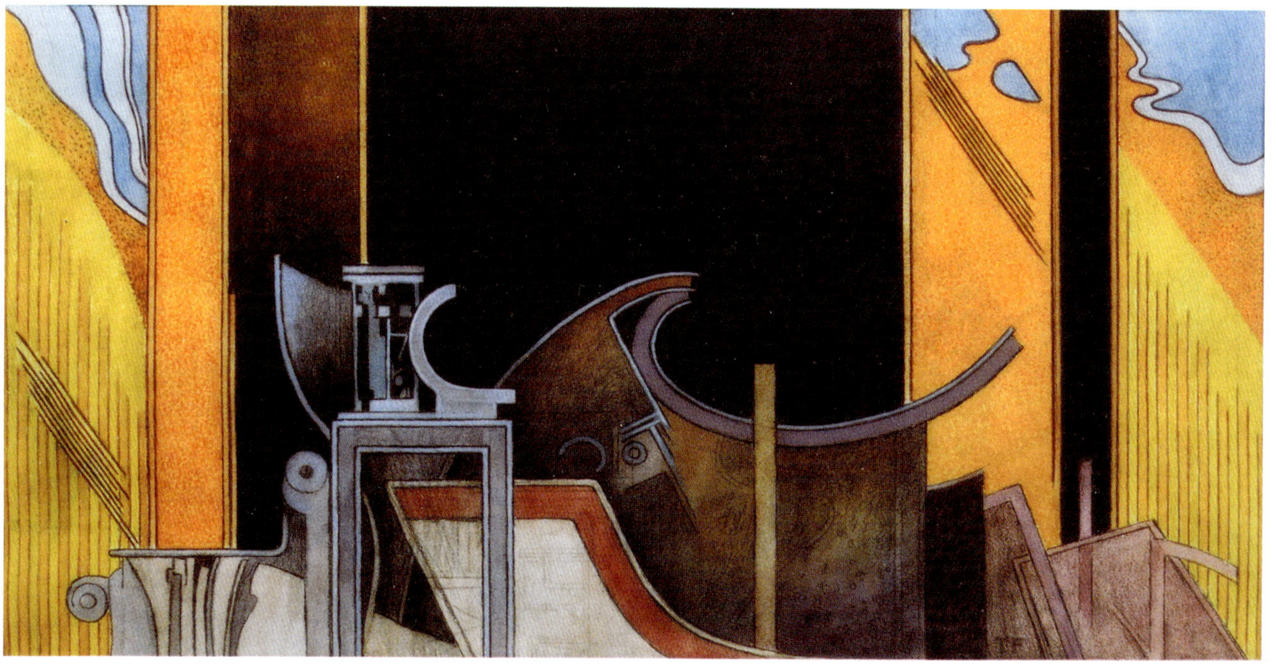

Neonlit Boat Yard Scrap

800 x 420 mm, watercolour, acrylic and conté crayon

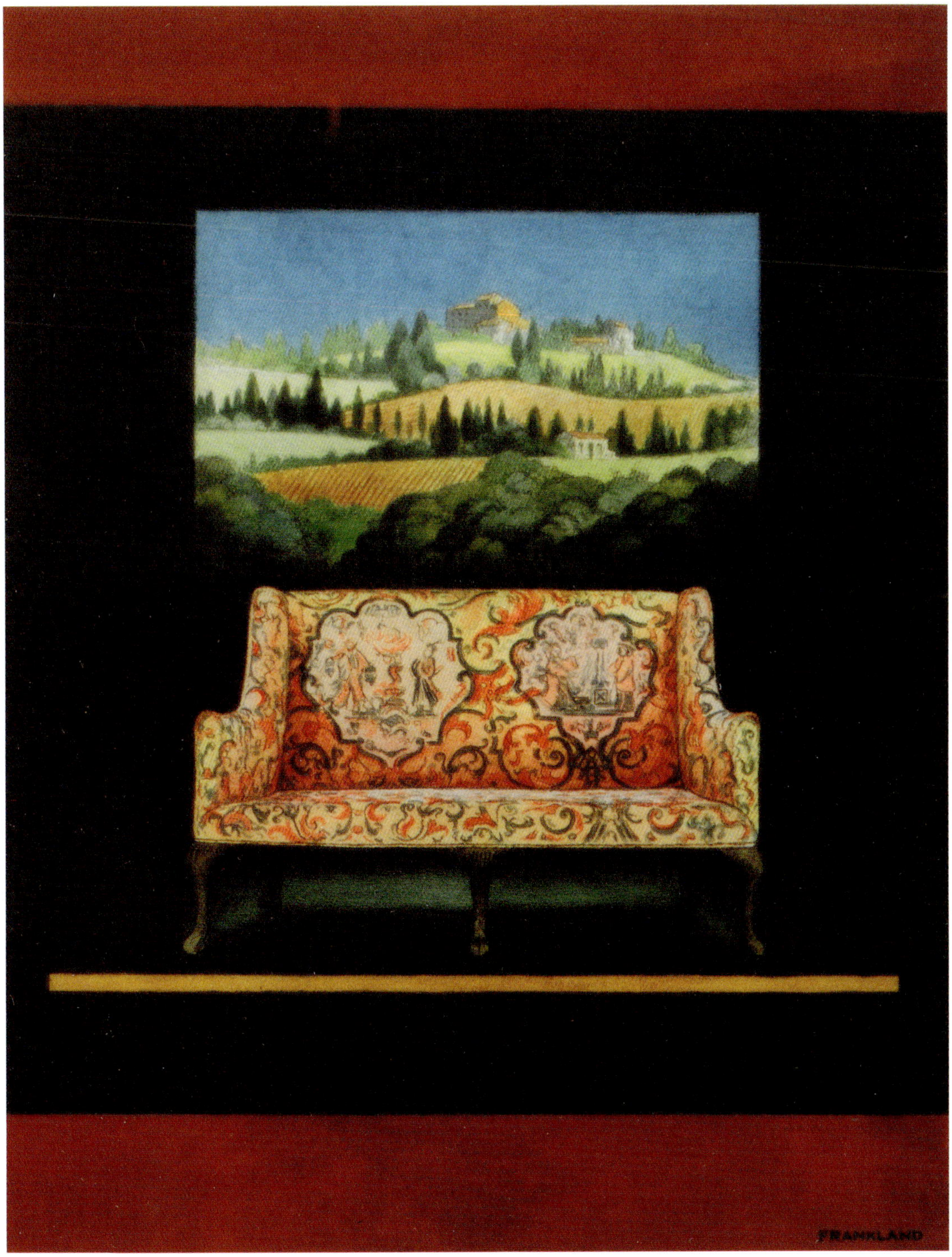

Time Suspended
740 x 900 mm, acrylic and conté pencil

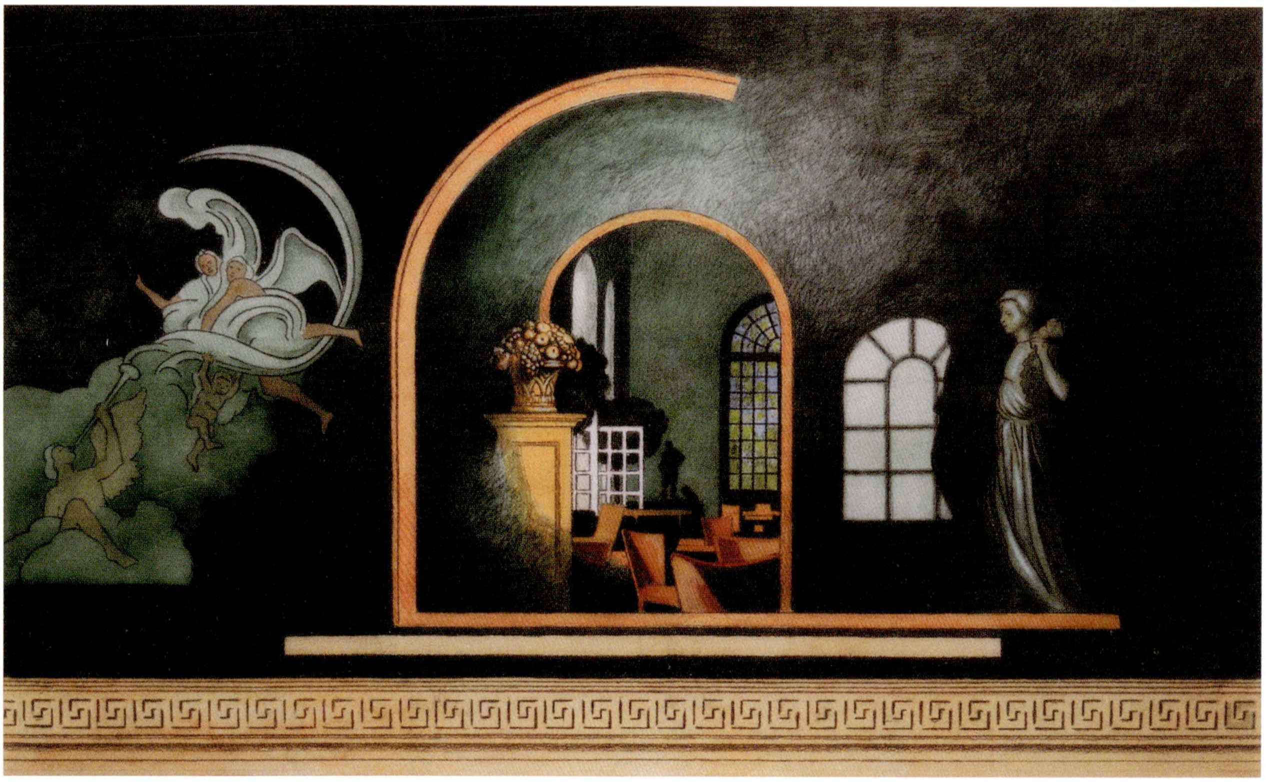

Summer in the Old City
840 x 520 mm, acrylic and conté pencil

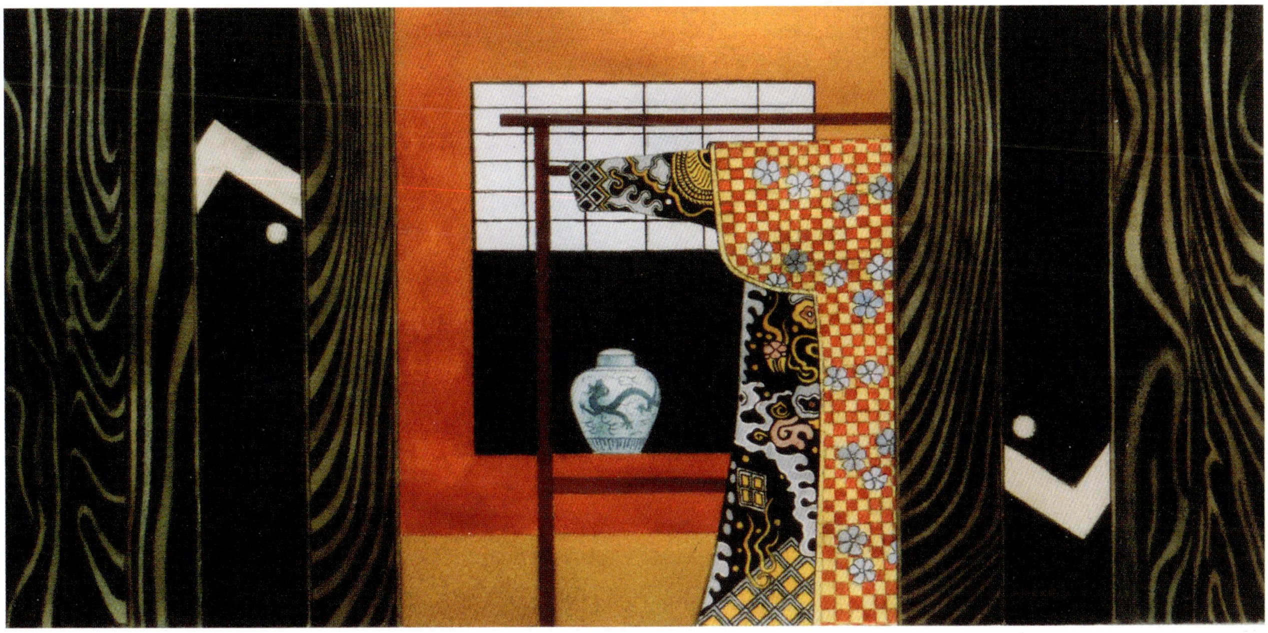

Measured Spaces and Passing Time
800 x 450 mm, acrylic and conté pencil

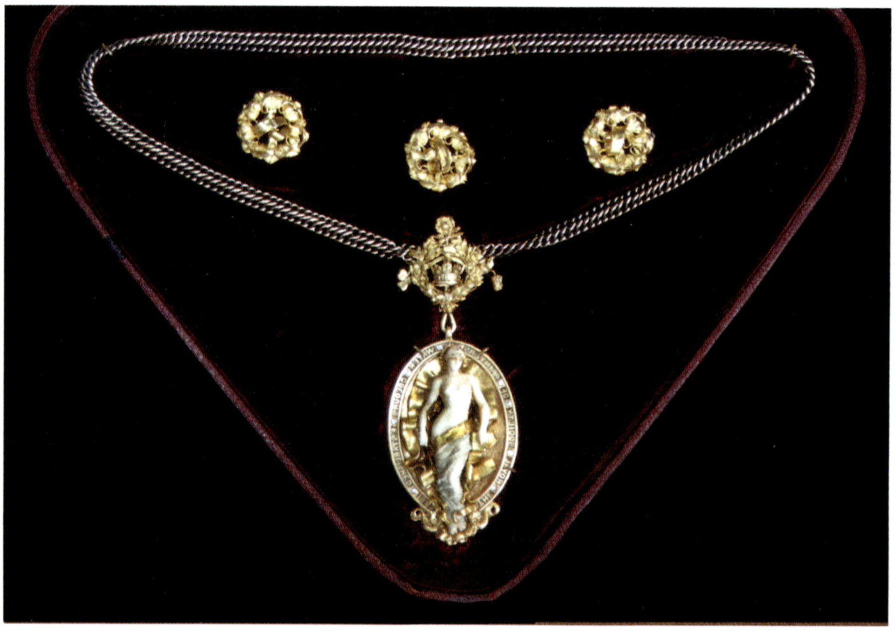

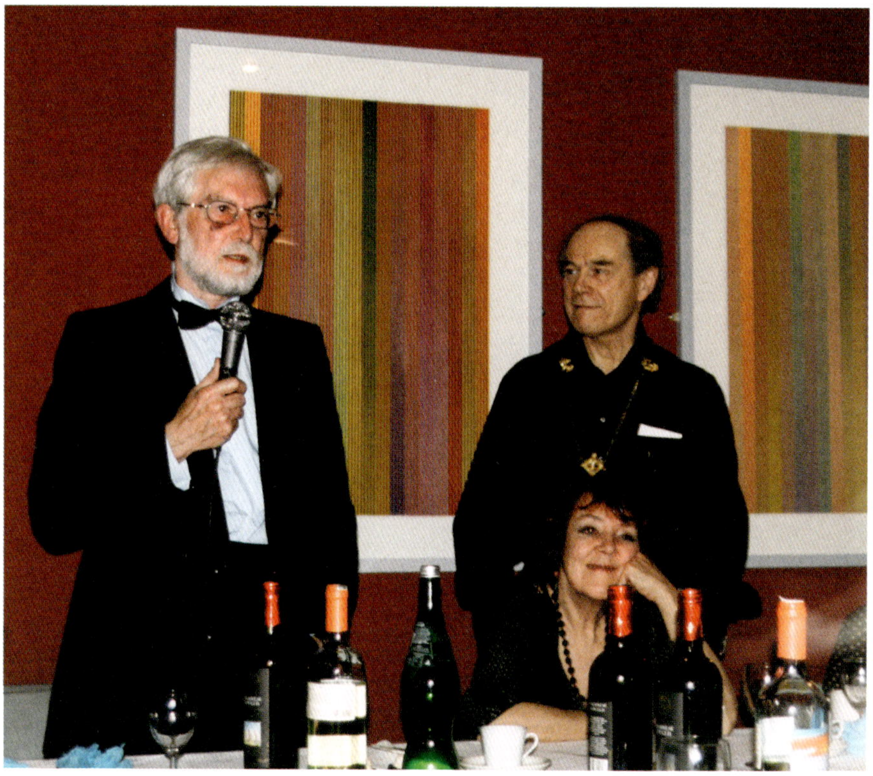

Jewel and Chain of Office of the President of the Royal Watercolour Society, designed by Sir Hubert von Herkomer and presented November 1896

Leslie Worth PPRWS, Trevor Frankland PRWS, and Dorothy Frankland, Royal Watercolour Society Annual Dinner 2003

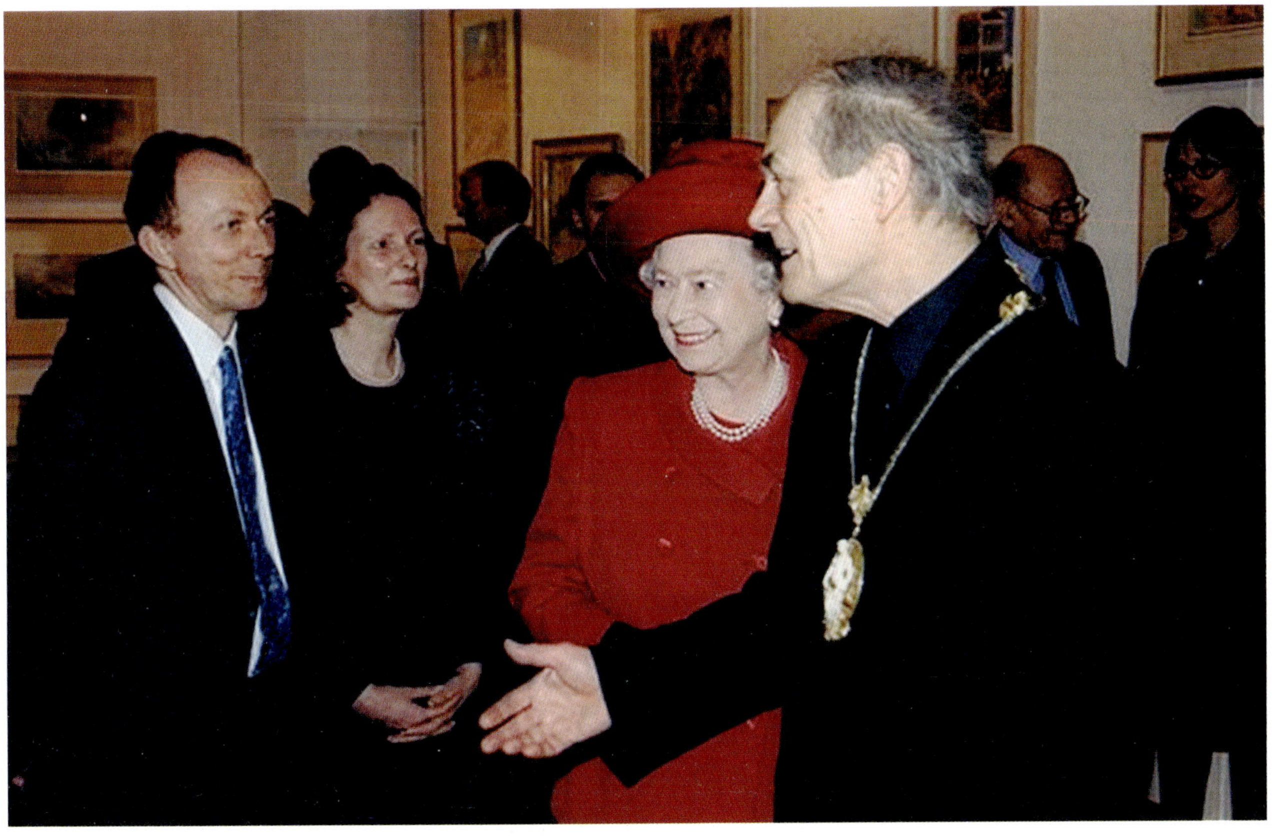

The Royal Visit to Bankside Gallery, February 2004. Trevor Frankland, RWS President, introducing Simon Fenwick and Angela Parker to HM the Queen (photograph courtesy of Dominic O'Neill)

President's Address

It gives me great pleasure as the President of the Royal Watercolour Society to introduce you to the present exhibition, *Then & Now,* which marks the beginning of our Bicentenary. The Society's first meeting was held in 1804 and the first exhibition of paintings in 1805, so our events will cover a two year period.

This current exhibition shows a selection of pictures from our Diploma Collection that have stimulated present Members of the Society to create related works. These form the major part of the exhibition and a more detailed account of the Diploma Collection can be found in the introduction.

The Society has had the strength and flexibility to survive 200 years of change. It has provided, and continues to provide, a solid base from which to create the new, and has parameters within which the present as well as the past can comfortably exist without conflict.

As Harold Rosenberg pointed out in his book, *The Tradition of the New,* "The vanguard steals the glamour of the profession...", and at the present time we can see that newspapers, magazines and television thrive on glamourising the activities of a few artists whom they promote as stars. We are confronted with a situation where a high level of state funding goes into promoting conceptual art at the expense of drawing and painting. This situation is affirmed by the practice in most institutions of higher education.

Plato said, "what is honoured in a country will be cultivated there." It is I believe, incumbent upon us to use our Bicentenary to emphasise that creativity comes in many forms and that the promotion of watercolour painting as a vehicle for expressing ideas is as valid now as it ever was in the past.

Then & Now is intended to introduce you to our past as well as our present, and we hope that various promotions throughout our Bicentenary will motivate more people to take an interest in the Society and its aims.

Trevor Frankland PRWS

2004
6 Feb - 7 March
'Then and Now' exhibition

President's Address

As President of the Royal Watercolour Society I would like to welcome you to our Spring Exhibition, which is the first of our annual shows to be held in the newly refurbished Bankside Gallery.

As you know, the Duke of Edinburgh and the Queen, who is our Patron, paid a visit to our Gallery on Wednesday the eighteenth of February. Her Majesty's visit during the first of our Bicentenary exhibitions has been a great help in drawing attention to the Gallery, as well as to the hopes and aspirations of our Society.

Over the years many of our Members have wished to modernise the space in which we exhibit our work, particularly to change the colour of the old red walls. But change relies on an alignment of just the right factors, like a fruit machine that has to line up a row of identical symbols before it will deliver the 'jackpot'. This year we have had just such an alignment, and the results, as you can see for yourselves, have been superb.

I believe the changes brought about in the appearance of the Gallery symbolise the rebirth of a society that has been in existence for two hundred years. By creating this new, thoroughly contemporary space we mark the seriousness of our intentions and avoid being associated with an image of times past.

Of course, as with any renaissance, communicating the change is vital. We have received some excellent press coverage this year that has drawn attention to the Society's Bicentenary and as part of our Bicentenary promotion works from this exhibition will be displayed in the Royal Cambrian Academy in Wales so that more people can become familiar with our work and understand that we promote watercolour as a versatile medium capable of being used to express a broad range of ideas. We have, as it were, nailed our colours to the mast for all to see.

I commend this show of paintings to you and hope that you will trumpet our drive forward to a wider audience.

Trevor Frankland PRWS

2004
18 March - 12 April
RWS Spring Exhibition

President's Address

My interest in the Royal Watercolour Society archive was stimulated by a letter that Ben Nicholson had written to a friend extolling the importance of getting information into various archives. The promotion of an artist and his work now relied on the written word being an integral part of that process and stored information was essential to achieve the desired result.

In the current exhibition, "Below the Surface: Secrets of the RWS", we celebrate our Bicentenary not only by looking forward to our future, but also by delving into our past. The Royal Watercolour Society archive, although not as comprehensive as one might hope, does contain a wealth of information that has enabled our archivist, Simon Fenwick, to 'swim beneath the surface' and bring to our gaze a selection of material that puts flesh on the dry bones of our past.

I commend to you the current exhibition on show as a fascinating glimpse into fragments of our past activities.

Trevor Frankland PRWS

2004
28 May - 20 June
'Below the Surface' exhibition

President's Address

Aqua Nova is a very suitable theme for an exhibition of paintings in watercolour, and coincidentally it also has an association with a poetic statement by J.M.W.Turner: 'Water, the image of the mind, clears as it runs and as it runs, refines'.

Looking around the gallery you can see how varied the response has been from Members to the idea of Aqua Nova. Some paintings show a direct link with the theme whilst others indicate a more oblique approach.

The theme of this exhibition was chosen to allow plenty of room for interpretation and in the process help to unite the display of work you now see on the walls. In the nineteenth century it would have attracted many paintings of storms and shipwrecks indicating an interest in the art of the sublime, but you will have to look very hard to find any shipwrecks in this show!

This exhibition also marks the launch of *The Watercolour Expert*, a book published by Cassell about Royal Watercolour Society Members and their work. It presents not only examples of their paintings but also descriptions written by each artist on his or her working procedure. I recommend this book to anyone who is curious to know what artists have to say about their paintings as well as to those who have an interest in the first printed overview of present RWS Members' work. It is a snapshot of the Society at this moment in time when we are celebrating our bicentenary.

Trevor Frankland PRWS

2004
8 - 31 October
RWS Autumn Exhibition

President's Address

It is my good fortune to be the President of the Royal Watercolour Society during our bicentenary and to have the opportunity to exhibit a body of work not only with colleagues whose paintings I know well but also with work by every other President since 1804.

The diverse nature of the work on show illustrates the individuality of each artist. It would be invidious of me to describe their working practices, as their own descriptions are printed in *The Watercolour Expert*, a book on the work of Society members.

Ever since Marcel Duchamp created the idea of 'ready-mades' in 1915 with his bicycle wheel, all artists have had to ask themselves: "How can a significant body of work be produced in an art world where diversity of approach is now king?" A choice has to be made. Many may gravitate towards the art forms that promise fame through art magazines and the cult of fashion, others may follow a time-honoured revolt against the past. There are also those who see the past as a springboard to the future, using, as a credo, the maxim, "he who ignores the past is bound to repeat the past."

The American psychologist A. Ames, referring to the visual world, said "what we see is our best guess as to what is out front." That best guess to which Ames refers allows the articulation of a psychic world where through the distortion of colour, form and mass, our inner response to things is conveyed.

The idea that a work of art should be more than how things appear to be has been around for a long time. Many artists working in the nineteenth and twentieth centuries have stated that the subject of a work of art was not to be found in trying to 'copy' nature, but in ourselves and this archaeology of the unconscious has proved to be a fertile source from which artists have created new work.

Diversity within a tradition requires invention, skill and a point of view. In so doing each artist will develop a strong 'signature style' which is well illustrated by the rich visual display you now see in the gallery. It deserves a prolonged look.

Trevor Frankland PRWS

2004
5 - 30 November
The Presidents' Exhibition

President's Address

We are now in the second year of our bicentenary celebrations. The Royal Watercolour Society was founded in 1804, as our Members' Diplomas declare, but the first society exhibition was not held until 1805, which is why the exhibition at the Dulwich Picture Gallery is entitled, 'The Triumph of Watercolour: The early Years of the RWS 1805 - 1850'. This is the last major historical show of our bicentenary and it will have its final showing at the Whitworth Art Gallery in Manchester from May to August of this year.

Whereas the show at Dulwich illustrates the early years of our Society, this current exhibition at the Bankside Gallery presents an excellent opportunity to see work by contemporary Members, thus creating a link across the two centuries. We are also delighted to present a large body of work in this exhibition from the year's featured artist, Salliann Putman.

As part of our policy of promoting the RWS outside the London area, over a hundred pieces of work will be transported, at the end of this spring show, to Martin's Gallery in Cheltenham. The gallery owner has been drawing attention to our contemporary Members as well as to those historical associations we are at present celebrating.

It was in February last year that we had a visit from Her Majesty the Queen and his Royal Highness The Duke of Edinburgh and in November His Royal Highness the Prince of Wales came to view 'The Presidents' exhibition. Our bicentenary dinner was held in the House of Lords and we have had three major publications: Simon Fenwick's *The Enchanted River*, a history of the Society; *The Watercolour Expert*, written and illustrated by the Members; and *The Triumph of Watercolour*, written by Timothy Wilcox, who curated our historical show at Dulwich Picture Gallery. We have also had several major shows here at the Bankside Gallery, with accompanying catalogues, in support of our bicentenary.

Meanwhile, at the end of this year when our bicentenary is over we will be able to look back to these memorable visits, exhibitions and other events, knowing that although these are now in the past, the three publications mentioned above will still continue to spread the name of the Society and the work of its Members across the world.

Trevor Frankland PRWS

2005
3 - 29 March
RWS Spring Exhibition

President's Address

The major exhibition of our bicentenary, 'The Triumph of Watercolour', which was on show at the Dulwich Picture Gallery, had nearly 25,000 visitors and did a great deal to publicise the Royal Watercolour Society.

The contemporary work of Members has also been and continues to be highlighted by the book entitled *The Watercolour Expert*, now into its second printing, to which will be added another book on the subject, *Then and Now*. This was the theme of one of our bicentenary exhibitions. This second book is due to be published next year.

It is difficult to imagine a better time than now for the Members to feel that they belong to a Society that has not only deep roots in the past but is also active in promoting a positive attitude to the ideas and work of current Members.

Francis Bacon said, "The past nourishes you and denying that source of nourishment is like cutting off an arm to make the other better. I have never felt the need to reject the past. I feel that I relate to tradition very seriously."

'High Life', the title of this present exhibition, has many connotations and this is exemplified by the work here on show. Many of the artists use the actual appearance of things from which to start their work, giving emphasis to things as they are known. Whilst others are interested in creating parallel realities opposed to those, which have been observed by other artists.

Fluctuat nec mergitur is the motto of Paris, but could be an appropriate motto for the Royal Watercolour Society to adopt, for in translation it means 'tossed by the waves but does not sink'.

Trevor Frankland PRWS

2005
6 - 30 October
RWS Autumn Exhibition. 'High Life'

Biographical Details

Born Middlesbrough

Studied

1952 – 1958 At the Laird School of Art Birkenhead and the Royal Academy Schools London.

1959 – 1960 Printmaking at the Royal Academy Schools with the assistance of a Leverhulme Fund Award.

Teaching

1960 – 1996 Various part-time posts, Medway College of Art, Hornsey School of Art, Middlesex Polytechnic and latterly at Middlesex University as an Associate Senior Lecturer

One-Person Exhibitions

1970 Billingham Art Gallery
1972 Shipley Art Gallery, Gateshead
1972 La Darsena Galleria, Milan
1976 Middlesbrough Art Gallery
1977 Calouste Gulbenkian Gallery, Newcastle upon Tyne
1978 Williamson Art Gallery and Museum, Birkenhead
1979 Northampton Central Museum and Art Gallery
1980 E.M. Flint Gallery, Walsall
1980 Worcester City Art Gallery
1980 Birmingham University
1981 Middlesbrough Art Gallery
1983 The New Gallery Hornsey Library, London
1983 Birmingham University
1988 Middlesbrough Art Gallery
1994 The Bedford Hill Gallery, London
1999 The Chelsea Arts Club
2006 The Dover Street Arts Club

Group Exhibitions

A large number of group shows including the RA, RWS, RBA, RE, RI, Singer and Friedlander, The Discerning Eye and The London Group, as well as exhibitions in America, France, Germany, Italy, Sicily, India, Mexico and Australia.

Awards

1954 – 1958
Landseer Scholarship
The Duff Greet Prize and Royal Academy Silver Medal for Drawing
Four David Murray Studentships
Landseer Prize (Drawing from the Antique)

1959 A Leverhulme Fund Award
1973 Medal Winner Premio Internazionale Di Grafica Del Pomero Rho Milano
1975 Arts Council Minor Award
1980 West Midlands Arts Grant Aid
1981 Northern Arts Grant Aid
1983 Greater London Arts Grant Aid
1983 Middlesex Polytechnic Grant Aid to attend a conference in Finland as one of the UK delegates of the International Association of Art, (UNESCO)
1988 Northern Arts Grant Aid
1992 John Purcel Paper Award
1994 Wandsworth Arts Grant Aid

2000 Fabbrica Prize (Joint winner)
2001 St Cuthberts Mill Award
2001 Awarded the RBA De Laszlo Medal
2002 Northbrook College Award
2006 RBA President's Choice

Collections

The Ashmolean Museum (RE Diploma Collection)
Birmingham University
Cleveland County Council
The Dover Street Arts Club
Middlesbrough Art Gallery
Middlesex University
The Rank Xerox Organisation
The Royal Academy of Arts (A. Hugill Fund Purchase)
The Royal Collection, Windsor
The Royal Watercolour Society Diploma Collection
The Scarborough Art Gallery Print Archive
The Shipley Art Gallery, Gateshead
The Special Trustees of Hammersmith Hospital
The United Grand Lodge of England Museum and Library
The Williamson Art Gallery, Birkenhead
Wolverhampton University

Private collections in England, Italy and America

Election to Societies etc.

1960 Elected a Fellow of the Royal Society of Arts, FRSA. (Life Member).
1992 Elected an Associate of the Royal Society of Painter Printmakers, ARE.
1993 Elected a full member of the Royal Society of Painter Printmakers, RE
1993 Appointed Honorary Treasurer of the RE. (1993 – 2003).
1993 Appointed to the Board of Directors Bankside Gallery Ltd. (1993 – 2006).
1995 Elected a member of the Royal Society of British Artists, RBA.
1996 Elected a member of The London Group.
1997 Appointed Honorary Treasurer of The London Group (1997 – 2005).
1997 Elected an Associate of the Royal Watercolour Society, ARWS.
1997 Appointed Honorary Curator of the RWS.
1998 Elected a full member of the Royal Watercolour Society, RWS.
1998 Elected a member of the Art Workers' Guild.
1998 Appointed Deputy Vice Chairman of the Royal Academy Schools Alumni Association (1998 – 2009).
2000 Appointed a Director, Trustee and Secretary of RBA Ltd.
2002 Elected a member of the Small Paintings Group.
2003 Elected President of the Royal Watercolour Society (2003- 2006).
2003 Elected an honorary member of the Royal Institute of Painters in Watercolour. Hon RI. Served on the UK Committee of the International Association of Art (affiliated to UNESCO), for several years led by Richard Carline and Morris Kestelman and in 1983 attended the 10th International Congress of the IAA, held in Helsinki, Finland, as a member of the UK delegation.

Garden Landscape – 'Summer River Bed Winter Flood Plain'

1979 Started to create a domestic landscape which has been the subject of four short films for television – Project Continuing.
1988 Channel 4 Television (state one).
1990 B/SKY/B Television (state two).

1992 London Weekend Television (state three).
1999 Channel 3 Carlton Television (state four).

Foreign Travel
1970 – onwards.

Visits to Italy, Turkey, Iran, Syria, Jordon, Iraq, Israel, Morocco, Algeria, India, Pakistan, Afghanistan, Tunisia, as well as Spain, Portugal, Finland, France, Holland and Greece.

Selected Bibliography

- *The Northern Echo,* Friday May 29 1970. Review of exhibition at Billingham Art Gallery by W.B.Johnson.
- *The Guardian,* Tuesday June 9 1970. Review of exhibition at Billingham Art Gallery by William Varley.
- *The Yorkshire Post,* June 11 1970. Review of exhibition at Billingham Art gallery by TCRB (Tom Bentley).
- *The Northern Echo,* Friday July 7 1972. Review of exhibition at The Shipley Art Gallery Gateshead by W.E. Johnstone.
- *The Guardian,* Friday July 14 1972. Review of exhibition at The Shipley Art Gallery Gateshead by William Varley.
- *The Journal* - Newcastle-upon-Tyne, July 27 1972. Review of exhibition at the Shipley Art Gallery Gateshead by William Feaver.
- Catalogue Introduction, to the La Darsena Galleria Di Milano Exhibition, October - November 1972, by Giuseppe Franzoso.
- La Darsena Galleria Di Milano, Vigevano 2000, Mostre in Cartello, 9 Dec 1972. Review of exhibition by Giuseppe Franzoso.
- XX11 Rasegna GB Salvi Piccola Europa Sassoferrato 1972 Exhibition Catalogue. Artist's statement and illustration, pages 74 and 75 under, 'Seven Artists De La Darsena Galleria Di Milano.'
- Luce Settimanale Cattolico Di Rho Milano, Dominica 27 Maggio 1973. Review of a five person show at La Viscontea Galleria Rho Milano.
- *Strutture Grafiche e Signi,* a book by Domenico Cara Published 1975 pages 357 & 472.
- *The Guardian,* May 3 1976. Review of a one-person show at Middlesbrough Art Gallery by William Varley.
- Catalogue Introduction to the Middlesbrough Art Gallery show, April - May 1976 by William Varley.
- *The Yorkshire Post,* May 11 1976. Review of a one-person show at Middlesbrough Art Gallery by TCRB (Tom Bentley).
- BBC Radio Teeside Programme 'Festival', May 1976, on the artist and his work. Interviewer Anne Horsted.
- *Gallery Focus North East,* Oct 1 - Nov 12 1977, Page 6, large illustration and details of a one-person show at the Calouste Gulbenkian Gallery, Newcastle-upon-Tyne.
- Sunderland Arts Centre Exhibition Cards. Part of a five-person show, June - July 1978 Illustration and artist's statement.
- *The Northern Echo,* Sat May 16 1981. Review of a one-person exhibition at Middlesbrough Art Gallery by W.E.Johnston.
- Catalogue Introduction, to the Middlesbrough Art Gallery Exhibition May 1981 by Matthew Collings.
- BBC Radio Cleveland Programme 'Roundabout' Wed 27 May 1981 on the artist and his work. Interviewer, Allan Wright.
- Catalogue Introduction, to a one-person exhibition at The New Gallery Hornsey, May - June 1983 by Matthew Collings.
- *The Artists' Day Book.* Compiled by Andrew Jones. (Preview of included images at Smith's Galleries Covent Garden London). Dec 1987.

- *Southside* Magazine, Nov 1987, 'Zen and the Art of Garden Maintenance,' three photographs plus an article on a domestic landscape construction.
- 'Summer Riverbed Winter Flood Plain', (state one) Interviewer Deborah Benady.
- *Living Magazine*, Oct 1988, pages 168 and 169, 'East meets West,' four photographs and an article on, 'Zen and a Domestic Landscape' (state one), by Gay Search.
- Artist's Statement in Catalogue, one-person show at Middlesbrough Art Gallery July - Aug 1988.
- Channel Four Television, 'A Bamboo Production,' Friday 16 Dec 9.30 pm 1988 an eight-minute film of the domestic landscape, 'Summer Riverbed Winter Flood Plain,' (state one).
- B/Sky/B Television, a 'New Era Production,' 28 March 1990, for the programme, 'Homeworks,' an eight-minute film of a domestic landscape, 'Summer Riverbed Winter Flood Plain', (state two).
- *Dictionary of British Art,* Vol vi '20th Century Painters and Sculptors,' by Frances Spalding. Published 1990 by The Antique Collectors Club, entry page 184.
- London Weekend Televlsion, 10 May 6pm 1992 . 'The Gardening Road Show - Unusual Gardens', an eight-minute film of, 'Summer Riverbed Winter Flood Plain', (state three).
- Carlton Television Channel 3. Programme, 'Planted,' July 1 5.30 pm 1999 An eight-minute film of, 'Summer Riverbed Winter Flood Plain', (state four). Visage T/V Ltd.
- *Gardens Illustrated* (Supplement), June 1999, Interview plus eight illustrations pages 14, 15, 16 and 17. Domestic Landscape, 'Summer Riverbed Winter Flood Plain' (state four).
- *Arts Review* Feb 2000 - A short statement by David Gluck on prints in the National Print Show, held at the Mall Galleries London.
- *The London Group*. Published 2003, illustrations and text, pages 102 and 103.
- *The Whistler*. Chelsea Arts Club Magazine, published 2003, an article on, 'Illusion in a Sculptured Space -The Garden as an Art Form,' pages 6 and 7.
- *SW Magazine*. Published October 2003, 'Controlled Experiment,' (domestic landscape), page 56.
- The Royal Watercolour Society. Exhibition catalogues 2004 - 2005, seven short essays, the President's Address to the members of the RWS.
- *The Enchanted River. A History of the Royal Watercolour Society,* by Simon Fenwick published by Sansom and Co. 2004. Preface to the book and mentioned pages 177, 183 and 191.
- *The Watercolour Expert*. Published 2004 by Cassell Illustrated. Essays on pages 78 - 79 and 86 - 87, also the Foreword.
- *The Times*. Feb 4 2004. ' Weathering Arts Stormy Waters', by Sue Corbett. A painting used to illustrate the article.
- *The Times* Register. Feb 21 2004. Photograph with HM the Queen at the Bankside Gallery London (RWS Bicentenary).
- The Singer and Friedlander / Sunday Times Watercolour Competition / Exhibition 2004. Catalogue Introduction relating to the RWS Bicentenary.
- *Modern and Contemporary Prints – a practical guide to collecting,* by Phoebe Phillips and Tom Robb. Published 2004 by The Antique Collectors Club. Full page illustration, page 57.
- 'The Triumph of Watercolour' A Dulwich Picture Gallery, London and Whitworth Art Gallery, Manchester, exhibition 2005. Preface to the catalogue.
- *The Artist* Magazine. Sept Issue 2005, 'Featured Artist', by Julian Halsby, pages 49, 50, and 51.
- 'The Artist and Radio Four - Sound and Vision'. A Bankside Gallery Exhibition 3 - 27 Nov 2005. Catalogue, photograph and text page 15.
- *Watercolour Masters - Then and Now*. Published by Cassell Illustrated, 2006. Text and illustration pages 30 and 31.
- *The Printmakers' Directory*. Published by A & C Black, 2006. Illustration and text, page 45.
- David Buckman's, *Artists in Britain Since 1945,* 2 volumes, Published by Art Dictionaries Ltd, 2006, entry page 543.
- *Who's Who in Art*. Published biannually by Hilmarton Manor Press.
- *Printmakers' Secrets* by Tony Dyson, published by A&C Black 2009, pages 58 and 59, illustrations plus text.